Praise for *World Class Learners*

"Professor Yong Zhao's latest book, *World Class Learners*, is unu[...] tive, and amusing. Dr. Zhao himself exemplifies the creative [...] roams across disciplines to synthesize new ideas based on insight and research. Having spent his youth in China and his adulthood in the United States gives him a clear-eyed view of the strengths and weaknesses of schooling in both the east and the west. His account of the unexpected consequences of well-intentioned policy should be read by every policy maker, from education secretaries to school board members. Teachers and parents will also benefit from his views on educating children to be creative, independent thinkers."

—Milton Chen, Former Executive Director
The George Lucas Education Foundation
Author of *Education Nation*

"Yong Zhao dares to challenge prevailing 'standardized' education policies and practices in favor of more individualized holistic approaches that tap into and enhance the talents of every child, enabling all children to be better prepared to live productively in a global-ized society. Zhao's book portrays a new global entrepreneurship paradigm for teaching and learning in our schools, and it imparts a sense of urgency and a call to action for education policy makers everywhere to shift away from standardization to globalization for the sake of our children and the well-being of our nation. Zhao's thoughtful and thought-provoking vision will inspire educators, and his global entrepreneurship para-digm is bound to intrigue, inform, and enhance their practice. The National Association of Elementary School Principals applauds Yong Zhao's vision and encourages educators to draw upon his new global entrepreneurship education paradigm for inspiration and practical ideas for engaging students and enhancing their talents and exceptionality."

—Gail Connelly, Executive Director
National Association of Elementary School Principals

"Zhao zeroes in on entrepreneurship and the sorts of open-ended learning that produce creative problem solvers most likely to succeed in the competitive world of business. Zhao shows us how, in spite of the obstacles our mania for test scores has put in the way, educators and students are succeeding on this path."

—Anthony Cody, Writer
"Living in Dialogue" Blog, *Education Week*

"Professor Zhao has provided a different and compelling view of what education can and should be if we want to remain a global, creative, entrepreneurial, and innovative nation. Policy makers at every level need to read and act on the ideas in this book as though our future depends on it. Because it does."

—Tom Watkins, Former Michigan Superintendent of Public Instruction

"Yong Zhao has provided the most compelling case I have read on how many (mainly Western) nations are on the wrong track in educational reform. The unrelenting focus on high-stakes testing, the narrowing of the curriculum, and the continuing faith in outdated models of schooling ensure that they are short-changing students and weakening their societies and economies. The good news, as this book shows, is that there are outliers of preferred practice in schools around the world. The challenge is to provide schools with the autonomy to innovate with an entrepreneurial spirit and to resist the pressures for more centralized command-and-control approaches to change in schools."

—Brian Caldwell, Professor, University of Melbourne
Principal Consultant, Educational Transformations

"Many of us who study innovation struggle with ways to domesticate the unruly habits of creative entrepreneurs into a useful framework for education and learning. Dr. Yong Zhao's *World Class Learners* brings the lessons of global entrepreneurs home to the 21st century classroom at a moment when those lessons are sorely needed. *World Class Learners* is a timely and important contribution to our understanding of the relationship between practical skills, creativity, and technology in preparing young people for an entrepreneurial world."

—Rob Salkowitz, Author
*Young World Rising: How Youth, Technology, and Entrepreneurship
Are Changing the World From the Bottom Up*

"Rarely do I read a well-written and engaging book that offers a research-based critique of current practices in education with a workable prescription for the future. *World Class Learners* is such a book. Moreover, its implications for the field of teacher preparation are profound, and the ideas presented in the book should become the basis for significant discussion within our field. As Zhao points out, the world is changing so rapidly, and the context that our schools and institutions of higher education confront is so dynamic, that we must embrace the need for change and make adjustments or potentially lose the franchise for preparing the next generation of educators. This book should be required for all those interested in education, but most significantly for those preparing for careers in the field."

—Rick Ginsberg, Dean of the School of Education
University of Kansas, Lawrence

"*World Class Learners* contains a clear call for teacher preparation to begin producing teachers capable of thinking differently about the purposes of schooling. If we ignore our opportunity to do so, our future is, at best, uncertain."

—Mark Girod, Chair, Division of Teacher Education
Western Oregon University, Monmouth

"Professor Zhao describes in rich detail how our world is rapidly being pushed by the triple forces of demographic change, economic globalization, and technological innovation toward evermore demanding requirements for educational improvement in our schools. He shows that focusing excessively on test scores undermines the very kinds of creativity and initiative that are most badly needed for economic success, social well-being, and environmental sustainability."

—Dennis Shirley, Professor of Education
Lynch School of Education, Boston College, Chestnut Hill, MA

"In this provocative book, Professor Zhao argues that creativity and entrepreneurship, rather than test scores, ought to be the goals that mobilize societies as they improve education. He suggests that policies aimed at improving test scores harm the development of creativity and entrepreneurial skills. This is a fresh and important contribution to the global conversation on education reform—a compelling call for systematically generalizing the opportunities to develop creativity that are at the root of child centered education."

—Fernando M. Reimers, Ford Foundation Professor of
International Education, Harvard Graduate School of Education

World Class
Learners

Educating Creative and Entrepreneurial Students

Yong Zhao

A Joint Publication

naesp™
Leading
Learning Communities

CORWIN
A SAGE Company

CORWIN
A SAGE Company

FOR INFORMATION:

Corwin

A SAGE Company

2455 Teller Road

Thousand Oaks, California 91320

(800) 233-9936

www.corwin.com

SAGE Publications Ltd.

1 Oliver's Yard

55 City Road

London EC1Y 1SP

United Kingdom

SAGE Publications India Pvt. Ltd.

B 1/I 1 Mohan Cooperative Industrial Area

Mathura Road, New Delhi 110 044

India

SAGE Publications Asia-Pacific Pte. Ltd.

3 Church Street

#10-04 Samsung Hub

Singapore 049483

Acquisitions Editor: Arnis Burvikovs

Associate Editor: Desirée Bartlett

Editorial Assistant: Kimberly Greenberg

Production Editor: Amy Schroller

Copy Editor: Terri Lee Paulsen

Typesetter: C&M Digitals (P) Ltd.

Proofreader: Barbara Johnson

Indexer: Judy Hunt

Cover Designer: Rose Storey

Permissions Editor: Karen Ehrmann

Copyright © 2012 by Corwin

Printed in the United States of America

Library of Congress Cataloging-in-Publication Data

Zhao, Yong

World class learners: educating creative and entrepreneurial students/Yong Zhao.

p. cm.
Includes bibliographical references and index.

ISBN 978-1-4522-0398-0 (pbk. : alk. paper)

1. Education—Aims and objectives. 2. Education—Curricula. 3. Education and state. 4. Education and globalization. I. Title.

LB41.Z47 2012
370.11—dc23   2012021035

This book is printed on acid-free paper.

13 14 15 16 10 9 8 7 6 5 4 3

Contents

Acknowledgments

This book is about creativity and entrepreneurship. Like all book projects, it is also the result of creativity and entrepreneurship. The creativity and entrepreneurship that led to the final product came from many individuals, who have along the way inspired and encouraged my creativity, supported and helped with my enterprise, as well as challenged and motivated me to create a better product. I am fortunate to have these individuals as friends, colleagues, and family, and I am grateful for their help and support.

Among all the people I wanted to thank first are my parents, who, despite their meager resources as peasants in a village in China, sent me to school instead of putting me in the rice field. More important, they did not act like stereotypical Chinese tiger moms and dads. They did not prescribe a destiny for me; nor did they force me to do what they believed to be right. They tolerated my crazy dreams, unusual behaviors, and unconventional pursuits as a farm boy. Whatever creativity or entrepreneurial spirit I have today I owe to my illiterate parents.

Rob Salkowitz's book planted the seed of the "student as entrepreneurs" idea and a later meeting with Rob in Seattle further convinced me to work on the book. The idea became stronger as I made presentations to educators around the world. Therefore I must thank the many educators who have allowed me to share my ideas in progress with them and given me invaluable feedback along the way. In particular, the U.K.-based iNET organized a number of events that allowed me to explore the idea with educators from different countries. I am indebted to Mike Bullis, my dean at the University of Oregon, for giving me the freedom to be creative and entrepreneurial. I am equally indebted to the anonymous donor who endowed the Presidential Chair at the University of Oregon that greatly facilitated my entrepreneurial activities, including the development of Oba.

I have particularly benefited from interacting with a number of outstanding thinkers around the world including Kathe Kirby of the Asian Education Foundation in Australia; Andy Hargreaves and Dennis Shirley of Boston College; Ken Frank of Michigan State University; Brian Caldwell of Education Transformations in Australia; Sue Williamson of the Schools Network in the United Kingdom; Sir Dexter Hutt of Ninestiles School in Birmingham, England; Tony MacKay and colleagues from the Global Education Leadership Program (GELP); David Berliner of Arizona State University; Chris Tienken of Seaton Hall University; Ken Dirkin of Michigan State University; and Xuyang Yao of Beijing Channel Consulting, China.

Larry Rosenstock, founder of High Tech High in San Diego; William Skilling, superintendent of Oxford Community Schools; Julie Stuart-Thompson of Cherwell School and her daughter Verity; and Steve Morse, principal of Roosevelt Elementary School, have generously offered me the opportunity to learn about their schools and projects. They have also helped read the first draft of all or parts of the book and provided insightful feedback.

Jing Lei of Syracuse University provided timely and high-quality assistance with data analyses, particularly those pertinent to the PISA and Global Entrepreneurship Monitor data. Wei Qiu of Webster University and Gaoming Zhang of the University of Indianapolis read drafts of all the chapters carefully and made excellent suggestions. I am grateful for their help.

There are a number of individuals who made the writing process much easier to manage. Lisa Payne of Michigan State University helped tremendously with my travel arrangements so I did not have to spend time worrying about where I should go. Brian Flannery and Connie Manley in my office at the University of Oregon managed the office with outstanding professionalism so I could travel and learn about education in different parts of the world.

My editor, Arnis Burvikovs, and his colleagues at Corwin have been extremely pleasant to work with. They provided timely and valuable suggestions along the way that greatly improved the book. The comments provided by the five anonymous reviewers were very insightful and helped enhance the final product.

This book would not have been possible without the support of my own family. My wife, Xi Chen, has always been the first reader of all my writings and the harshest yet most encouraging critic of my ideas. My son, Yechen, and his friends at the University of Chicago have been a constant source of ideas and inspiration. Yechen also reviewed and edited parts of the manuscript. Of course, I must thank my daughter, Athena. She keeps me updated with the trendiest trends for teens. She challenges my assertions about how children learn. She reminds me that I am too old to know Lady Gaga well. Most important, she keeps me smiling all the time.

Yong Zhao
Eugene, Oregon
April 2012

About the Author

 Yong Zhao is Presidential Chair and associate dean for Global and Online Education at the College of Education, University of Oregon. His recent books include *Catching Up or Leading the Way: American Education in the Age of Globalization* and *Handbook of Asian Education.*

Introduction

To Create Is Human

This book started with a story I read in *Young World Rising: How Youth, Technology, and Entrepreneurship Are Changing the World From the Bottom Up,* a book about young entrepreneurs in developing countries, authored by Rob Salkowitz (Salkowitz, 2010). The book begins with the story of Suhas Gopinath, the Indian teenage entrepreneur who started his company developing websites for businesses in the United States at the age of 14 (Salkowitz, 2010). Born in 1986, Gopinath began his career as a freelance Web developer when he was 13, using skills he learned while minding the local cyber café in Bangalore. When he decided to found his own company, Globals Inc., he had to register it in California because Indian laws did not permit him to do so. A decade later, Globals Inc. is a multimillion-dollar global company with operations in a dozen countries. Gopinath has been recognized as the world's youngest CEO, with awards from various organizations including the World Economic Forum, the European Parliament, and the International Association for Human Values.

The story got me thinking. At a time when even college graduates are having a hard time finding a desirable job, or any job at all, how could Suhas Gopinath, a teenager from a family without a business tradition in one of the poorest countries on earth, create a job he apparently loves for himself and many others? Why don't the college graduates in developed countries who supposedly have better education and more resources than Gopinath create jobs for themselves?

THE NEED FOR ENTREPRENEURSHIP

Youth unemployment has become an urgent challenge facing the global society. In 2011, nearly 75 million youth aged

1

15 to 24 were unemployed worldwide. The majority of the world's youth (87%) living in developing countries "are often underemployed and working in the informal economy under poor conditions," according to the 2012 *The World Youth Report* of the United Nations (United Nations, 2011). But the situation is not much better in the developed countries. In the 34 member countries of the Organisation for Economic Co-operation and Development (OECD), which include the world's wealthiest and most developed countries, "22.3 million young people—were inactive in the fourth quarter of 2010, neither in jobs nor in education or training" (United Nations, 2011).

Entrepreneurs like Gopinath are what the world wants to solve the unemployment problem. Numerous international organizations have produced reports about the importance of entrepreneurship and issued calls for countries to develop entrepreneurship (Schoof, 2006; World Economic Forum, 2011). The World Economic Forum, for example, has identified entrepreneurship education as the core of its Global Education Initiative (World Economic Forum, 2009, 2011) because "[I]nnovation and entrepreneurship provide a way forward for solving the global challenges of the 21st century, building sustainable development, creating jobs, generating renewed economic growth and advancing human welfare" (World Economic Forum, 2009, p. 7). "Entrepreneurs are recognized as important drivers of economic and social progress, and rapidly growing entrepreneurial enterprises are viewed as important sources of innovation, employment and productivity growth," says another report of the World Economic Forum (World Economic Forum, 2012).

To raise awareness of the importance of entrepreneurship and celebrate entrepreneurs, U.K. Prime Minister Gordon Brown and Carl Schramm, the president and CEO of the Ewing Marion Kauffman Foundation, kicked off the annual Global Entrepreneurship Week (GEW) initiative in 2008. Since then GEW has become "the world's largest celebration of the innovators and job creators who launch startups that bring ideas to life, drive economic growth and expand human welfare" with

115 countries participating (Global Entrepreneurship Week, 2012). In his 2009 Presidential Proclamation of the GEW in the United States, President Barack Obama spoke highly of entrepreneurs: "Throughout our history, American entrepreneurs have been an effective force for innovation at home and around the world. . . . Entrepreneurs are the engine of job creation in America, generating millions of good jobs" (Obama, 2009). The European Roundtable on Entrepreneurship Education wrote in a report:

> Europe is facing challenges in terms of competitiveness as well as economic and sustainable growth. . . . Europe must invest in developing entrepreneurial and innovative skills to build sustainable economic development, create jobs, generate renewed economic growth and advance human welfare. (European Roundtable on Entrepreneurship Education, 2010)

THE REDEFINITION OF ENTREPRENEURSHIP

While Gopinath may epitomize traditional entrepreneurship, that is, the ability to start a business and make a profit, the meaning of entrepreneurship has expanded significantly in its current use. The World Economic Forum defines entrepreneurship as

> a process that results in creativity, innovation and growth. Innovative entrepreneurs come in all shapes and forms; its benefits are not limited to startups, innovative ventures and new jobs. Entrepreneurship refers to an individual's ability to turn ideas into action and is therefore a key competence for all, helping young people to be more creative and self-confident in whatever they undertake. (World Economic Forum, 2009, p. 9)

Entrepreneurs are no longer only those who start a business and try to maximize profits. There are social entrepreneurs who recognize a social problem and apply entrepreneurial principles to achieve social change (Martin & Osberg, 2007). There are intrapreneurs who bring significant innovative changes from within an organization (Swearingen, 2008). There are also policy entrepreneurs, whose enterprise is to bring innovative improvement in policy from within public and government institutions (Harris & Kinney, 2004).

With the expanded definition, entrepreneurs are believed to have more power to solve the complex problems facing human beings and bring prosperity to humanity than governments and international organizations, according to Philip Auerswald, senior fellow in Entrepreneurship of the Kauffman Foundation and associate professor at George Mason University. In his 2012 book *The Coming Prosperity: How Entrepreneurs Are Transforming the Global Economy*, Auerswald argues that "the vast majority of alleged threats to humanity are, in fact, dwarfed by the magnitude of opportunities that exist in the twenty-first century" (Auerswald, 2012b, location 133–136). These opportunities will be harnessed by entrepreneurs, more so than governments, to transform the human society:

> if anything is more naïve than an unquestioning belief in the transformative power of entrepreneurs, it is an unquestioning belief in the power of national governments, international organizations, and multinational corporations to address complex twenty-first century challenges. In many parts of the world where change is most urgently needed, governments are as likely to be a part of the problem as a part of the solution. In such environments, all institutions structured to work through national governments face serious handicaps. The relevance, much less effectiveness, of the UN and the World Bank—the two institutions most clearly tasked in the post–World War II order with addressing global challenges—is less assured today than that of entrepreneurs. (Auerswald, 2012b, location 136–139)

THE MISSING LINK

The world needs entrepreneurs and great entrepreneurs like Henry Ford, Thomas Edison, Steve Jobs, Richard Bronson, and Mark Zuckerberg, who are admired, envied, celebrated, and in great demand. But how come we don't have more of them?

The missing link is "an entrepreneurial mindset—a critical mix of success-oriented attitudes of initiative, intelligent risk-taking, collaboration, and opportunity recognition," says a report by the Aspen Institute Youth Entrepreneurship Strategy Group (Aspen Youth Entrepreneurship Strategy Group, 2008). It is hard to imagine someone without an entrepreneurial mindset to engage in entrepreneurship activities. Moreover, the entrepreneurship mindset as defined by the Aspen Institute is also needed for working in existing businesses and organizations. It is a frustrating and sad irony that with so many unemployed in the world, business leaders are complaining that they cannot find qualified workers (Auerswald, 2012b; Zhao, 2009). "The number of workers with adequate skills has decreased," says the Manpower Group, a global consulting firm with offices in over 80 countries (Manpower Group, 2012).

Why is the "entrepreneurial mindset" missing in our society in general and among our youth in particular?

Our schools don't teach entrepreneurship seems to be a logical answer. It is generally true that "entrepreneurship" has not been part of the formal curriculum in the majority of schools around the world. Even in the United States, a country that has been typically or stereotypically viewed as the land of entrepreneurship, "there is no system in place that offers Entrepreneurship Education as an option for all students" (Aspen Youth Entrepreneurship Strategy Group, 2008, p. 19). As a result, "youth Entrepreneurship Education programs are in place in some communities, but most American youths have little or no access to such training," writes the Aspen Institute Youth Entrepreneurship Strategy Group in its 2008 *Policy Maker's Action Guide* for youth entrepreneurship education

(Aspen Youth Entrepreneurship Strategy Group, 2008). According to a *Survey of Entrepreneurship Education Initiatives* conducted by the Science and Technology Policy Institute, although 18 states in the United States have taken legislative actions to support entrepreneurship education in K–12 schools, some simply require the inclusion of the entrepreneurship concept. "None of these programs has been rigorously evaluated, so beyond the establishment of a program or concept, the impact of these initiatives remains unclear" (Peña, Transue, & Riggieri, 2010, p. 9).

IT'S NOT ABOUT TEACHING ENTREPRENEURSHIP

Thus a seemingly natural step is to teach entrepreneurship formally in schools by making entrepreneurship education part of the curriculum. "The first and most important step would involve state and school district adoption of a formal Entrepreneurship Education curriculum," followed by teacher professional development, community partnerships, and effective and accurate evaluation (Aspen Youth Entrepreneurship Strategy Group, 2008, p. 19). Governments are then called to develop and adopt standards for entrepreneurship education and provide funds to support teacher development so they can teach entrepreneurship to students. "Including Entrepreneurship Education in formal statewide education standards is the first and most important reform that can occur at the state level," recommends the Aspen Institute (Aspen Youth Entrepreneurship Strategy Group, 2008, p. 22). The Science and Technology Policy Institute suggests the U.S. federal government should "assume the role of setting program standards and curricula guidelines for entrepreneurship education" and "creating a national system for accreditation and certification" (Peña et al., 2010, pp. 24–25).

This seemingly natural action to produce more entrepreneurs is unlikely to work. Gopinath apparently did not take an entrepreneurship education course in his school before starting his business. He was not even a good student, according to his mother and the traditional educational criteria. He failed his exams and had to miss classes often in order to run his business. Apparently, it was not his school learning that made him successful in business. It was not his homework and exams that gave him the ability to create value for society and job opportunities for many people globally. Steve Jobs did not take an entrepreneurship course before he started Apple, nor did Bill Gates before starting Microsoft. What's perhaps in common across these entrepreneurs is that they succeeded *despite of*, not because of, their school experiences. Some poorly implemented, standardized, required entrepreneurship education course could have damaged their entrepreneurial activities.

Furthermore "there are no definitive studies that clearly and unequivocally demonstrate the impact and benefits of entrepreneurial education" (Peña et al., 2010, p. 15). In fact, making entrepreneurship education a part of the formal curriculum may do more harm than good. The curriculum standards, guidelines, assessment, and evaluation that will likely be put in place for a formal course or program are antithetical to the entrepreneurial mindset.

The real problem is that our "educational system continues to push students through career services offices around the country toward the same pathways followed by their parents, rather than encouraging students to map out new pathways that correspond to current realities," writes Auerswald (2012a). "Our education system is designed to turn out 'good employees,' not 'good entrepreneurs,'" Tom of Dayton, Ohio, wrote to Steve Strauss, a *USA Today* columnist who specializes in small business and entrepreneurship (Strauss, 2006). Strauss agreed, adding: "We have an education system that was created around the time of the Industrial Revolution when we needed to turn rural kids into urban employees capable of working in assembly line, mass-market factories. As a result, we ended up with a school system focused on rote memorization and measurable, predictable results" (Strauss, 2006).

Entrepreneurs, in the broad sense, are not only a select few. Everyone needs to be entrepreneurial in the 21st century. Entrepreneurs today are the "black-collar workers," a term coined by Auerswald with inspiration from Steve Jobs' black turtleneck (Auerswald, 2012b). A teacher who does not believe we need all to be entrepreneurs asked me the same question that Auerswald answers:

> From where we sit now, it seems improbable that an entire economy could be built of such workers. Where are the drones in this picture? Where are the undifferentiated masses of the unfulfilled? Try asking yourself this question instead: from the standpoint of a 15th-century peasant, how likely is the reality of the present day? . . . Just as former farmers were compelled to convert themselves into blue-collar workers to realize their potential in the economy of the 20th century, so will former factory workers (and retooling economic drones of all types) convert themselves into black-collar workers to realize their potential in the economy of the 21st century. (Auerswald, 2012a)

"Entrepreneurship refers to an individual's ability to turn ideas into action and is therefore a key competence for all, helping young people to be more creative and self-confident in whatever they undertake" (World Economic Forum, 2011, p. 5). The entrepreneurial skills and mindset are similar to the new survival skills in the 21st century discussed in *The Global Achievement Gap: Why Even Our Best Schools Don't Teach the New Survival Skills Our Children Need—And What We Can Do About It,* by Tony Wagner, co-director of the Change Leadership Group at Harvard Graduate of School of Education. The new survival skills—effective communication, curiosity, and critical-thinking skills—"are no longer skills that only the elites in a society must muster; they are essential survival skills for all of us" (Wagner, 2008, p. xxiii). But even our best schools don't teach these skills.

What can and should we do then? What can we learn from Gopinath and his fellow entrepreneurs? Are the Gopinaths born or made? Are they simply great happy accidents, lovely exceptions, or can we find a way to produce more?

TO ENTERPRISE IS HUMAN

The Loss of Entrepreneurship and Creativity

To borrow Duke University engineering professor and prolific author Henry Petroski's notion that "to engineer is human," I suggest to enterprise is human and to create is human. "While educators are currently wrestling with the problem of introducing technology into conventional academic curricula, thus better preparing today's students for life in a world increasingly technological," writes Petroski in his book *To Engineer Is Human: The Role of Failure in Successful Design*, "I believe, and I argue in this essay, that ideas of engineering are in fact in our bones and part of our human nature and experience" (Petroski, 1992, p. vii).

Entrepreneurship is fundamentally about the desire to solve problems creatively. The foundation of entrepreneurship—creativity, curiosity, imagination, risk taking, and collaboration—is, just like the ideas of engineering, "in our bones and part of our human nature and experience." Human beings are born with the desire and potential to create and innovate, to dream and imagine, and to challenge and improve the status quo. We are also born with propensity to be social, to communicate, and to collaborate. For thousands of years, bees have kept the same design of their dwellings, the honeycomb, but the design of human buildings has been changing constantly. "It is the human tastes, resources, and ambitions that do not stay constant" (Petroski, 1992, p. 2). And sometimes, we just like to change things.

The potential can be suppressed or amplified by our experiences. Some experiences enhance our creativity, while others suppress it. Some experiences encourage risk taking, while others make us risk aversive. Some experiences strengthen our desire to ask questions, while others instill compliance. Some experiences foster a mindset of challenging the status quo, while others teach us to follow orders. Human beings are adaptable and our nature malleable. The experiences we have play a significant role in what we become.

Schools are the primary institution for our children besides family, and therefore the primary place that shapes the experiences our children have. There is no definitive research to show to what degree school experiences in general increase or decrease creativity and entrepreneurial capacities because of the differences in definitions and measures of creativity and the differences in the experiences different schools offer (Claxton, Pannells, & Rhoads, 2005). But one well-known longitudinal study by George Land and Beth Jarman found a decline in creativity as children became older. In their 1992 book *Breakpoint and Beyond: Mastering the Future—Today*, Land and Jarman (1992) describe a longitudinal study on creativity beginning in the 1960s. Land administered eight tests of divergent thinking, which measure an individual's ability to envision multiple solutions to a problem. NASA had used these tests to measure the potential for creative work by its employees. When the tests were first given to 1,600 three- to five-year-olds, Land found 98% of them to score at a level called creative genius. But five years later when the same group of children took the tests, only 32% scored at this level and after another five years, the percentage of geniuses declined to 10%. Figure 0.1 illustrates the sharp decline in one measure of creativity as children get older. By 1992, more than 200,000 adults had taken the same tests and only 2% scored at the genius level. The Harvard psychologist Howard Gardner also noted a decline in artistic creativity once children enter school (Gardner, 1982). Tony Wagner also "observed that the longer our children are in school, the less curious they become" (Wagner, 2008, p. xxiii).

While to varying degrees all schools squelch creativity and entrepreneurship (Zhao, 2009), some do so more effectively

Figure 0.1 Decline of Ceativity by Age

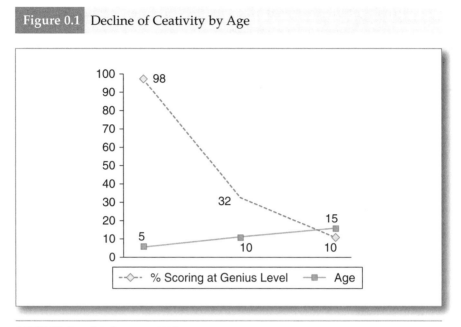

SOURCE: Land & Jarman, 1992.

than others. This partially explains the uneven distribution of entrepreneurial activities across different regions and nations globally. Some countries seem to have more entrepreneurial and creative talents than others. The annual Global Entrepreneurship Monitor (GEM) Survey that tracks various aspects of entrepreneurship activities in over 50 countries shows significant differences in terms of entrepreneurial capabilities and activities across different countries of similar economic conditions (for example, Bosma, Wennekers, & Amorós, 2012; Kelley, Bosma, & Amorós, 2010). The number of patents per capita, an indicator of a nation's innovation endeavors and innovative talents, also varies a great deal across different nations (World Intellectual Property Organization [WIPO], 2007).

What is intriguing is that countries that show a low level of entrepreneurship are countries that have been high performers on international tests. For example, high-scoring countries on the Programme for International Student Assessment (PISA) and the

Trends in International Mathematics and Science Study (TIMSS), such as Singapore, Japan, Korea, and Taiwan, scored much lower than Australia, the United Kingdom, and the United States in the category of perceived entrepreneurship capabilities of the Global Entrepreneurship Monitor Survey in 2011 (Bosma et al., 2012). Correlational analyses show a statistically significant negative relationship between test scores in math, reading, and sciences and aspects of entrepreneurship. Figure 0.2 shows the ranking of 23 countries (regions) that participated in both the 2009 PISA and 2011 Global Entrepreneurship Monitor survey in PISA math performance and reported entrepreneurial capabilities. All 23 countries (regions) are considered developed economies and thus are categorized as "innovation-driven economies" by the GEM study.

Figure 0.2 Ranking by PISA Math Score and Perceived Entrepreneurial Capability

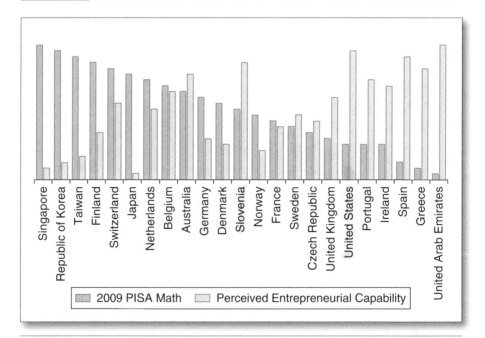

SOURCES: Bosma, Wennekers, & Amorós, 2012; Organisation for Economic Co-operation and Development (OECD), 2010.

This inverse relationship between test scores and entrepreneurship does not necessarily mean high test scores caused the loss of entrepreneurial capabilities or vice versa, but it does suggest that education systems that produce good test scores more often than not have lower entrepreneurship activities and capabilities. It also suggests the possibility that the mechanisms that lead to higher test scores could lead to lower levels of entrepreneurship. The possibility becomes more certain when other evidence, such as differences in educational policy, curriculum, pedagogical practices, and student activities, are taken into consideration. For example, the United States has seen a significant decline in creativity among its youth over the past two decades, which coincides with its waves of educational changes to boost student test scores.

THE DECLINE OF CREATIVITY AND EDUCATION REFORM IN THE UNITED STATES AND NCLB

In July 2010, *Newsweek* published "The Creativity Crisis," an article about the decrease in creativity in the United States. The article cites research by Kyung Hee Kim, an educational psychology professor at the College of William & Mary. Kim analyzed performance of adults and children on a commonly used creativity measure known as the Torrance Tests of Creative Thinking. The results indicate a creativity decrease in the last 20 years in all categories. Fluency scores (a measure of the ability to produce a number of ideas) decreased by 7% from 1990 to 2008, while Originality scores (ability to produce unique and unusual ideas) decreased by 3.74% from 1990 to 1998. Although it remained static between 1998 and 2008, Kim says, "Originality scores have actually significantly decreased, but the decrease has been deflated through the use of outdated scoring lists." Creative strengths (creative personality traits) decreased by 3.16% from 1990 to 1998 and by 5.75% from 1990 to 2008. Elaboration scores (ability to develop and elaborate upon ideas, detailed and reflective thinking, and motivation) decreased by 36.80% from 1984 to 2008. Scores in Abstractness of Titles (ability to produce the thinking process of synthesis and organization, to know what is important) increased until 1998, but decreased by 7.41% from 1998 to 2008. Scores in Resistance to Premature Closure (intellectual curiosity and open-mindedness) decreased by 1.84% from 1998 to 2008 (Britannica Editors, 2010a).

When asked to explain this decline, Kim proposed several societal, home, and school factors. For example, "contemporary parenting styles may create overly programmed lives for children, by overprotecting them and overscheduling them, which has the effect of denying children opportunity to discover for themselves," Kim told editors of the Encyclopedia Britannica. Schools certainly play a significant role. "Teachers claim to value creativity in children, but in fact it is proven that they generally dislike creative behaviors and characteristics in the classroom because they are inconvenient and hard to control" (Britannica Editors, 2010b). Then she talks about the impact of No Child Left Behind (NCLB) on creativity: "NCLB has stifled any interest in developing individual differences, creative and innovative thinking, or individual potential" because:

> Teaching to this test [mandated by NCLB—author] discourages purposeful creativity development and stifles children's creativity in schools. Standardized testing forces emphasis on rote learning instead of critical, creative thinking, and diminishes students' natural curiosity and joy for learning in its own right. Further, NCLB may stifle teachers' creativity because the high pressure to cover the content required to produce passing test scores override the desire (and time) to stimulate children's imagination and curiosity. . . . The standardized testing movement created by NCLB has led to the elimination of content areas and activities, including gifted programs, electives, arts, foreign languages, and elementary science

and recess, which leaves little room for imagination, critical and creative thinking. This may eliminate the opportunities for creative students to release their creative energy in school. . . . Those who preserve and develop their creative abilities despite the odds will be adversely affected. . . . Further, research shows that high school students who exhibit creative personalities are more likely to drop out of school than other students. (Britannica Editors, 2010b)

THE FUTURE OF EDUCATION

Schools in general reduce instead of enhance creativity and the entrepreneurial spirit because they have been designed to prepare good employees. And the qualities of a good employee in the traditional sense are drastically different from what makes a good entrepreneurial worker today. The majority of schools in the world today are facing increasing pressure to produce good employees and thus working hard at what is believed to produce good employees with prescribed standardized curricula, lock-step pacing guides, and standardized tests that encourage memorization and compliance.

The possibility that measures to raise *test scores* or to improve *academic achievement* reduce entrepreneurial capability has significant implications for the directions of education. There is general agreement among policy makers, government and business leaders, educators, parents, and the general public across the world that we need to provide high-quality education to all children so they can be prepared for the future—the globalized world that is constantly and rapidly transformed by technology. There is also an agreement at the conceptual level that a well-prepared citizen of the future needs to be creative, entrepreneurial, and globally competent. As well, agreement exists that the current version of education offered in most countries is not sufficient to meet the needs of the future and reform is necessary.

However, when it comes down to educational policy and practice that actually affect students, there are significant differences. At the system level, standing on one side are the standard-lovers and test-addicts represented by the so-called education reformers championed and backed by government and business leaders in mostly Western developed countries such as the United States, the United Kingdom, Australia, and New Zealand, which traditionally have had a relatively decentralized and less standardized education. Although these countries have generally performed well economically and had more entrepreneurial and creative endeavors, they have not necessarily consistently held top places on international tests. These countries have been in recent years pursuing an educational approach characterized by centralizing curriculum standards, narrowing the school curriculum, increasing the stakes on test scores for teachers and students, and reducing variation in educational pathways for students. *NCLB* and *Race to the Top* of the U.S. federal government and the Common Core State Standards Initiative are good examples of measures pursued by this group.

In stark contrast are the veterans of standards and testing represented by mostly Eastern Asian education systems such as China, Korea, Singapore, Hong Kong, and Japan, which have had a long tradition of fairly centralized and standardized education. These countries have over the past few decades evolved into new economic powerhouses and have consistently held top places on the international test score league tables. These countries have begun to travel down a different path characterized by less centralization and standardization, less emphasis on test scores, broader curriculum, more autonomy for schools and teachers, and more choices for students.

Which group will eventually win is not certain, but existing evidence suggests at least that tightly controlled standardized curriculum, a uniformly executed teaching approach, narrowly prescribed and carefully planned learning activities, and rigorously watched and frequently administered high-stakes tests do not produce creative and entrepreneurial talents, although they may lead to higher test scores. I am not certain about the winner because I am not sure how far and fast can the latter group move away from their tradition of standards and testing, while I very much appreciate their desire and conviction. I am not certain also because I don't know how much more evidence of damage the Western group needs to see before they may want to stop and rethink.

This book is written in the spirit of showing my appreciation of and support for the efforts that have been undertaken by China, Korea, Singapore, Hong Kong, and other systems that have seen the damages of standards and testing. It is also written to provide more evidence and reason to help convince the new converts to standards and testing that the road has been traveled before, and it does not lead to the future—according to those who have been there.

To prepare global, creative, and entrepreneurial talents, that is, everyone in the future, education should at first not harm any child who aspires to do so or suppress their curiosity, imagination, and desire to be different by imposing upon him or her contents and skills judged to be good for him or her by an external agency and thus depriving of the opportunities to explore and express on their own. In other words, we should at least allow Suhas Gopinath and the likes to exist without punishing them or locking them up in a classroom in the name of helping them to become successful. The most desirable education, of course, is one that enhances human curiosity and creativity, encourages risk taking, and cultivates the entrepreneurial spirit in the context of globalization.

This book is about the why and how of the most desirable education.

PLAN OF THE BOOK

The book includes 10 chapters.

Chapter 1 presents a summary of the concerted efforts toward standardization and homogenization of learning experiences undertaken by governments and international organizations. It discusses the intentions, outcomes, and why these efforts are futile in saving the past and harmful to the future.

Chapter 2 presents arguments of "mass entrepreneurship," or reasons for why everyone needs to and can become global, creative, and entrepreneurial. It brings evidence from a broad array of sources to show that dramatic population increase, accumulation of wealth, technological advances, and economic globalization have created a new world that demands and supports everyone to become entrepreneurs or entrepreneurial employees.

Chapter 3 presents the essential elements of entrepreneurial capabilities or the entrepreneurial spirit. It also follows the debate about whether entrepreneurs are born or made and suggests that they are probably both and more with evidence from research in entrepreneurship, economics, cognitive psychology, and evolutionary psychology.

Chapter 4 connects entrepreneurship to education. Starting with the observation that commonly believed education giants such as China and Singapore are entrepreneurial and creative dwarfs, this chapter studies the test score gap and the entrepreneurship gap. By analyzing the inverse relationship between test scores on international assessments and entrepreneurship capacities, this chapter presents evidence to show that high test scores come at the cost of creativity and the entrepreneurial spirit.

Chapter 5 uses education in China and the United States as a case study to further illustrate how an education that produces high test scores does damage to creativity and entrepreneurship. Through microlevel analyses of educational policies and practices, this chapter shows that the "flaws" in the U.S. education system happen to be the mechanisms that lead to the successes of Steve Jobs and Lady Gaga, while what helps China's students in Shanghai to be No. 1 in the PISA rankings is also what causes its lacking of innovative entrepreneurial giants. However, the U.S. capability to produce more creative entrepreneurs is an accident, an imperfect execution of an old education paradigm that is shared by China and other countries.

Chapter 6 discusses how we must have a paradigm shift in order to turn the happy accidents of the U.S. education system into a designed approach. The chapter contrasts two educational paradigms that exist: the employment-oriented vs. the child-centered. Although the child-centered paradigm has existed for a long time and has accumulated abundant evidence to prove its success, it has not been widely adopted. The chapter discusses why we need the paradigm shift and the obstacles to making the shift.

Chapters 7, 8, and 9 together present the components of the new paradigm: the what, the how, and the where. Chapter 7 uses Summerhill School in England as a case of the principle of student autonomy in deciding what learning experience they have in a school. It brings evidence to show why respecting student voice, self-governance, and passion are not only morally right but also educationally sound.

Chapter 8 uses High Tech High in San Diego as an example to show engaging students in creating products is an effective way to cultivate creativity and entrepreneurship. The chapter discusses the different models and incarnations of project-based learning and proposes a new concept—product-oriented learning—as a way to prepare the talents we need. It also makes specific recommendations about implementing product-oriented learning.

Chapter 9 uses the Cherwell School in England and Oxford Community Schools in the United States as examples of why and how students can become global entrepreneurs and schools global enterprises. This chapter discusses the components of global competency for entrepreneurs and different ways schools can become global enterprises that not only provide rich global experiences for their students but also take advantage of global resources to provide a better education for their students and students in other places.

Chapter 10 presents the triad model of education that unifies the three principles discussed in the previous chapters.

The chapter proposes a comprehensive list of indicators of a world class school ready to prepare their students to become global, creative, and entrepreneurial.

References

Aspen Youth Entrepreneurship Strategy Group. (2008). *Youth Entrepreneurship Education in America: A Policy Maker's Action Guide.* Washington DC: The Aspen Institute.

Auerswald, P. (2012a, March 11). Bliss is on the way: Black-collar workers and the case for economic optimism. *Good.* Retrieved April 5, 2012, from http://m.good.is/post/bliss-is-on-the-way -the-case-for-economic-optimism

Auerswald, P. (2012b). *The coming prosperity: How entrepreneurs are transforming the global economy.* New York, NY: Oxford University Press.

Bosma, N., Wennekers, S., & Amorós, J. E. (2012). *Global entrepreneurship monitor: 2011 extended report: Entrepreneurs and entrepreneurial employees across the globe.* London, England: Global Entrepreneurship Research Association.

Britannica Editors. (2010a, April 20). The decline of creativity in the United States: 5 questions for educational psychologist Kyung Hee Kim. Retrieved from http://www.britannica.com /blogs/2010/10/the-decline-of-creativity-in-the-united-states -5-questions-for-educational-psychologist-kyung-hee-kim/

Britannica Editors. (2010b, April 20). Explaining the decline of creativity in American children: A reply to readers. Retrieved from http://www.britannica.com/blogs/2010/12/explaining -the-decline-of-creativity-in-american-children-a-reply-to-readers/

Claxton, A. F., Pannells, T. C., & Rhoads, P. A. (2005). Developmental trends in the creativity of school-age children. *Creativity Research Journal, 17*(4), 327–335.

European Roundtable on Entrepreneurship Education. (2010). Manifesto. *Global Education Initiative.* Retrieved April 5, 2012, from http://www3.weforum.org/docs/WEF_GEI_European Roundtable_Manifesto_2010.pdf

Gardner, H. (1982). *Art, mind, and brain: A cognitive approach to creativity.* New York, NY: Basic Books.

Global Entrepreneurship Week. (2012). About. *Global Entrepreneurship Week.* Retrieved April 4, 2012, from http://www.unleashingideas .org/about

Harris, M., & Kinney, R. (Eds.). (2004). *Innovation and entrepreneurship in state and local government.* Lanham, MA: Lexington Books.

Kelley, D. J., Bosma, N., & Amorós, J. E. (2010). *Global entrepreneurship monitor.* London, England: Global Entrepreneurship Research Association.

Land, G. T., & Jarman, B. (1992). *Breakpoint and beyond: Mastering the Future—Today.* New York, NY: Harper Business.

Manpower Group. (2012). *How to navigate the human age: Increasing demand for better skills assessment and match for better results.* Milwaukee, WI: Author.

Martin, R. L., & Osberg, S. (2007). Social entrepreneurship: The case for definition. *Stanford Social Innovation Review, 2007,* 29–39.

Obama, B. (2009, November 19). Presidential proclamation—National Entrepreneurship Week. Retrieved April 5, 2012, from http://www.whitehouse.gov/the-press-office/presidential -proclamation-national-entrepreneurship-week

Organisation of Economic Co-operation and Development (OECD). (2010). OECD Programme for International Student Assessment (PISA). Retrieved January 10, 2010, from http://www.pisa.oecd .org/pages/0,2987,en_32252351_32235731_1_1_1_1_1,00.html

Peña, V., Transue, M., & Riggieri, A. (2010). *A survey of entrepreneurship education initiatives.* Washington, DC: Institute for Defense Analyses, Science and Technology Policy Institute.

Petroski, H. (1992). *To engineer is human: The role of failure in successful design.* New York, NY: Vintage Books.

Salkowitz, R. (2010). *Young world rising: How youth, technology, and entrepreneurship are changing the world from the bottom up.* Hoboken, NJ: Wiley.

Schoof, U. (2006). *Stimulating youth entrepreneurship: Barriers and incentives to enterprise start-ups by young people.* Geneva, Switzerland: International Labor Organization.

Strauss, S. (2006, June 26). Education for entrepreneurs. *USA Today.* Retrieved April 8, 2012, from http://www.usatoday.com /money/smallbusiness/columnist/strauss/2006-06-26 -education_x.htm

Swearingen, J. (2008, April 10). Great intrapreneurs in business history. Retrieved January 14, 2012, from http://www.cbsnews .com/8301-505125_162-51196888/great-intrapreneurs-in -business-history/

United Nations. (2011, November 24). The world youth report. Retrieved April 8, 2012, from http://www.unworldyouthreport

.org/index.php?option=com_k2&view=itemlist&layout=category&
task=category&id=1&Itemid=67

Wagner, T. (2008). *The global achievement gap: Why even our best schools don't teach the new survival skills our children need—and what we can do about it.* New York, NY: Basic Books.

World Economic Forum. (2009). *Educating the next wave of entrepreneurs: Unlocking entrepreneurial capabilities to meet the global challenges of the 21st century.* Geneva, Switzerland: Author.

World Economic Forum. (2011). *Unlocking entrepreneur capabilities to meet the global challenges of the 21st century: Final report on the entrepreneurship education work stream.* Geneva, Switzerland: Author.

World Economic Forum. (2012). Global entrepreneurship. *World Economic Forum.* Retrieved April 5, 2012, from http://www .weforum.org/issues/global-entrepreneurship

World Intellectual Property Organization (WIPO). (2007). *WIPO patent report: Statistics on worldwide patent activity (2007 edition).* Geneva, Switzerland: World Intellectual Property Organization.

Zhao, Y. (2009). *Catching up or leading the way: American education in the age of globalization.* Alexandria, VA: ASCD.

1

The Wrong Bet

Why Common Curriculum and Standards Won't Help

Education is what remains after one has forgotten what one has learned in school.

—Albert Einstein

In the books lies the House of Gold; in the books lies the Beautiful Wife you desire.

—Song Dynasty Emperor Zhao Heng

June 2, 2010, was a symbolically big day for American education. From this day on, the United States of America theoretically and technically ended its history of no national curriculum, for on this day, a national curriculum was born with the official launch of the Common Core State Standards (Common Core) by the National Governors Association (NGA) and the Council of Chief State School Officers (CCSSO). The press conference was held at Peachtree Ridge High School in Suwanee, Georgia, a nice suburb of Atlanta. Why this newly built popular suburban school with little poverty and excellent facilities was picked as the launch site is unknown, but the cast of participants was masterfully chosen to represent the broad range of support for the

Common Core: Governors Sonny Perdue (Georgia) and Jack Markell (Delaware) for political leaders; state education chiefs Steven Paine (West Virginia) and Eric Smith (Florida) for state-level education leaders; Randi Weingarten, president of the American Federation of Teachers (AFT), and Lily Eskelsen, vice president of the National Education Association (NEA), for teacher unions; Leah Luke, Wisconsin Teacher of the Year, for teachers; Andres Alonso, CEO of Baltimore Public Schools, for local education leaders; Byron Garrett, CEO of the national Parent-Teacher Association (PTA), for parents; and Steve Rohleder, an executive of consulting firm Accenture, for business (National Governors Association Center for Best Practices [NGA Center] & Council of Chief State School Officers, 2010).

This selection of participants reflects the political smartness of the proponents of the Common Core. For fear of political resistance that stems from the deep-rooted suspicion of federal encroachment of state rights in education, they have been very careful not to call their initiative "national standards" or "national curriculum" while working very hard to create a national curriculum. They have avoided using any federal funds to develop the standards and repeatedly emphasized the role states have played in the process. "The year-long process was led by governors and chief state school officers in 48 states, 2 territories and the District of Columbia," stated the press release of the event (National Governors Association Center for Best Practices [NGA Center] & Council of Chief State School Officers, 2010). From the very beginning, the initiative has been suggested to be state led and demanded by a broad spectrum of stakeholders, and the participants at the launch event reflected that breadth. In that spirit, the Common Core initiative website features a large collection of videos and statements of support from representatives of virtually all sectors of America.

But the avoidance of "national" in the name of the initiative is merely a thin mask that cannot hide the intention of the initiative to create a national curriculum for the United States, nor can it deny the fact of the involvement of the federal government in helping making them the core of American children's education diet. The fact that 45 states and the District of Columbia have adopted these standards and are pouring a tremendous amount of resources to implement them suggests unequivocally that America has more than embarked on the journey toward a national curriculum. The nearly $5 billion federal Race to the Top program has without question served to bait many states to adopt the Common Core by making adopting "common standards" a prerequisite for application (U.S. Department of Education, 2009). To reinforce the intention, the U.S. Department of Education required that "a State must have already adopted college- and career-ready standards in reading/language arts and mathematics" if a state wished to be relieved of the unrealistic expectations of No Child Left Behind (NCLB) (The White House, 2011).

The Common Core State Standards are not just academic standards. They are quickly evolving into curriculum and assessment. With $330 million of Race to the Top money, all but five states formed two consortia intended to design common assessments for the Common Core. When developed, such common assessment will no doubt drive the nation's schools to teach to the Common Core. Moreover, with an additional $15.8 million, the two consortia have announced plans to provide curriculum resources, instructional materials, and professional development for teachers to teach to the Common Core (Gewertz, 2011).

The release of the standards on June 2, 2010, was not a huge news item, judging from the lack of major media coverage of the event, but it sent the majority of American schools on an unprecedented journey—a journey toward a common, almost national, curriculum. It "marks the conclusion of the development of the Common Core State Standards and signals the start of the adoption and implementation process by the states," announced the press release about the June 2 event by NGA and CCSSO (National Governors Association Center for Best Practices [NGA Center] & Council of Chief State School Officers, 2010). The journey will be expensive. While no one knows exactly what the cost will be, "based on a range of state estimates, a reasonable estimate of the total nation-wide cost 'would be $30 billion,'" writes Rachel Sheffield (2011). The Pioneer Institute, a Boston-based think tank, esti-mated that over seven years, the national implementation of the Common Core to be $15.8 billion across participating states. "This constitutes a 'mid-range' estimate that only addresses the basic expenditures required for implementation of the new standards" (AccountabilityWorks, 2012, p. 1).

Why is America, a traditionally extremely decentralized education system with some 15,000 school districts and a con-stitution that delegates the responsibility of education to its 50 states, putting so much resource, at a time of economic recession, into a national curriculum? More important, how could such an effort have garnered so much support in a nation that has long valued local control of education and worked to limit the reach of the federal government?

"To compete successfully in the global economy" is the answer given in the Mission Statement of the Common Core Initiative:

> The Common Core State Standards provide a consistent, clear understanding of what students are expected to learn, so teachers and parents know what they need to do to help them. The standards are designed to be robust and relevant to the real world, reflecting the knowledge and skills that our young people need for success in college and careers. With American students fully prepared for the future, our communities will be best positioned to compete successfully in the global economy. (Common Core State Standards Initiative, 2011b)

The Common Core standards are purportedly going to make all students ready for college and career in the global economy by addressing three ills that have long plagued American education: equity, quality, and efficiency (Common Core, 2009; Goertz, 2010; Mathis, 2010). "We need standards to

ensure that all students, no matter where they live, are prepared for success in postsecondary education and the workforce. Common standards will help ensure that students are
receiving a high quality education consistently, from school to
school and state to state" (Common Core State Standards
Initiative, 2011a). Common standards are also needed because
they "provide a greater opportunity to share experiences and
best practices within and across states that will improve our
ability to best serve the needs of students" (Common Core
State Standards Initiative, 2011a). Furthermore, they make test
results across schools in different places more comparable,
thus making it easier to hold schools and teachers more
accountable for learning (Tienken & Zhao, 2010; Zhao, 2009).
Most important, the Common Core standards are supposedly
internationally benchmarked so that they embody the highest
expectation for students. "The Common Core State Standards
have been built from the best and highest state standards in
the country. They are evidence-based, aligned with college
and work expectations, include rigorous content and skills,
and are informed by other top performing countries"
(Common Core State Standards Initiative, 2011a).

NATIONAL HOMOGENIZATION

Increased Centralized Prescription of Student Learning

The Common Core State Standards Initiative represents the
increasing trend of national homogenization of student learning in the world. The homogenization is achieved through
increased national control of what children should learn. Such
control is exercised through three interconnected measures:
(1) the identification of core subjects, (2) the development of
centralized curriculum standards, and (3) the use of high-
stakes testing to enforce standards of core academic subjects.

The movement toward more central government control of
student learning is evidenced in both traditionally centralized

education systems and traditionally decentralized systems. Roughly speaking, there are two types of educational systems in the world. The first has a central government education authority that prescribes and enforces what students should learn through national or state curriculum and assessment programs. China, Singapore, and Korea are examples of this first type. Most of the world's education systems fall into this category. The second type has no national control of student learning experiences, leaving much of the curriculum decision to local education authorities. The local can be instantiated at the state or provincial level. In some contexts, the local has been defined in an even more granular or grass-roots policy grid that places the determinative decision making at the community or even school level. The United States, Canada, and Australia are traditionally the prime examples of the second category.

While some of the educational systems that have traditionally practiced national centralized curricula have attempted to decentralize parts of their curricula, the proportion remains small and the extent of success uncertain (Zhao, 2009). In comparison, efforts to develop centralized curriculum in traditionally decentralized educational systems are gaining momentum. As a result, the number of decentralized education systems, which was small to begin with, is quickly dwindling.

Australia is a telling example. On December 9, 2010, Australia marked a turning point in its educational history with the endorsement by Australian education ministers of a national curriculum that includes content descriptions for Foundation to Year 10 in English, mathematics, science, and history (McGaw, 2010). To be expanded to include other subjects, the "Australian Curriculum sets out what all young Australians are to be taught, and the expected quality of that learning as they progress through schooling." The rationale behind the Australian Curriculum, according to the Australian Curriculum Assessment and Reporting Authority (ACARA), are similar to that in the United States: equity, efficiency, and quality for all students "to compete successfully in the global economy":

1. School and curriculum authorities can collaborate to ensure high quality teaching and learning materials are available for all schools.

2. Greater attention can be devoted to equipping young Australians with those skills, knowledge and capabilities necessary to enable them to effectively engage with and prosper in society, compete in a globalised world and thrive in the information-rich workplaces of the future.

3. There will be greater consistency for the country's increasingly mobile student and teacher population. (Australian Curriculum Assessment and Reporting Authority, 2010)

Countries that already have a more flexibly defined national curriculum have been working on standards to specify in more detail what students should learn at what grade level. For example, New Zealand, which had a more flexible national curriculum framework, published its national standards in 2010. The national standards "set clear expectations that students need to meet in reading, writing, and mathematics in the first eight years at school" (Ministry of Education [NZ], 2011). They describe specifically what students should know and be able to do at different points of their schooling. And the reason:

National Standards are a tool to help teachers and schools understand the expected levels of achievement at stage/ year-appropriate levels, know how to measure the achievement of each student in relation to the expectations, and to improve teaching and learning for better student learning and progress in all areas of the curriculum. (Ministry of Education [NZ], 2010)

Another example is England. England is in the midst of another round of review of its national curriculum, initially established in 1988 (Department for Education, 2011; Oates, 2010). More specification and focus are what is needed, according to Michael Gove, England's secretary of state for Education. "While other countries have developed coherent national curricula that allow for the steady accumulation of knowledge and conceptual understanding, our National Curriculum has, sadly, lost much of its initial focus," writes Gove in the Foreword of a report on the review of the national curriculum by Tim Oates of Cambridge Assessment (Oates, 2010). "What is crucial is first identifying the crucial concepts and ideas that each year group should learn," he adds.

The objectives of this round of review of the English national curriculum are many, but international comparison and efficiency feature prominently:

- ensure that the content of our National Curriculum compares favourably with the most successful international curricula in the highest performing jurisdictions, reflecting the best collective wisdom we have about how children learn and what they should know;
- set rigorous requirements for pupil attainment, which measure up to those in the highest performing jurisdictions in the world;
- enable parents to understand what their children should be learning throughout their school career and therefore to support their education. (Department for Education, 2011)

In a nutshell, these efforts, if successful, will not only prescribe what students learn, but also when they should learn what. Enforced with high-stakes assessment, either for individual students or for schools, these common standards and curricula in essence push teachers to ration learning to all students (Booher-Jennings, 2006). In the pursuit of efficiency, equity, and national consistency, these standards and curricula essentially homogenize children's learning, serving the same educational diet within a nation.

GLOBAL HOMOGENIZATION: INTERNATIONAL BENCHMARKING

The attempt to homogenize children's learning goes beyond national borders and is becoming global. England's objective to ensure the content of its national curriculum "compares favourably with the most successful international curricula in the highest performing jurisdictions" is a common theme across the various national curriculum and standards efforts. International benchmarking, that is "the alignment of standards, instruction, professional development and assessment to those of the highest-performing countries" (Education Commission of the States [ECS], 2008, p. 5), has become the buzzword among educational reformers around the world. The U.S. Common Core initiative, the Australian Curriculum, and England's National Curriculum review all strive to create standards and curriculum that match the best in the world.

In the United States, the nation's state education policy makers pledged to use international benchmarking as a way to make the "efforts to raise standards, advance teaching quality, and improve low-performing schools" more effective (National Governors Association, Council of Chief State School Officers, & Achieve, Inc., 2008, p. 6). A report jointly released by the National Governors Association (NGA), Council of Chief State School Officers (CCSSO), and Achieve, Inc. called on state leaders to take five actions to ensure a world class education for American students. The No. 1 recommended action is to "upgrade state standards by adopting a common core of internationally benchmarked standards in math and language arts for grades K–12 to ensure that students are equipped with the necessary knowledge and skills to be globally competitive" (National Governors Association, Council of Chief State School Officers, & Achieve, Inc., 2008, p. 24). Writing about the Australian curriculum, Barry McGaw, chair of the Australian body that oversees the development of its national curriculum, says, "The Australian curriculum has been benchmarked against curricula in high-performing countries to ensure that we expect no less of our students than they do of theirs" (McGaw, 2010).

International benchmarking has effectually the result of developing a globally homogenous learning experience for all students. When the content and standards are aligned across different countries, students learn the same thing at the same time. And when professional development and pedagogy are aligned, teachers are asked to deliver the same content in the same method. When international assessments are applied, nations have even more reason to teach the same thing to their children.

This push toward a globally homogenous education has one obvious rationale: global competition, as argued by the National Center for Education and the Economy (NCEE) in its 2007 report *Tough Choices or Tough Times:*

> The best employers the world over will be looking for the most competent, most creative, and most innovative people on the face of the earth and will be willing to pay them top dollar for their services. This will be true not just for top professionals and managers, but up and down the length and breadth of the workforce. Those countries that produce the most important new products and services can capture a premium in world markets that will enable them to pay high wages to their citizens. (The New Commission on the Skills of the American Workforce, 2007)

International assessment programs have added fuel to the global homogenization movement in the new age of globalization by showing the relative standings of different nations. While the International Association for the Evaluation of Educational Achievement (IEA) has been conducting international comparative studies in mathematics and sciences regularly, and literacy and other subjects occasionally, for half a century, the newly developed Programme for International Student Assessment (PISA) by the Organisation for Economic Co-operation and Development (OECD) has come to the scene with even more force. Both IEA's Trends in International Mathematics and Science Study (TIMSS) and OECD's PISA have captured the attention of national and local education leaders, researchers, and the media. Because many view the results of TIMSS and PISA as indicators of national education quality and global competitiveness, TIMSS and PISA are now viewed as the gold standards of education. The relative standing of each nation on these assessments is automatically equated with the quality of education in each nation and consequently the nation's future competitiveness in the global economy. A recent report by OECD makes the direct and explicit connection between PISA scores and economic gains:

> A modest goal of having all OECD countries boost their average PISA scores by 25 points over the next 20 years . . . implies an aggregate gain of OECD GDP of USD 115 trillion over the lifetime of the generation born in 2010. Bringing all countries up to the average performance of Finland, OECD's best performing education system in PISA, would result in gains in the order of USD 260 trillion. (Hanushek & Woessmann, 2010, p. 6)

It should then come as no surprise that nations want to improve their PISA scores. The best way to improve performance on the PISA is then naturally to align one's curriculum and standards with the top-performing nations on the PISA.

International assessments such as PISA and TIMSS have certainly served as a major motivator for the homogenization of curriculum, observed Professor Geoffrey Howson of the University of Southampton in the case of the English National Curriculum a decade ago, saying that it "was probably expedited by the nation's poor showing in the Second International

Math Study (SIMS) and in similar, smaller, studies undertaken in the 1980s" (Howson, 2001, p. 261). Joel Spring, a prolific education author and professor at the City University of New York, made a similar observation about the role of PISA:

> OECD has played a major role in the global standardization of education through its assessment program PISA. By becoming an international standard, PISA has the direct potential for determining the curriculum content in the areas tested, which are mathematics, reading, and science. (Spring, 2008, p. 62)

Moreover, international studies have helped identifying curriculum and standards to align with. Top ranking nations in TIMSS and PISA have been viewed as nations with excellent educational systems that are worth emulating (Common Core, 2009; National Research Council, 1999). A recent report by the National Center for Education and the Economy, entitled *Standing on the Shoulders of Giants: An American Agenda for Education Reform,* called for learning from Canada (Ontario), China (Shanghai), Finland, Japan, and Singapore because they are the world's education giants, at least according to their performance on the PISA (Tucker, 2011). And TIMSS held Singapore, Korea, and Japan as the world's example of educational excellence due to their outstanding showing. The Singaporean math curriculum, in particular, has been the target of alignment by many countries.

The outcome of international benchmarking is inevitably a globally homogenized learning experience for all students. And if all goes as planned by the advocates, students will be taught the same thing at the same pace by the same methods. This is of course a stretch given the diversity of educational systems around the world, but it is certainly a goal of many governments and policy makers. Regardless of the degree to which policy makers can successfully align their own nations' education to top-performing nations on PISA or TIMSS, various governments are working diligently toward the goal that one day all their students will enjoy internationally benchmarked content, be held to internationally benchmarked standards and expectations, and be taught with internationally benchmarked teaching methods. And that is, according to the advocates, a world class education, which will prepare their students "to succeed in the global economy."

PLACING THE BET

The Core Subjects

The efforts to define what students should learn are not a free exercise of governments or well-intentioned policy makers. They have cost—huge cost. It costs money to define and develop curriculum and standards. It costs political and social capital to debate what should be included for what age. Once developed, it costs money and energy to have them adopted and implemented by schools and teachers. It costs to develop assessments and other mechanisms to ensure that schools and teachers teach accordingly, students learn accordingly, and parents provide assistance accordingly. There is also the opportunity cost. When all energy and resources are poured into defining and enforcing the common curriculum and standards, nothing is left to pursue anything else.

But it is not the money, energy, or political and social capital that should be of most concern, although they are so high that they cannot be ignored. The most important is the children's future. Asking a child to devote 12 years of his life to the study of something is akin to placing a bet for his future. It is a promise to the innocent child and his parents that if the prescribed curriculum is mastered, he will have a bright future because he will be ready for college and career and able to succeed in the global economy. What if the bet is misplaced and the promise broken? That cost is unbearable and can never be recovered.

The stakes are high; how good is the bet then?

Before questioning the bet, a description of what exactly the advocates are betting on, that is, what is included in the internationally benchmarked curriculum and standards, is in order. *Mathematics, literacy/reading,* and *science* are the primary subjects most countries have placed their bet on. In the United States, the Common Core State Standards Initiative has put out standards in mathematics and English Language Arts as the core for all students. Science is in the works. In England, "the core subjects of English, mathematics and science will remain subjects within the National Curriculum" (Department for Education, 2011), meaning that the inclusion of these three subjects are not subject to discussion during the review and will form the core of the new national curriculum. The Australian Curriculum pledges to include a variety of subjects but for now includes English, mathematics, science, and history, to be "followed by geography, languages, the arts, economics, business, civics and citizenship, health and physical education, and information and communication technology and design and technology" (Australian Curriculum Assessment and Reporting Authority, 2010).

While many countries may have on paper a broad range of subjects included in their national curriculum, what carries the most stake become the core subjects. For example, Singapore's primary education curriculum is comprised of languages, mathematics, science, social studies, arts and crafts, and music (Ministry of Education, 2011). But what really matters are languages (English and mother tongue), mathematics, and science because they are the subjects of the Primary School Leaving Exam (PSLE) that determines what type of secondary school a child can enter, and subsequently their future (Singapore Examinations and Assessment Board, 2011). The same is true for Korea. While students may be offered a wide range of subjects, the core subjects required of all students and counted the most on the high-stakes Korean College Scholastic Ability Test are Korean language, mathematics, and English (as a foreign language). Over a dozen other subjects in social studies and sciences are offered as electives (Korea Institute for Curriculum and Evaluation, 2011). China follows the same practice. A broad range of subjects are offered in the national curriculum, but the College Entrance Exam, which practically determines one's future life, tests Chinese, English, and mathematics as the core subjects for all students, while students can pick and choose other subjects.

The popular international assessments such as PISA and TIMSS further affirm the core status of math, literacy/reading, and science. PISA tests 15-year-olds' abilities in mathematics, science, and reading, while TIMSS, as its name tells, tests mathematics and science. IEA, the same organization that offers TIMSS, also conducts the Progress in International Reading Literacy Study (PIRLS).

In fairness, advocates of internationally benchmarked standards are intelligent people with good intentions. They recognize that a child's education should be much more than the core subjects, but what they fail to recognize is the reality that the subjects that carry the most stakes for students and schools are the ones that receive the most attention and resources. Other subjects become peripheral and disposable. It has also been argued that the core curriculum only prescribes the essential knowledge and skills and should be the foundational knowledge and skills a child needs, thus it is not the ceiling, rather the floor. Unfortunately, due to the differentiated status and stakes, the floor usually becomes the ceiling. The basic becomes the ultimate goal. This is what has been referred to as *curriculum narrowing.*

Curriculum narrowing happens on two levels. First, when high stakes are attached to a limited number of subjects, they take precedence over other subjects. Consequently, time and efforts are taken away from other subjects in order to ensure the high-stakes or core subjects are taught well. There is mounting evidence that NCLB has caused widespread reduction of opportunities for students to learn subjects besides the assessed math and reading (McMurrer, 2007, 2008). Although technically NCLB does not impose a national curriculum or national standards, it forced states to use common assessments in math and reading to hold schools accountable. Thus, in order to ensure that their students performed well on the common assessments, schools increased instructional time for math and reading and reduced time for other subjects such as arts, music, social studies, science, and even lunch and recess (McMurrer, 2007, 2008). A study by the Center on Education Policy (CEP) published in 2007 found that five years after the implementation of NCLB, over 60% of school districts reported that they have increased instructional time for math and English language arts, while 44% reported that they have reduced time for other subjects or activities such as social studies, science, art and music, physical education, and lunch and/or recess. The decrease was significant: an average of 32% in total instructional time devoted to these subjects (McMurrer, 2007). Table 1.1 summarizes the findings of the CEP study about decreases in instructional time devoted to subjects that are not tested under NCLB since the implementation of NCLB. As Table 1.1 suggests, while instructional time devoted to non-NCLB subjects decreased across the board, the decrease was more significant in school districts that had difficulty meeting the NCLB mandates.

A separate study by the Council for Basic Education (CBE) had similar findings by surveying school principals in 2004, only two years after the implementation of NCLB. The study found that three-quarters of surveyed principals reported increases in instructional time for math and English language arts, 25% reported decreases in time for the arts, and 33% anticipated future decreases (Zastrow & Janc, 2004).

The second level of curriculum narrowing happens within the "favored" subjects. Teaching to the test and learning to test, that is, teach and learn only what is likely to be tested, in the formats most likely presented on the tests, have been frequently observed around the world. China's education has been officially labeled a "test-oriented" education and so has Korea's (Zhao, 2009). In the United States, a CEP study found that NCLB has compelled most school districts to narrow their reading and math curricula to what is covered on the state tests (McMurrer, 2007). The study found that 84% of districts reported that they changed their curriculum

Table 1.1 Decreasing Instructional Time for Non-NCLB Subjects in Elementary Schools Since NCLB (2001–2006)

Subjects	Percentage of Districts Decreasing Time		Average Decrease in Minutes Per Week	
	Districts With No Identified School	Districts With Identified School*	Districts With No Identified School	Districts With Identified School*
Social Studies	31%	51%	70	90
Sciences	23%	43%	67	94
Art & Music	12%	30%	55	61
Physical Education	7%	14%	32	57
Lunch	6%	4%	**	**
Recess	19%	22%	47	60

SOURCE: McMurrer, 2007, Table 4.

*Districts that had at least one school identified for improvement, corrective action, or restructuring under NCLB.

**Sample size too small to allow reporting.

"somewhat" or "to a great extent" to put greater emphasis on tested content in elementary level reading: 79% in middle school, and 76% in high school. A similar pattern was found in math: 81% of districts changed their curriculum at the elementary and middle school level to emphasize tested content and skills, and 78% in high school math.

Classroom instruction has been transformed into test preparation. Studies found that since the implementation of NCLB, rigid curriculum objectives and mechanistic preparation for state standardized testing hijacked curricular diversity and pedagogical exploration and flexibility. "Teachers felt compelled to match closely what they taught to what would be tested and worried about how well aligned the district curriculum was with state test's content, language, and format" (Valli & Buese, 2007, p. 531). Consequently, instructional quality and opportunities to access a diverse curriculum deteriorate. Cognitively complex teaching becomes more basic-skill oriented and students ultimately become less cognitively nimble. Another study by CEP on the influence of federal and state accountability polices on curriculum and instruction in Rhode Island, Illinois, and Washington found classroom instruction to be focused on test preparation, and teachers generally focused their instruction on content they thought most likely to be tested (Srikantaiah & Kober, 2009).

As a result, what is prescribed as the core subjects truly becomes the core and in many cases the only thing that truly matters to students, teachers, and schools. A broad curriculum remains simply on paper, as exemplified by England's national curriculum experiment. England replaced a largely locally controlled curriculum with a national curriculum in the early 1990s. The curriculum is broader than math and literacy including many other subjects, but only math, literacy, and science are considered core subjects and attached more significance through testing. According to a recent report receiving heavy media coverage, the national curriculum has essentially deprived public school children in England of a real education. The report, titled *The Cambridge Primary*

Review, summarizes the problems of the national curriculum, among them are

- The loss, for whatever reason, of the principle of children's entitlement to a broad, balanced, and rich curriculum, and the marginalization, in particular, of the arts, the humanities and—latterly—science.
- The test-induced regression to a valuing of memorization and recall over understanding and enquiry, and to a pedagogy which rates transmission more important than the pursuit of knowledge in its wider sense.
- The use of a narrow spectrum of the curriculum as a proxy for the quality of the whole, and the loss of breadth and balance across and within subjects as a result of the pressures of testing, especially at the upper end of the primary school.
- The continuing and demonstrably mistaken assumption that high standards in "the basics" can be achieved only by marginalizing much of the rest of the curriculum. (Alexander, 2009, p. 21)

It is clear that defining a common curriculum and enforcing it through high-stakes testing results in an educational experience aligned with the curriculum. The core curriculum, however defined, becomes the de facto full curriculum. The floor, that is the basic essential knowledge, becomes the ceiling. Perhaps this is what the reformers intend and expect to have.

QUESTIONING THE BET

But the bet that many governments are placing on behalf of millions of children around the world will have little chance to prepare future generations to live successfully in the era of globalization. Even in the most optimistic situation when all wishes become true, which is unlikely, the outcomes will not be globally competitive citizens. At best all these exercises will be a futile waste of resources and opportunities. At worst, these actions will lead to irreversible damages. This is because our children will face a society that has been fundamentally changed by globalization and technology while the efforts to develop and implement nationally and internationally homogenized curriculum are working on fixing an educational paradigm that has outlived its utility.

The paradigm evolved at a time when the world was separated by geographical distance, when most societies were insular, and when changes happened much slower than today and tomorrow. For most of human history, before this wave of globalization and massive technological changes, economies were mostly local and slow changing. In those economies, most people undertook similar jobs that satisfied the local needs. And in many cases, the jobs and their required knowledge and skills did not change very fast, making it possible to predict and thus prescribe a curriculum that by and large could prepare children to find employment. Furthermore, the knowledge and skills required of workers were fairly basic and most people could be asked or forced to acquire them. Only a relatively small number of individuals were engaged in jobs that require creativity, uniqueness, and high-level cognitive skills.

As a result, the dominant paradigm of modern mass education has been about producing employees with similar skills to meet the demand of the local economy and a common citizenry with similar values compatible with the local society. The primary function of this paradigm has been to reduce human diversity into skillful workers through prescribed content and experiences in the form of curriculum. It is also about passing on cultural values of the local society. The starting point of this education is to identify the essential skills and knowledge a society wishes to pass on for the sake of cultural continuity and gainful economic life of future generations. That is, to formulate a sensible curriculum.

But the world is drastically different now. First, with only a few exceptions (e.g., North Korea), geographical distance and political boundaries no longer divide the world in terms of economical activities. Virtually all economies are globally interconnected and interdependent. Employment opportunities are thus no longer isolated to specific locations. Jobs can be outsourced to distant places physically or performed by individuals remotely. In a world where jobs can be and have been moved around globally, anyone could potentially go after any job he or she desires. Whether she can be employed depends largely on two factors: qualifications and price. All things being equal, those asking for a lower price for the same qualifications will receive the job.

With over seven billion people living on earth today, there is plenty of competition for everyone. But due to the vast economic disparities in the world, there exist tremendous differences in labor cost. The hourly compensation costs in manufacturing in 2010 varied from $1.90 in the Philippines to $57.53 in Norway, according to data released by the U.S. Bureau of Labor Statistics in 2011 (Bureau of Labor Statistics, 2011). If a Norwegian were doing exactly the same job as a Filipino, it is very probable that his job will be gone soon. For the Norwegian to keep his job, he'd better be doing something that the Filipino is unable to do.

Here lies the first problem of the global homogenization of learning. If all children are asked to master the same knowledge and skills, those who cost less will be much more competitive than those who cost more. There are many poor and hungry people in the developing world willing to work for a fraction of what workers in developed countries need. Thus for those in developed countries to be globally competitive, they must offer something qualitatively different, that is, something that cannot be obtained at a lower cost in developing countries. And that something is certainly not great test scores in a few subjects or the so-called basic skills, because those can be achieved in the developing countries.

Second, old jobs are being rapidly replaced by new ones as old industries disappear due to technological changes or existing jobs move around the globe. For example, existing firms lost on average over one million jobs annually in the period from 1977 to 2005, according to a report of the

Kauffman Foundation, while an average of three million jobs were created annually by new firms (Kane, 2010). As a result, there is no sure way to predict what jobs our children will have to take in the future. As the head of PISA, Andrea Schleicher recently said: "Schools have to prepare students for jobs that have not yet been created, technologies that have not yet been invented and problems that we don't know will arise" (Schleicher, 2010). Here lies the second problem of the move to prescribe knowledge and skills. If one does not know what careers are there in the future, it is difficult, if not impossible, to prescribe the knowledge and skills that will make today's students ready for them.

Third, jobs that require routine procedure skills and knowledge are increasingly automated or sent to places where such skills and knowledge are abundant with lower cost. As a result, as best-selling author Daniel Pink observed, what will be of more value is traditionally neglected talents, which he refers to as right-brain directed skills, including design, story, symphony, empathy, play, and meaning (Pink, 2005). And these are just antagonistic to the core subjects that are being prescribed by many governments and tested on international assessments such as PISA and TIMSS, which are mostly left-brained cognitive skills. This is the third problem of the movement to prescribe knowledge and skills for all schools, because what they are prescribing is not necessarily what is needed.

Fourth, the world our children will live in is global, not local as before. Given the interconnectedness and interdependence of economies, the rise of global challenges such as climate change, and the ease of movement across national borders, one's birthplace no longer determines his or her future living space or whom he or she may be working for or with. Thus, to be ready to live in this global world requires the knowledge and abilities to interact with people who are not born and raised in the same local community. But the core curriculum of most nations does not include an element to prepare the future generations to live in this globalized world and interact with people from different cultures. The focus on local values and the need of the local society represents the fourth problem of a national core curriculum and a global curriculum that narrowly focuses on numeracy and literacy.

Last, globalization and technological changes, while presenting tremendous challenges, bring vast opportunities. Globalization, for example, vastly expands the pool of potential customers for products and services. Niche talents that used to be of only interest to a small fraction of people may not be of much value locally because the total population is small in a given community. In the globalized world, the potential customers could be seven billion people. Even a small fraction of seven billion can be significant. Additionally, talents that may be of little value in a given location can be very valuable in another. Globalization and technology today enables products and services to reach almost any corner of the world. But the traditional paradigm, by forcing children to master the same curriculum, essentially discriminates against talents that are not consistent with the prescribed knowledge and skills. Students who are otherwise talented but do not do well in the prescribed subjects are often sent to spend more time on the core subjects, retained for another grade, or deprived of the opportunity to develop their talents in other ways.

In summary, the traditional education paradigm may have worked before but is no longer adequate for the changed world. The efforts to develop common curriculum, nationally and internationally, are simply working to perfect an outdated paradigm. The outcomes are precisely the opposite of the talents we need for the new era. It is the wrong bet for our children's future.

References

AccountabilityWorks. (2012). *National cost of aligning states and localities to the Common Core Standards: A Pioneer Institute and American Principles Project white paper.* Boston, MA: Pioneer Institute.

Alexander, R. J. (2009). *Towards a new primary curriculum: A report from the Cambridge Primary Review. Part 2: The future.* Cambridge, England: University of Cambridge Faculty of Education.

Australian Curriculum Assessment and Reporting Authority. (2010). A curriculum for all young Australians. Retrieved December 2, 2011,

from http://www.acara.edu.au/verve/_resources/Information
_Sheet_A_curriculum_for_all_young_Australians.pdf

Booher-Jennings, J. (2006). Rationing education in an era of accountability. *Phi Delta Kappan, 87*(10), 756–761.

Bureau of Labor Statistics. (2011, December 21). International comparisons of hourly compensation costs in manufacturing, 2010.
Retrieved January 2, 2012, from http://www.bls.gov/news
.release/pdf/ichcc.pdf

Common Core. (2009). *Why we are behind: What top nations teach their
students but we don't.* Washington, DC: Common Core State
Standards Initiative.

Common Core State Standards Initiative. (2011a). Common Core
State Standards Initiative. Retrieved November 24, 2011, from
http://www.corestandards.org/

Common Core State Standards Initiative. (2011b). Mission statement.
Retrieved May 20, 2011, from http://www.corestandards.org/

Department for Education. (2011, November 16). Review of the
National Curriculum in England. Retrieved December 2, 2011,
from http://www.education.gov.uk/schools/teachingand
learning/curriculum/b0073043/remit-for-review-of-the
-national-curriculum-in-england

Education Commission of the States (ECS). (2008). *From competing to
leading: An international benchmarking blueprint.* Denver, CO: Author.

Gewertz, C. (2011, February 21). Common-assessment consortia
expand plans: Extra federal funds will go toward curricula,
teacher training. *Education Week.* Retrieved from http://www
.edweek.org/ew/articles/2011/02/11/21consortia.h30.html

Goertz, M. E. (2010). National standards: Lessons from the past,
directions for the future. In B. Reys, R. Reys, & R. Rubenstein
(Ed.), *Mathematics curriculum: Issues, trends, and future direction,
72nd yearbook* (pp. 51–64). Washington, DC: NCTM.

Hanushek, E. A., & Woessmann, L. (2010). *The high cost of low educational performance: The long-run economic impact of improving PISA
outcomes.* Paris, France: OECD.

Howson, G. (2001). What can we learn from international comparisons? In L. Haggarty (Ed.), *Teaching mathematics in secondary
schools: A reader* (pp. 259–272). London, England: Routledge.

Kane, T. (2010). *The importance of startups in job creation and job
destruction.* Kansas City, MO: Kauffman Foundation.

Korea Institute for Curriculum and Evaluation. (2011). College
Scholastic Ability Test. Retrieved December 2, 2011, from
http://www.kice.re.kr/en/resources/abillityTest.jsp

Mathis, W. J. (2010). *The "Common Core" Standards Initiative: An effective reform tool?* East Lansing, MI: The Great Lakes Center for Education Research & Practice.

McGaw, B. (2010, December 9). A historic moment: The first Australian curriculum endorsed. Retrieved December 12, 2010, from http://www.acara.edu.au/default.asp

McMurrer, J. (2007). *Choices, changes, and challenges: Curriculum and instruction in the NCLB era.* Washington, DC: Center on Education Policy.

McMurrer, J. (2008). *Instructional time in elementary schools: A closer look at changes for specific subjects.* Washington, DC: Center on Education Policy.

Ministry of Education. (2011). What will primary education be like for my child? Retrieved December 2, 2011, from http://www.primaryeducation.sg/

Ministry of Education (NZ). (2010). National standards: Key information—questions and answers. Retrieved December 2, 2011, from http://nzcurriculum.tki.org.nz/National-Standards/Key-information/Questions-and-answers

Ministry of Education (NZ). (2011). National standards. Retrieved December 1, 2011, from http://nzcurriculum.tki.org.nz/National-Standards

National Governors Association, Council of Chief State School Officers, & Achieve Inc. (2008). *Benchmarking for success: Ensuring U.S. students receive a world-class education.* Washington, DC: National Governors Association.

National Governors Association Center for Best Practices (NGA Center) & Council of Chief State School Officers. (2010, June 2). National Governors Association and state education chiefs launch common state academic standards. Retrieved November 20, 2011, from http://www.corestandards.org/articles/8-national-governors-association-and-state-education-chiefs-launch-common-state-academic-standards

National Research Council. (1999). *Global perspectives for local action: Using TIMSS to improve U.S. mathematics and science education.* Washington, DC: National Academy Press.

The New Commission on the Skills of the American Workforce. (2007). *Tough choices or tough times.* Washington, DC: National Center on Education and the Economy.

Oates, T. (2010). *Could do better: Using international comparisons to refine the National Curriculum in England.* Cambridge, UK: Cambridge Assessment.

Pink, D. H. (2005). *A whole new mind: Moving from the Information Age to the Conceptual Age.* New York, NY: Riverhead Books.

Schleicher, A. (2010). The case for 21st-century learning. Retrieved January 2, 2012, from http://www.oecd.org/document/2/0,37 46,en_2649_201185_46846594_1_1_1_1,00.html

Sheffield, R. (2011, November 28). Implementing Common Core could cost states $30 billion. Retrieved December 2, 2011, from http://news.heartland.org/newspaper-article/2011/11/28 /implementing-common-core-could-cost-states-30-billion

Singapore Examinations and Assessment Board. (2011). Primary school leaving examination. Retrieved December 2, 2011, from http://www.seab.gov.sg/psle/psle.html

Spring, J. (2008). *Globalization of education: An introduction.* London, England: Routledge.

Srikantaiah, D., & Kober, N. (2009). *How state and federal accountability policies have influenced curriculum and instruction in three states: Common findings from Rhode Island, Illinois, and Washington.* Washington, DC: Center on Education Policy.

Tienken, C. H., & Zhao, Y. (2010). Common Core national curriculum standards: More questions . . . and answers. *AASA Journal of Scholarship and Practice, 6*(4), 3–14.

Tucker, M. S. (2011). *Standing on the shoulders of giants: An American agenda for education reform.* Washington, DC: National Center on Education and the Economy.

U.S. Department of Education. (2009). *Race to the Top Fund.* Retrieved from http://www2.ed.gov/programs/racetothetop/index.html

Valli, L., & Buese, D. (2007). The changing roles of teachers in an era of high-stakes accountability. *American Educational Research Journal, 44*(3), 519–558.

The White House. (2011, September 23). Obama Administration sets high bar for flexibility from No Child Left Behind in order to advance equity and support reform. Retrieved November 20, 2011, from http://www.ed.gov/news/press-releases/obama -administration-sets-high-bar-flexibility-no-child-left-behind -order-advanc

Zastrow, C. V., & Janc, H. (2004). *Academic atrophy: The condition of the liberal arts in America's public schools.* Washington, DC: Council for Basic Education.

Zhao, Y. (2009). Comments on the Common Core standards initiative. *AASA Journal of Scholarship and Practice, 6*(3), 46–54.

2

The Changed World

The Need for Entrepreneurs

All changes, even the most longed for, have their melan-
choly; for what we leave behind us is a part of ourselves;
we must die to one life before we can enter another.

—Anatole France

Everyone thinks of changing the world, but no one thinks
of changing himself.

—Leo Tolstoy

Burn your resume, and create a job," is the message serial entrepreneur Scott Gerber has been sending to his fellow Generation Y members all over the world (Martin, 2011; Wilson, 2011). In 2005 "after graduating from New York University with a film degree and thousands of dollars in student loans, Scott Gerber moved back in with his parents on Staten Island. He then took out more loans to start a new-media and technology company, but he didn't have a clear market in mind; the company went belly up in 2006," says a *New York Times* article (Seligson, 2010). But he persisted despite the failure and his mother's nagging him to find a real job, one with a salary and boss. He started more businesses and some became successful. He "isn't a millionaire, but he's paid off his loans and doesn't have to live with his parents" (Seligson, 2010).

The Gerber story as yet one more young entrepreneur who became successful could end here if he had not come out to actively share his story and encourage others to follow his suit. He has written a book *Never Get a "Real" Job: How to Dump Your Boss, Build a Business, and Not Go Broke* (Gerber, 2011). He has shared his stories on blogs and websites. He has founded the Young Entrepreneur Council, a nonprofit organization aimed to "create a shift from a résumé-driven society to one where people create their own jobs" (Seligson, 2010).

"Now more than ever, youth unemployment is a devastating epidemic globally. When our parents graduated from college there were a few million students. Now you have tens of millions, plus online students, all competing," answered Gerber when asked what inspired him to write the book. "The average open position today around the world is getting between 75 and 1,000-plus resumes. So you have at any one time less than a 1 per cent chance of getting that employment opportunity" (Wilson, 2011).

No jobs! Gerber is right.

NO JOBS

The Dire Youth Unemployment Situation

"The individual stories are familiar. The chemistry major tending bar. The classics major answering phones. The Italian studies major sweeping aisles at Wal-Mart," writes Catherine Rampbell in the *New York Times* recently (Rampbell, 2011). Her story is about the miserable job market facing college graduates today in the United States.

In fact, these students are lucky. They have jobs. Many of their peers don't even have the opportunity to tend bars, answer phones, or sweep aisles at Walmart. Millions of Americans with college degrees do not have jobs or are employed only part time.

According to a 2011 study by the John J. Heldrich Center for Workforce Development of Rutgers University, only 53% of those who graduated from college between 2006 and 2010 hold full-time jobs (Godofsky, Zukin, & Horn, 2011).

The dire unemployment situation for youth has reached a crisis level, not only in the United States, but globally. In July 2011, there were over four million unemployed youth in the United States, meaning that more than 18% of 16- to 24-year-old Americans were unemployed (Bureau of Labor Statistics, 2011a). In the United Kingdom, over one million youth did not have a job in 2011 (Allen, 2011). The situation in other European countries is worse. Youth unemployment rate in Spain and Greece were approaching 50%, and even in Ireland over 30% of youth under the age of 25 were unemployed in 2011 (Salmon, 2011). The average unemployment rate in OECD (Organisation for Economic Co-operation and Development) member countries, 34 of the richest nations on earth, was over 16% in 2010 (OECD, 2011) and was expected to reach 18% in 2011 (OECD, 2010).

The 2008 economic crisis certainly exacerbated the employment situation for many but even before that the world had way more people than employment opportunities. In 2004, more than half or over 80 million of the youth available for work did not have jobs globally (Schoof, 2006). The number of young people who will be looking for jobs is on the rise as the world's population grows. In 2015, it is estimated that approximately 660 million young people in the world will either be working or looking for work (Schoof, 2006).

The specific causes of this massive unemployment may vary in different regions and countries, but in general they come down to increased productivity thanks to technological advancement, the global redistribution of work resulting from global economic integration, and the rapid growth of human population and an increase in life expectancy, hence years in the workforce. Interestingly, the same forces that created unemployment are potentially the same forces that may help create jobs.

Increased Productivity

Human beings have become increasingly more productive over the years. They are able to generate a lot more value in the same amount of time today than ever before. The late economist Angus Maddison of the Organisation for Economic Co-operation and Development (OECD) documented the stunning human progress in economic productivity and welfare in his best-selling book *The World Economy: A Millennial Perspective* published in 2001 (Maddison, 2001). Worldwide per capita GDP, that is the approximate value of goods produced by a person, was around $400 in the year AD 1000, about the same as the year AD 1, which means there was not much growth at all during the first millennium after the birth of Jesus Christ. But during the second millennium, from AD 1000 to AD 2000, the increase was staggering. Per capita GDP rose to nearly $6,000 in 1998, a 14-fold increase. And most of that growth took place in the last 200 years, after 1820. In 2012, the world's per capita GDP grew to $11,200, more than double what it was in 1998, according to the *CIA World Factbook* (Central Intelligence Agency [CIA], 2011).

The productivity increase has not been uniform across the world. Certain regions and countries, such as Western Europe, the United States, and Japan, for example, grew much faster than other regions. In 1999, GDP per capita in the United States reached $33,900 and $47,200 in 2010. In the United Kingdom, per capita GDP in 1999 was $21,800 and in 2010 the figure was $34,800. But in Africa and certain countries in Asia, the per capita GDP remains under $10,000. For example, Uganda's per capita GDP was $1,900 in 2010, and Chad's was $1,600 in the same year. And there are more countries, such as China, India, and Brazil, that are growing fast. Over the past decade China's per capita GDP rose from $3,800 in 1999 to $6,700 in 2009 (CIA, 2011).

Increased productivity has led to rising standard of living, longer life expectancy, better health, and more leisure time, which is good. In the meantime, it also means a surplus of labor. It simply does not need as many people to produce the same amount of goods and services as before. For example, according to University of Michigan–Flint's economics professor Mark Perry, although there was a 32.5% reduction in factory employment in the U.S. manufacturing industry between 2000 and 2010, manufacturing output actually increased by more than 5%, which means a significant improvement in productivity and an equally significant loss in the number of jobs. "Manufacturing worker productivity has doubled in the last 17 years since 1993, and that has contributed to the loss of more than 11 million jobs," Perry wrote in a blog post in 2010 (Perry, 2010).

The bottom line is that as human beings become more productive, through the advancement of technology, more efficient organization of production, and more powerful energy sources, there will be even more people freed from existing jobs. Hence more people will be unemployed within the existing framework unless they find something else valuable to do.

More People and Longer Work Life

Rising living standards have led to longer life expectancy and better health. Angus Maddison estimated that the average life expectancy at birth was 26 years in 1820 and 31 years in 1900. It increased to 49 years in 1950. By the end of last millennium, it had reached 66 years. This is the world average. In developed countries today, the average life expectancy at birth is about 77 years, compared with about 46 years just a century ago (Maddison, 2001). This means many people can work much longer in their life than their ancestors.

Human population has grown significantly as well. It reached the first billion around 1800 and took about 130 years to add another billion. The third billion came in less than 30 years, in 1959. Only another 15 years later, human population reached four billion in 1974. Thirteen years later, in 1987, came the fifth billion. And today we have over seven billion people living on earth (United Nations Population Fund, 2011).

Increased productivity reduces the number of workers needed to produce the same amount of goods, longer life expectancy enables more people to stay in their jobs longer, and the billion people added over the last decade will enter the workforce soon. In fact, almost half of the 7 billion people are 24 years old or younger, with 1.2 billion between the ages of 10 and 19, according a United Nations Population Fund report published in 2011. It is no surprise that the world is hungry for jobs.

Global Redistribution of Jobs

The unemployment issue may appear to be locally confined to a community, country, or region, but in a world that has become flat (Friedman, 2005), that is not the case. Geographical and political boundaries can still confine people to where they are born, but they have become much easier to cross and definitely no longer protect jobs. Thanks to technological advancement and the collapse of political barriers, the time and efforts to move across geographical distances have dramatically shrunk over the years. What used to take years and significant efforts and resources can be achieved today with much less, for example, talking with someone 2,000 miles away. What used to be impossible can be done with little effort. For instance, merely 40 years ago, it would have been impossible to sell Coca-Cola in China. Just 30 years ago, the cost would have been prohibitive for most people to have video conferencing across the Atlantic Ocean or even within the American continent.

Furthermore, over the last several decades, digital technology has matured and become ubiquitous. The digital revolution (Negroponte, 1995) has transformed almost every sector of our society, from banking to transportation, from work to entertainment, from communication to education, and from politics to socializing. Digital technologies have freed us from being constrained by the physical aspects of our world. As a result, physical co-location and presence have become nonessential for many human activities. For example, we conduct banking transactions without going to the bank, exchange ideas with others without being in the same place, or take classes without going to the physical campus.

As a result, a job that used to be in one location and expected to be had by some person born in the same location could be taken by someone from other places in a number of ways. First, the job can be outsourced or physically shifted to another location. Second, the job can be performed remotely online. And finally, a person from another location could migrate to the location. All these have happened and will only continue in the future. The result is what Gary Gereffi, professor of sociology and director of the Center on Globalization, Governance and Competitiveness at Duke University, calls "the great global job shift" (Gereffi, 2005).

The shift is first through offshoring or offshore outsourcing. To reduce cost and maximize profit, businesses began to shift parts or the whole of their production to places where the labor cost is lower or simply hire overseas companies to produce what used to be produced in house. Starting in the 1960s, low-level manufacturing jobs in shoes, clothing, toys, and cheap electronics were moved from developed countries to developing regions. Routine service work followed. Basic computer coding, credit-card processing, airline reservations, and other such jobs were sent overseas. The 1990s, with increasingly ubiquitous access to high-speed network and improved communication and information technologies, saw another wave of jobs moving overseas, and this time it included a wide-range of knowledge-intensive jobs (Gereffi, 2005).

As a result, millions of jobs have left the developed countries for poorer developing countries since the 1960s. The exact number of jobs that have been offshored is not available and hotly debated. A study by the research firm Forrester Group suggested that over one million jobs in Europe would move offshore by 2015. Nearly 760,000 of these jobs are in the United Kingdom. In other words, each year about 3% of the U.K.'s total jobs will move offshore. The situation is worse for the United States, which is expected to have about 3.4 million service jobs moved to other countries (McCarthy, 2004). On the manufacturing side, the number cited by labor advocates is much more staggering. In an Op-Ed piece published by *USA Today*, Richard Trumka, president of the AFL-CIO, America's largest labor union, claims "57,000 U.S. manufacturing facilities shut down in the last 10 years, costing us five-and-a-half million good-paying jobs, nearly half of those to China alone" (Trumka, 2010).[1]

"This process of job transfer ('outsourcing') is a central aspect of contemporary entrepreneurship and globalization," writes Harvard professor emeritus of economics David Landes in his 2010 book *The Invention of Enterprise, Entrepreneurship from Ancient Mesopotamia to Modern Times* (Landes, Mokyr, & Baumol, 2010, p. 4). As such, most economists and trade experts agree that offshoring of jobs is a trend that will continue at an even more accelerated pace. For the developed countries, that means more jobs will be sent to other places. Alan S. Blinder, a professor of economics at Princeton University and former vice chairman of the Federal Reserve, estimated that "between 22% to 29% of all U.S. jobs are or will be potentially offshorable within a decade or two" in a widely cited paper first appearing as a working paper in 2007 (Blinder, 2007) and later published by *World Economics* in 2009 (Blinder, 2009). Earlier, he had given a much higher percentage:

> My brave-but-crude guesstimate of the number of potentially offshorable jobs was 42–56 million, of which 14 million are in manufacturing and 28–42 million (a large range, to be sure) are in the various non-manufacturing

---

[1]But University of Michigan–Flint's economics professor Mark Perry does not agree. Citing productivity statistics, Perry contends: "Manufacturing worker productivity has doubled in the last 17 years since 1993, and that has contributed to the loss of more than 11 million jobs" (Perry, 2010).

("service," for short) sectors. In round numbers, the total represents roughly 30–40% of all the jobs in the United States at present. (Blinder, 2007, p. 4)

The other aspect of this global job redistribution is through migration. Non-offshorable jobs are not necessarily guaranteed for the local natives because others move in. And there are plenty of people who would risk anything for better opportunities than provided within the location of their birth. Today, there are over 240 million people living in a country in which they were not born, a staggering number and on the increase. Migration also happens within a country, and frequently. China, a country that used to strictly limit people to where they are born and still carries discriminatory practices and policies against migrant workers, has 260 million migrants within the country in 2010. That number was only six million in 1980. It is projected to reach 350 million in 2050, according to a UN report (United Nations Population Fund, 2011).

Not a Zero-Sum Game

This "great global job shift" essentially compels us to seek solutions to unemployment from a global perspective. With increased productivity reducing the number of workers needed for existing jobs, more people needing jobs, and the removal of geographical and political boundaries as job protections, the only solution is to create more jobs in the world. And governments all over the world are trying to strengthen their economy and create jobs.

Job creation, for example, is a major theme in U.S. President Barack Obama's 2012 State of the Union address. In the speech, he sent a "simple" message to American business leaders: "Ask yourselves what you can do to bring jobs back to your country, and your country will do everything we can to help you succeed" (Obama, 2012). He promised to give tax incentives to businesses that create jobs in the United States and punish those who send jobs to other countries.

How well will Mr. Obama's plan work to bring jobs back to the United States is uncertain, but what is certain is that in the long term such nationalistic and retrospective approach is not going to create more jobs for the billions of people on earth, nor will it for Americans. Jobs could be brought back to America, but that means no jobs in other countries. And these jobs have generated wealth, thus consumers who can afford to buy more products and services—which can be invented in America. Moreover, moving jobs back to the United States could mean higher prices for certain products, and that may force other countries to create their own with less cost and out-compete American products. Or they could become so expensive that few can afford them any longer. Furthermore, Americans may not even want some of the jobs that are done in other countries. The beloved iPhones and iPads from Apple are a telling example.

Kenneth Kraemer and his colleagues at the Personal Computer Industry Center of the University of California–Irvine conducted multiple microeconomic studies about the distribution of values of Apple products, including the iPod, iPhone, and iPad (Kraemer, Linden, & Dedrick, 2011). Their findings show that despite the hundreds of thousands of Chinese workers who put the Apple gadgets together inside China, Apple's 14,000 employees in the United States and its shareholders, mostly American, capture the lion's share of the profit. Chinese workers keep about $10 out of the $229 to $275 devices. Based on this analysis, they conclude:

> our study also shows that "manufacturing" is not necessarily the path back to "good jobs." . . . Our analysis here and elsewhere makes clear that there is simply little value in electronics assembly. The gradual concentration of electronics manufacturing in Asia over the past 30 years cannot be reversed in the short- to medium-term without undermining the relatively free flow of goods, capital, and people that provides the basis for the global economy. And even if high-volume assembly expands in North

America, this will likely take place in Mexico where there is already a relatively low-cost electronics assembly infrastructure. (Kraemer et al., 2011, p. 8)

Moreover, as University of California–Berkeley Professor Ann Harrison and Tufts University professor of economics Margaret McMillan found through their analysis of U.S. manufacturing multinational companies' foreign employment, offshoring can actually create jobs for the United States (Harrison & McMillan, 2009). In fact, they concluded that "job losses would have probably been even greater in the absence of offshoring expansion by US multinationals" (Harrison & McMillan, 2009, p. 24). Further, they found:

For firms most likely to perform the same tasks in foreign affiliates and at home ("horizontal" foreign investment), foreign and domestic employees appear to be substitutes. For these firms, lower wages in affiliate locations are associated with lower employment in the US. However, for firms which do significantly different tasks at home and abroad ("vertical" foreign investment), foreign and domestic employment are complements. . . . For vertical foreign investment, lower wages abroad are associated with higher US manufacturing employment. (Harrison & McMillan, 2009, pp. 24–25)

Harrison and McMillan suggest something crucial to policy makers and governments: The global distribution of jobs does not have to be a zero-sum game. The number of jobs is not finite, carved in stone at one time. It is not about keeping jobs home and preventing others from taking the jobs away, rather, it is about creating new jobs.

POTENTIAL FOR NEW JOBS

Paradoxically, the forces that resulted in unemployment are also the forces that will lead to the creation of jobs. Technology advancement, globalization, and abundance of unemployed youth are all building blocks of a new economy. Increased productivity resulted in more free time and wealth and thus increased capacity to pursue previously unrecognized or unmet human needs, which in turn provide new opportunities for jobs. The new way of production also creates opportunities for jobs. Furthermore, globalization and digitization together have created a new platform that helps create new jobs. This platform delivers a global customer base, a global capital pool, and a global workforce—all easily accessible.

Previously Unmet or Unrecognized Human Needs

Increased productivity has resulted in a growth of wealth, more disposable income, and more free time for humans to pursue needs that could not have been met or even recognized previously. In the United States, for example, the average yearly household income increased by 67-fold from $750 in 1901 to $50,302 in 2002, while the average family size almost halved from 4.9 to 2.5 persons per household, which means per person income has increased even more. Even after adjusted for inflation, the average income in the United States would have increased three- to four-fold. Increased income resulted in increased expenditure. The average U.S. household had $769 in expenditures in 1901. A hundred years later, these expenditures increased 53-fold to $40,748 in 2002. More significantly, the percentage of expenditures for necessities (food, clothing, and housing) has fallen dramatically, from nearly 80% in 1901 to just about 50% in 2002. In 1901, a large chunk (42.5%) of the family income was spent on food and in 2002, the average American family spent only 13.2% on food. Moreover, almost half of the 13.2% was spent eating out. This means Americans today can allocate a lot more of their income (49.9% vs. 20%) on nonnecessities, such as entertainment, charity, reading and education, personal care, vacationing and travel, and health, than they did 100 years ago. In 2002, the average American family spent over $2,000 on entertainment and health care, in contrast to $12 and $40, respectively, in 1901 (U.S. Bureau of Labor Statistics, 2006).

The increased spending power on nonnecessities, such as entertainment, presents new opportunities for new jobs. Coupled with technological development, a host of new industries have emerged and flourished. The film industry, the video and TV industry, the computer gaming industry, the music industry, and many more that did not even exist 100 years ago are now employing millions of people and making a significant contribution to the world's economy. The entertainment and media industry is projected to reach $555 billion in the United States and $1.9 trillion worldwide by 2015, according to a study by PriceWaterhouseCoopers (2011), an international consulting firm. In a nutshell, while an increasing number of traditional jobs will be lost due to increased productivity, many more jobs can be created because more people will have the income to consume more and more diverse products and services.

Emerging Needs

Globalization presents new challenges to all sectors of society, and hence new needs for people to address these challenges, and hence new opportunities for jobs. For example, to ensure that a globalized company operates smoothly, we need global supply chain managers, language interpreters, cultural consultants, and people to manage the global workflow and the global workforce. Immigration creates opportunities for jobs that provide social services, legal assistants, language education, and a series of other tasks to help immigrants settle in the new community. It is well known that the information technology industry has created whole new lines of jobs that never existed before—online social presence managers, Web designers, search engine optimizers, security and privacy managers, and many more. Undoubtedly there will be even more needs emerging in the future that will create jobs and occupations that we do not even have titles for.

Global Customer Base

Not only are there human needs that are potential opportunities for jobs and employment, but also there are tools that have become mature and accessible for the ordinary people to make job creation a reality through entrepreneurial activities. Globalization and the digital revolution have created a platform that enables anyone to potentially reach a global customer base of seven billion people; hence, there are more opportunities for new jobs that meet the needs of people beyond the local community. With the advent of online banking, microtransaction services such as PayPal, all-purpose global shipping systems such as UPS and FedEx, and easy-to-use trading platforms such as eBay and Amazon, anyone today can run a business that is automatically global. No need to rent space in a shopping mall that only serves local customers. Running a global store that runs 24/7 is simple, easy, and inexpensive—especially compared with operating a physical store. If you have something to sell, it costs next to nothing to open a store on the numerous online shopping platforms such as eBay, Amazon, and now even on Facebook.

Millions of people have taken advantage of this new opportunity to operate retail businesses online. eBay, for example, has over 200 million active users globally. Technically, all of these 200 million-plus users can sell any items to the others. Certainly while not all of them consider selling on eBay a full-time job or business, there are millions who do. In 2008, eBay hosted more than 1.2 million small businesses (Massad, 2010). There are a few who have made millions of dollars as well (Dahl, 2011). In China, a developing country, nearly 15 million individuals operated an online store in 2011, according to statistics released by China e-Business Research Center (Zhongguo Dianzi Shangwu Yanjiu Zhongxin [China e-Business Research Center], 2011).

While it is difficult to find accurate data about the scale of individual or small-business activity in online businesses because of the rapid changes and diversity of platforms, there is no question that "e-commerce has been the growth engine for retailers in mature markets for the past 10–15 years," according to a report by Cisco Systems (Bethlahmy, Popat, & Schottmiller, 2011). The same report expects global e-commerce to reach almost $1.4 trillion in 2015. And to participate in this global economy, one only needs a computer or iPhone and, of course, the knowledge, skills, and entrepreneurial spirit.

Operating an online store is just one of the many entrepreneurial activities one can engage in easily. If you are good at taking pictures, upload your photos on Flickr and you have an online photo store to sell your products. If you are musically talented, record your songs and sell them on iTunes. If you are good at computer programming, develop apps for mobile devices and sell them on iTunes or Android market. If you are into making videos or films, there are YouTube and Vimeo to serve as your broadcast station. If you want to teach, any subject, become a tutor at tutors.com and work from home to teach your students. If you are really good, become an instructor for many online schools, colleges, and teaching services.

Globalization and the digital revolution not only have brought a global market to any individual with a computing device connected to the Internet, enabling ordinary people to engage in entrepreneurial activities as individuals with very low startup costs, but also have brought potential investors, partners, collaborators, and employees from all parts of the world to individuals who may otherwise have no such access. Here are some examples.

Crowdfunding: A Global Capital Pool

If you have a bright idea and want to turn it into a product or business but lack the capital, conventionally you would have to put up your own money or convince your relatives and friends for the initiative investment. You could, of course, try to sell the idea to venture capitalists or borrow from a bank. But the Internet has brought another option that is rapidly gaining traction. Crowdfunding is quickly emerging as a way of attracting initial funding for businesses. Simply speaking, crowdfunding is a way for people anywhere ("the crowd") to finance endeavors they want to support. It has been used by various startups to raise seed money.

A 2008 *Time* magazine article reported a number of successful efforts of crowdfunding in the entertainment industry (Dell, 2008). For example, British filmmaker Franny Armstrong raised over $800,000 to finance the documentary film *The Age of Stupid.* Those who invested over $9,000 would get a share of the profit. Another film, *The Cosmonaut,* was also financed through crowdfunding. Nearly 4,000 people from around the world put up nearly half a million dollars to become the film's producers.[2] Dedicated platforms have emerged to facilitate crowdfunding. SellaBand.com, for example, provides a platform for unsigned artists to raise funds, bypassing the labels. Artists register on the site and indicate the amount of funding they need. Individuals invest and receive the music and a share of the profit, if any. Since its launch in 2006, SellaBand .com has raised over $4 million to finance about 100 independent bands (SellaBand.com, 2012). Kickstarter is another popular crowdfunding platform that represents "a new way to fund and follow creativity" in art, journalism, solar energy, or anything else. In 2011, its second year of operation, Kickstarter reached $100 million in pledges from over one million "backers" (i.e., investors), funding approximately 1,000 projects each month, according to statistics released by the website (Kickstarter, 2012).

Crowdsourcing: A Global Workforce

If you are looking for ideas, projects, or talents for your business, there is crowdsourcing. Contributing editor of *Wired* magazine and author of the book *Crowdsourcing: Why the Power of the Crowd Is Driving the Future of Business,* Jeff Howe (2008), wrote about the new phenomenon of crowdsourcing in an article "The Rise of

---

[2]https://shop.thecosmonaut.org/en/producers

Crowdsourcing in 2006: Remember outsourcing? Sending jobs to India and China is so 2003. The new pool of cheap labor: everyday people using their spare cycles to create content, solve problems, and even do corporate R&D" (Howe, 2006).

The basic idea of crowdsourcing is fairly simple yet very powerful: You seek ideas, solutions, products, and services from the crowd, that is, everyone on the Internet. Large corporates can do this. For example, the Canadian gold mining company Goldcorp Inc. used crowdsourcing to find more gold. In March 2000, the company launched the "Goldcorp Challenge," with a total of $575,000 prize money available to anyone in the world with the best methods and estimates of locations of gold in its mining area, after its own employees failed to find more. The company released all information about its 55,000-acre property on its website. Thousands of people from over 50 countries participated in this gold-finding mission. They were not only geologists, but also graduate students, consultants, mathematicians, and military officers. In the end, the "crowd" identified 110 targets, 50% of which had not been previously identified by the company. And over 80% of the new targets yielded gold. The contest helped the company find eight million ounces of gold (Tapscott & Williams, 2008). Netflix, the online video store, obtained a much better algorithm for recommending movies to users through crowdsourcing, with $1 million (Lohr, 2009). As with outsourcing, crowdsourcing enables all businesses or individuals to find talents, skills, ideas, solutions, and services globally without first identifying or creating full-time jobs for those talents.

Crowdfunding and crowdsourcing are examples of a new kind of economy. It is the Wiki-economy. Don Tapscott and Anthony Williams coined the term *Wikinomics* to describe this new economy in their best-selling book, *Wikinomics: How Mass Collaboration Changes Everything* (Tapscott & Williams, 2008). Just like Wikipedia—the online encyclopedia written, edited, updated, and maintained by unorganized individuals scattered in every corner of the world—this economy is driven by the mass of individuals.

In this globalized economy, traditional geographical and organizational barriers are removed. Individuals can raise capital from anyone anywhere on earth. Individuals can easily market their talents, skills, products, and services to a global pool of consumers. Individuals can also find partners and employees globally. It is thus realistic for anyone to become an entrepreneur, a global entrepreneur, with relatively little resources to start with.

A SHIFT OF MINDSET

From Finding Jobs to Creating Jobs

We can take a variety of approaches to address the global unemployment challenge, including short-term economic policies and trade regulations. But in the long run, we simply need more people to become entrepreneurs who seek to take advantage of what has been made possible by globalization and technological changes to create jobs. As the World Economic Forum, the global body of political and business leaders and celebrities, pointed out:

> entrepreneurship has never been as important as it is today when the world is confronted with big challenges that extend well beyond the global economy. Entrepreneurship is a tremendous force that can have a big impact in growth, recovery, and societal progress by fuelling innovation, employment generation and social empowerment. (World Economic Forum, 2012)

Entrepreneurs have always existed in human history, and they have been a major driving force for economic prosperity (Landes et al., 2010). But their numbers have remained small in most of human history. Their social status has varied across time and societies. Sometimes revered, respected, and celebrated in some places, other times they were despised, prohibited, and ignored. Even in societies that have a tradition of celebrating entrepreneurship, starting one's own business has been considered a risky lifestyle or requires a lot more resources or special talent than many people would consider having. Thus the traditional mentality has been getting an education and finding a job. Most people have avoided entrepreneurship if at all possible. For example, in the United States where there is a general positive attitude toward entrepreneurship, only about 5% of college graduates consider starting their business, even at a time when finding a job has become rather difficult (Godofsky et al., 2011).

Running one's own business may still be risky, but the massive changes over the last few decades that I have discussed in this chapter have accumulated into a perfect storm for mass entrepreneurship, making it not only a necessary but also a viable alternative of economic life. The shift in mindset is beginning to happen, starting with the gradual decline in the perceived stability and benefits of traditional jobs.

The attractiveness of traditionally defined jobs, the 40 hours a week for 40 years of employment with the same company, has been gradually but steadily decreasing. Finding employment with a real boss, preferably a large company, has always been considered safer than starting one's own business. That belief was partially built on the idea of job security or life-time employment. But that has been proven to be an urban myth. Historical data, for example, suggest that in the United States, long-term employment with one employer never existed for the majority of the population. Only about 10% of Americans had jobs that lasted 20 or more years, according to research by the Employee Benefits Research Institute during the period from 1983 to 2008 (Copeland, 2010). The same study found that the median job tenure for the lowest age group (25–34) has been hovering around two years since the 1960s, and about nine years for the highest for those aged 55 to 64. The median for all age groups has been about four years. The United States is not alone in developed countries in this regard: Fewer than 30% of workers in Anglo-Saxon countries and about 35% in Western European countries held their job for more than a decade (Hobijn & Sahin, 2007). Even in Japan, a country that has life-long employment minted in its business culture and social psyche, the practice has been called into question and has not protected all workers all the time, particularly younger workers at difficult times (Moriguchi & Ono, 2006).

Even if a business is committed to life-long employment, because employee stability brings a number of benefits to companies (Moriguchi & Ono, 2006), situations can force firms to let go of their employees. Such situations include improved productivity through automation or outsourcing, decreased demand for the firm's products or services, and bankruptcy of the firm. The average life expectancy of Fortune 500 companies is only 40 to 50 years, and many smaller-size firms only survive about a decade (De Geus, 1997).

Many of the benefits of working with large corporations have disappeared. Labor unions, for example, once a major mechanism to provide job security and good compensation for workers, have been on the decline steadily over the past half a century (Mayer, 2004; Wachter, 2007). In 2010, only 11.9% of all American wage and salary workers belonged to a union, down from over 20% in 1983, when comparable data were available. And most of the union members were public sector workers. Only 6.9% of private sector workers belonged to a union in 2010, according to the latest statistic released by the Bureau of Labor Statistics (Bureau of Labor Statistics, 2011b). Many Americans now work longer hours but earn less than two decades ago, according to a study of the Center for American Progress (Williams & Boushey, 2010). Consequently, "most Americans are well aware that the social contract associated with work in America is going through a period of profound change," says a report by the Pew Research Center in 2006, "with the industrial-era model of secure jobs with good wages and benefits that predominated until roughly a generation ago giving way to a more cost-conscious and globally-competitive workplace marked by stagnant real wages, cutbacks to health benefits and retirement plans, and growing threats of having jobs outsourced abroad" (Pew Research Center, 2006, p. 1).

Accompanying these changes is a shift in the conceptualization of jobs, particularly job security. Brenda Kowske and her colleagues at the Kenexa Research Institute studied job-related issues of tens of thousands of individuals across different generations and found a possible fundamental shift in the definition of job security. For the older generations "cradle-to-grave" jobs are secure, but the Millennials have few expectations upon entering the workforce. They are content as long as they can keep their position until the next round of downsizing (Kowske, Rasch, & Wiley, 2010). In essence, frequently changing jobs (involuntarily) has become the new norm.

THE MISSING LINK

Lack of Entrepreneurial Spirit

However, the change in mindset is not fast enough. Scott Shane, a professor of entrepreneur studies at Case Western University, documents in his book *The Illusion of Entrepreneurship: The Costly Myths That Entrepreneurs, Investors, and Policy Makers Live By* that despite the popular belief, entrepreneurship has declined in the United States and other developed countries over the past two decades (Shane, 2008). The Global Entrepreneurship Research Association (GERA), a not-for-profit organization that conducts research on entrepreneurship around the globe, has been publishing the Global Entrepreneurship Monitor (GEM) since 1999 (Kelley, Bosma, & Amorós, 2010). This annual publication reports findings of entrepreneurial activities in over 80 economies in the world. The 2010 report contains data from nearly 60 economies that cover over 50% of the world's population and 84% of the world's GDP. The study found a very low level of entrepreneurship activities in developed countries. According to the report, in 2010:

- Only 5.6% of individuals between the ages of 18 and 64 were actively engaged in business start-ups in the 22 developed countries included in the study, ranging from 2.3% in Italy, 3.3% in Japan, and 3.7% in Germany, to 10.6% in Iceland, 7.8% in Australia, and 7.6% in the United States.
- Only 3.0% of individuals in these countries were actively working toward establishing a firm, ranging from 1.3% in Italy and 1.8% in Japan and Korea, to 4.4% in Ireland, 4.8% in the United States, and 7.4% in Iceland.
- An average of 8.2% of individuals in the developed countries intended to start a business in the next three years. With 15.7%, Iceland had the largest proportion of people intending to start a business, while Japan had the smallest, with only 2.9%. The percentage is 7.7% for the United States. (Kelley et al., 2010)

These figures are consistent with other sources. For example, the survey conducted of college graduates by Rutgers University found that about 5% of college graduates in the United States intended to start their own business (Godofsky et al., 2011). A 2011 Gallup poll of 83 countries found on average 8% of the population planned to start a business in the next 12 months in all 83 countries, with 7% in North America, 4% in the European Union, 8% in Asia, and 20% in Sub-Sahara Africa (Badal & Srinivasan, 2011).

Why—at a time when entrepreneurship is so urgently needed and strongly promoted by governments and social organizations, the potentials are so great, the tools are readily available, and traditional jobs are disappearing and have become as risky as entrepreneurship—aren't there more people who want to become entrepreneurs? The answer lies with the lack of entrepreneurial spirit. And the lack of entrepreneurial spirit is a result of an educational tradition that has been focused on producing employees who are taught to look for jobs and wait for orders. The next few chapters explore the elements of the entrepreneurial spirit and how education works to suppress it.

References

Allen, K. (2011, 16 November). Youth unemployment hits 1 million. *The Guardian.* Retrieved from http://www.guardian.co.uk/business/2011/nov/16/youth-unemployment-hits-1m-uk

Badal, S., & Srinivasan, R. (2011). *Mentor support key to starting a business.* Washington, DC: Gallup Poll.

Bethlahmy, J., Popat, B., & Schottmiller, P. (2011). *The global e-commerce gold rush: How retailers can find riches overseas.* San Jose, CA: Cisco Systems.

Blinder, A. S. (2007). How many U.S. jobs might be offshorable? *Princeton University CEPS Working Paper No. 142.* Retrieved from http://www.princeton.edu/~blinder/papers/07ceps142.pdf

Blinder, A. S. (2009). How many U.S. jobs might be offshorable? *World Economics, 10*(2), 41–78.

Bureau of Labor Statistics. (2011a, August 24). Employment and unemployment among youth summary. Retrieved January 4, 2012, from http://bls.gov/news.release/youth.nr0.htm

Bureau of Labor Statistics. (2011b, January 21). Union members—2011. Retrieved January 10, 2012, from http://www.bls.gov/news.release/pdf/union2.pdf

Central Intelligence Agency (CIA). (2011). The world factbook. Retrieved January 26, 2011, from https://www.cia.gov/library/publications/the-world-factbook/

Copeland, C. (2010). Employee tenure, 2008. *EBRI Notes, 31*(1), 2–12.

Dahl, D. (2011, March 3). Meet the eBay millionaires: From iPods to African collectibles, savvy entrepreneurs are making big money selling just about everything on eBay. Retrieved January 4, 2012, from http://smallbusiness.aol.com/2011/03/23/meet-the-ebay-millionaires/

De Geus, A. (1997). *The living company: Habits for survival in a turbulent business environment.* Cambridge, MA: Harvard Business School Press.

Dell, K. (2008, September 4). Crowdfunding. *Time.* Retrieved January 10, 2012, from http://www.time.com/time/magazine/article/0,9171,1838768,00.html

Friedman, T. L. (2005). *The world is flat: A brief history of the twenty-first century.* New York, NY: Farrar, Straus and Giroux.

Gerber, S. (2011). *Never get a "real" job: How to dump your boss, build a business and not go broke.* Hoboken, NJ: John Wiley & Sons.

Gereffi, G. (2005). *New offshoring of jobs and global development.* Geneva, Switzerland: International Institute for Labour Studies.

Godofsky, J., Zukin, C., & Horn, C. V. (2011). *Unfulfilled expectations: Recent college graduates struggle in a troubled economy.* New Brunswick, NJ: John J. Heldrich Center for Workforce Development, Rutgers University.

Harrison, A., & McMillan, M. (2009). Offshoring jobs? Multinationals and US manufacturing employment. *Discussion Papers Series, Department of Economics, Tufts University.* Retrieved from http://ideas.repec.org/p/tuf/tuftec/0741.html

Hobijn, B., & Sahin, A. (2007). *Job-finding and separation rates in the OECD.* New York, NY: Federal Reserve Bank of New York.

Howe, J. (2006, June). The rise of crowdsourcing: Remember outsourcing? Sending jobs to India and China is so 2003. The new pool of cheap labor: everyday people using their spare cycles to create content, solve problems, even do corporate R & D. *Wired, 14.06.*

Howe, J. (2008). *Crowdsourcing: Why the power of the crowd is driving the future of business.* New York, NY: Three Rivers Press.

Kelley, D. J., Bosma, N., & Amorós, J. E. (2010). *Global entrepreneurship monitor.* London, England: Global Entrepreneurship Research Association.

Kickstarter. (2012). 2011: The stats. Retrieved January 11, 2012, from http://www.kickstarter.com/blog/2011-the-stats

Kowske, B. J., Rasch, R., & Wiley, J. (2010). Millennials' (lack of) attitude problem: An empirical examination of generational effects on work attitudes. *Journal of Business and Psychology, 25*(2), 265–279.

Kraemer, K. L., Linden, G., & Dedrick, J. (2011). *Capturing value in global networks: Apple's iPad and iPhone.* Irvine, CA: Personal Computer Industry Center, UC–Irvine.

Landes, D. S., Mokyr, J., & Baumol, W. J. (Eds.). (2010). *The invention of enterprise: Entrepreneurship from ancient Mesopotamia to modern times.* Princeton, NJ: Princeton University Press.

Lohr, S. (2009, July 19). Unboxed: The crowd is wise (when it's focused). *The New York Times,* p. 4. Retrieved from http://www.nytimes.com/2009/07/19/technology/internet/19unboxed.html

Maddison, A. (2001). *The world economy: A millennial perspective.* Paris, France: OECD Publishing.

Martin, M. (Host). (2011, 2012). Burn your resume, and create a job. In NPR (Producer), *Tell Me More* [Radio program]. Retrieved from http://www.npr.org/2011/01/18/133021321/Burn-Your-Resume-And-Create-A-Job

Massad, V. J. (2010). Understanding the online selling environment: A segmentation approach to profiling eBay sellers. *ABD Journal, 2,* 1–9.

Mayer, G. (2004). *Union membership trends in the United States.* Ithaca, NY: Cornell University ILR School.

McCarthy, J. (2004). *Near-term growth of offshoring accelerating.* Cambridge, MA: Forrester Research.

Moriguchi, C., & Ono, H. (2006). Japanese lifetime employment: A century's perspective. In M. Blomstrom & S. L. Croix (Eds.), *Institutional change in Japan* (pp. 152–176). New York, NY: Routledge.

Negroponte, N. (1995). *Being digital.* New York, NY: Vintage Books.

Obama, B. (2012). *Remarks by the president in State of the Union Address.* Retrieved from http://www.whitehouse.gov/photos-and-video/video/2012/01/25/2012-state-union-address-enhanced-version#transcript

Organisation for Economic Co-operation and Development (OECD). (2010). *Off to a good start? Jobs for youth.* Paris, France: OECD Publishing.

Organisation for Economic Co-operation and Development (OECD). (2011). *Youth unemployment rate, employment and labour markets: Key tables from OECD, No. 2.* Paris, France: Author.

Perry, M. (2010, October 4). Increases in U.S. worker productivity, more than China's currency, responsible for loss of U.S. jobs. Retrieved from http://www.dailymarkets.com/economy/2010/10/03/increases-in-u-s-worker-productivity-more-than-chinas-currency-responsible-for-loss-of-u-s-jobs/

Pew Research Center. (2006). *Public says American work life is worsening, but most workers remain satisfied with their jobs.* Washington, DC: Author.

PriceWaterhouseCoopers. (2011). Global entertainment and media outlook 2011–2015. Retrieved January 29, 2012, from http://www.pwc.com/us/en/industry/entertainment-media/publications/global-entertainment-media-outlook.jhtml

Rampbell, C. (2011, May 19). Many with new college degree find the job market humbling. *The New York Times.* Retrieved from http://www.nytimes.com/2011/05/19/business/economy/19grads.html?_r=1&hp

Salmon, F. (2011, December 22). The global youth unemployment crisis. Retrieved January 4, 2012, from http://blogs.reuters.com/felix-salmon/2011/12/22/the-global-youth-unemployment-crisis/

Schoof, U. (2006). *Stimulating youth entrepreneurship: Barriers and incentives to enterprise start-ups by young people.* Geneva, Switzerland: International Labor Organization.

Seligson, H. (2010, December 12). No jobs? Young graduates make their own. *The New York Times,* p. BU1. Retrieved from http://www.nytimes.com/2010/12/12/business/12yec.html?pagewanted=all

SellaBand.com. (2012). *About us.* Retrieved January 11, 2012, from https://www.sellaband.com/en/pages/about_us

Shane, S. A. (2008). *The illusions of entrepreneurship: The costly myths that entrepreneurs, investors, and policy makers live by.* New Haven, CT: Yale University Press.

Tapscott, D., & Williams, A. D. (2008). *Wikinomics: How mass collaboration changes everything.* London, England: Penguin Books.

Trumka, R. (2010, September 30). Opposing view on international trade: "It's time for action." *USA Today.* Retrieved from http://www.usatoday.com/news/opinion/editorials/2010-10-01-editorial01_ST1_N.htm

United Nations Population Fund. (2011). *State of world population 2011: People and possibilities in a world of 7 billion.* New York, NY: United Nations Population Fund.

U.S. Bureau of Labor Statistics. (2006). *100 years of U.S. consumer spending: Data for the nation, New York City, and Boston.* Washington, DC: U.S. Department of Labor.

Wachter, M. (2007). The rise and decline of unions. *Regulation, Summer 2007,* 23–29.

Williams, J. C., & Boushey, H. (2010). *The three faces of work-family conflict: The poor, the professionals, and the missing middle.* Washington, DC: Center for American Progress.

Wilson, D. (2011, February 9). Burn your resume: Secrets to avoiding a real job. Retrieved January 5, 2012, from http://www.smh.com.au/small-business/entrepreneur/burn-your-resume-secrets-to-avoiding—a-real-job-20110209–1amc0.html

World Economic Forum. (2012). Education. Retrieved January 14, 2012, from http://www.weforum.org/issues/education

Zhongguo Dianzi Shangwu Yanjiu Zhongxin (China e-Business Research Center). (2011). *Zhongguo dianzi shangwu shichang suju jianche baogao (China e-Business market statistics).* Hangzhou, China: Author.

3

What Makes an Entrepreneur

The Entrepreneurial Spirit

Why join the Navy if you can be a pirate?

—Steve Jobs

Failure is simply the opportunity to begin again, this time more intelligently.

—Henry Ford

The world knows entrepreneurs like Henry Ford, Steve Jobs, and Bill Gates, but few people know Woodrow Campbell, or Woody. In 2008 Woody started the Green Cab Company in Lansing, Michigan (Hughes, 2008). I used Woody's services frequently when I lived in Michigan. On a number of long rides with Woody to the Detroit and Grand Rapids airports, I had the opportunity to talk with him about his business. I was very impressed with his decision to start a business in such an economically difficult time in Michigan, when many people were laid off and waiting to find jobs. Woody said the idea of a green cab company, one that uses only hybrid vehicles, came from his wife, who saw a similar taxi service in Toronto, Canada. Then he told me that he saw a need in Lansing, where Michigan State University is located. The concept of an environmentally friendly taxi company would be attractive to the students and faculty. But "green" is not his only selling point. He was the first to use meters and published the rate so "people would know how much they were paying." This may be a small and simple thing but ultra important for cost-conscious students, especially international students and visitors new to the United States who prefer to have a meter to being told by the driver or company of the fare. And he saw an increase of international students and visitors to Michigan State University. Woody also strives to keep his cars clean and his drivers friendly. Green Cab Company has been a huge success. Woody started with only one Honda Civic hybrid in 2008 with himself as the owner, driver, and dispatcher. In less than three years, his fleet expanded to include four cars, all hybrid, and his company expanded to about 20 employees.

Woody is not Steve Jobs, but they have something in common. They both are entrepreneurs. The term entrepreneur originated from French, with the original meaning being someone who undertakes a significant project or activity (Dees, 1998). It was used to refer to someone who undertakes a business venture by the 16th century (Sobel, 2008). Two economists, the French Jean-Baptiste Say and the British John Stuart Mill, have been credited for popularizing the academic usage of the word in the 19th century. The term was further refined by the economist Joseph Alois Schumpeter in the 20th century (Dees, 1998; Martin & Osberg, 2007; Sobel, 2008). Today, the term is generally used to refer to individuals who organize, manage, and assume the risks of a business or enterprise (Martin & Osberg, 2007; Sobel, 2008). Both Woody and Steve Jobs are individuals who have organized, managed, and assumed the risks of a business.

THE DIFFERENT FORMS OF ENTREPRENEURSHIP: REDEFINING ENTREPRENEURS

The conventional definition of entrepreneurs has often been associated with owning a business to pursue profit, but the term has acquired an expanded set of meanings to encompass a lot more than business owners (Florida, 2002; Landes, Mokyr, & Baumol, 2010; Pink, 2002). To begin with, an entrepreneur does not have to own a business with employees in the traditional sense. One can just work for herself or she *IS* the business. Author Daniel Pink provides an insightful discussion about the growing trend of self-employment in his best-selling book *Free Agent Nation: The Future of Working for Yourself.* Although not all of his upbeat observations of freedom from full-time employment with a company a decade ago has been supported by data and other observers (Florida, 2002), a large number of people have become free agents, their own bosses and employees. According to data released by the U.S. Census Bureau in 2011, there were over 21 million business establishments that did not have employees in 2009 (U.S. Census Bureau, 2011). Data from the Internal Revenue Service (IRS) confirm this figure. In 2009, nearly 23 million tax returns were from "sole proprietorships," meaning individuals who operated a business but without any employees (IRS, 2011). An entrepreneur is simply someone who creates a job or employment for him or herself in this case.

Social Entrepreneurs

Financial profit does not have to be the sole pursuit of an entrepreneur. Social entrepreneurship, for example, aims to create social values, benefits to the society, rather than financial values. Roger Martin, dean of Rotman School of Management of the University of Toronto, and coauthor Sally Osberg, president and CEO of the Skoll Foundation, an organization dedicated to fostering social entrepreneurship, wrote recently, "the social entrepreneur aims for value in the form of large-scale, transformational benefit that accrues either to a significant segment of society or to society at large" (Martin & Osberg, 2007, p. 35). This, however, does not mean social entrepreneurs do not make money or consider making a profit. "Ventures created by social entrepreneurs can certainly generate income, and they can be organized as either not-for-profits or for-profits. What distinguishes social entrepreneurship is the primacy of social benefit" (Martin & Osberg, 2007, p. 35). One of the best-known examples of social enterprises is perhaps Muhammad Yunus, the Nobel Peace Prize winner who founded the Grameen Bank in Bangladesh in 1983 to provide microcredit and financial lessons to poor villagers. His enterprise has had tremendous success in helping people escape poverty and has inspired many around the world to undertake similar actions. In his new book *Building Social Business: The New Kind of Capitalism that Serves Humanity's Most Pressing Needs*, he recounts his story and provides advice to those "dedicated to change the world" through entrepreneurial activities (Yunus & Webber, 2010).

Intrapreneurs

Entrepreneurs do not have to manage a business. She can be an employee of a corporate. In this case, she is called an intrapreneur. The *American Heritage Dictionary of English* defines intrapreneur as "a person within a large corporation who takes direct responsibility for turning an idea into a profitable finished product through assertive risk-taking and innovation."[1] The basic idea of intrapreneurship is to "allow employees of large corporations to behave within the company as they would as individual entrepreneurs in the outside world," noted Henry Petroski in his book *The Evolution of Useful Things* (Petroski, 1994, pp. 83–84). Thus an intrapreneur in essence is an entrepreneur within an organization or entrepreneurial employees (Bosma, Wennekers, & Amorós, 2012).

Art Fry and Spencer Silver, co-creators of the Post-it notes, are called "model intrapreneurs" by Petroski in his recount of how Post-it notes came into existence and became such a huge success. Art Fry, a chemical engineer at 3M, had a problem with his bookmarking procedure. He had been using scraps of paper to mark the pages in his hymnal so he could quickly locate the songs. But the loose scraps of paper would fall out

---

[1]http://www.intrapreneur.com/MainPages/History/Dictionary.html

of their places after the first use, which naturally resulted in problems locating the songs as Fry had planned. Fry certainly was not the only human being who had encountered such a problem, but he was the first person who came up with a solution. He remembered a product created by Spencer Silver, also a 3M researcher. Silver came upon an adhesive that is strong and yet easily removed several years earlier, but no one had come up with a use of it despite Silver's belief in its commercial value. Connecting his dissatisfaction with his bookmarking method and Silver's adhesive, Fry came up with the idea of making sticky bookmarks that could be easily removed without damaging the book. Thanks to 3M's "bootlegging" policy, a practice that allows its employees to devote a certain percentage of their work time to work on their own projects, Fry got to work on his idea, which eventually led to the ubiquitous Post-it notes (Petroski, 1994).

Fry and Silver are not the only intrapreneurs who have made a tremendously successful product, although the contributions of intrapreneurs are not typically known to the outside world like the successful entrepreneurs. In fact, intrapreneurs create values and jobs for others the same way as entrepreneurs. A CBS News 2008 story gives a sense of the magnitude of contribution of intrapreneurs. The story listed five of the "greatest intrapreneurs" in business history that include Silver and Fry for creating Post-it notes at 3M; Ken Kutaragi for making the PlayStation at Sony; Patrick Naughton, James Gosling, and Bill Joy for developing the Java language at Sun Microsystems; Larry Hornbeck for developing digital light processing technology at Texas Instrument; and Dave Myers and John Spencer for inventing the ELIXIR guitar strings at W. L. Gore (Swearingen, 2008).

Policy Entrepreneurs

Entrepreneurship can also happen and is needed in the public sector. Governments need policy entrepreneurs for innovations in public policy and management so as to maximize the value of public services. "People who seek to initiate dynamic policy change" are policy entrepreneurs, according to Michael Mintrom, a professor of political science at the University of Auckland in New Zealand (Mintrom, 1997, p. 738). In a study published by the *American Journal of Political Science,* Mintrom showed the key role policy entrepreneurs play in promoting innovative public policy. An edited book by political science professors Michael Harris and Rhonda Kinney of Eastern Michigan University includes empirical studies of entrepreneurship and innovation in state and local governments. These studies show that "policy entrepreneurs oftentimes play central roles in catalyzing the demand for change into a drive to innovate in a more specific fashion," but "not enough attention is given in the literature on public sector innovation as to the role of the entrepreneur" (Harris & Kinney, 2004, p. 184).

Thus, entrepreneurs come in different shapes and forms. They can be solo business owners, freelancing writers, or technological innovators. They can also be leaders of social institutions, organizers of social movements, or even government employees. They may be well-known and ultra successful such as Steve Jobs and Muhammad Yunus, but they can also be unknown small enterprise starters. Calvin A. Kent, former dean and distinguished professor at the Lewis College of Business of Marshall University and twice elected president of the National Association of Economic Educators, concludes in a book he edited on entrepreneurship education:

> Entrepreneurship is more than just starting a small business. Despite the traditional focus on small business startup, entrepreneurship is vastly more than that. While often the entrepreneurial urge results in the formation of a new business venture, to limit entrepreneurship in that way misses its true character. Entrepreneurship can take place within corporations, nonprofit organizations, and even government bureaucracies. The essence of entrepreneurship is bringing about change that is beneficial in its result. Those who bring about these changes are the entrepreneurs. (Kent, 1990, p. 283)

The same expansion of definition of entrepreneurs is applied in the 2011 global report on youth entrepreneurship by the World Economic Forum:

> Entrepreneurship is about growth, creativity and innovation. Innovative entrepreneurs come in all shapes and forms and their impact is not limited to start-ups—they also innovate in the public, private, academic and non-profit sectors. Entrepreneurship refers to an individual's ability to turn ideas into action and is therefore a key competence for all, helping young people to be more creative and self-confident in whatever they undertake. (World Economic Forum, 2011, p. 5)

WHAT MAKES AN ENTREPRENEUR

The Entrepreneurial Spirit

While entrepreneurs may differ in what they do and the context in which they undertake entrepreneurship activities, there are some fundamental commonalities among all entrepreneurs: They are dissatisfied with an existing condition, be it the centralized computing system for Steve Jobs or the lack of access to loans for Muhammad Yunus, then they see an opportunity and take the risk to change the condition with ingenuity, and finally they persist to make it successful, despite the ups and downs (Martin & Osberg, 2007). These common characteristics form the core of the entrepreneurial spirit.

The entrepreneurial spirit captures the common qualities shared by entrepreneurs: "inspiration, creativity, direct action, courage, and fortitude" (Martin & Osberg, 2007, pp. 32–33). Whereas Steve Jobs was inspired to change how computing was done, Woody was inspired to use energy-efficient vehicles to provide environmentally friendly taxi services. The entrepreneur also has to be creative and apply the creativity to develop new solutions. Jobs used his creativity earlier on to bring aesthetically appealing personal computers to solve the problem of the inflexible centralized mainframe computing, and for Woody he used hybrid cars and added taxi meters. After the inspiration to develop a creative solution and once the solution is identified, the entrepreneur must take direct actions. "Rather than waiting for someone else to intervene or trying to convince somebody else to solve the problem, the entrepreneur takes direct action by creating a new product or service and the venture to advance it" (Martin & Osberg, 2007, pp. 32–33). Jobs and Steve Wozniak developed Apple IIs and Macintosh and formed Apple Computers, while Woody set up his Green Cab Company.

The process of innovation, developing products and services, and managing a business or project is not smooth, thus entrepreneurship requires courage. That is even when others may think it unwise, unreasonable, and unrealistic, the entrepreneur has the courage to take the risk, known or unknown. It was certainly risky for Jobs to develop new products, but it was as risky for Woody to quit his job and invest his time and savings in a green cab company. Finally, entrepreneurship is not a one-time deal, a short process, but rather a long, bumpy journey. Thus the entrepreneur needs fortitude or perseverance to see their solution to fruition and market acceptance.

With some variations in the terms used, these characteristics— inspiration, creativity, courage, direct actions, and fortitude— have been generally identified as personal attributes of entrepreneurs by researchers of entrepreneurship. Other terms that have been used to refer to the qualities of entrepreneurs include alertness to opportunities, foresight, ambition, passion, confidence, innovation, risk taker, creativity, social networker, and persistence (Kent, 1990; Rabbior, 1990).

WHERE DO ENTREPRENEURS COME FROM?

Born or Made?

"The entrepreneurial mystique? It's not magic, it's not mysterious," the management guru Peter Drucker once wrote, "and it has nothing to do with the genes" (Drucker, 1985). But Scott Shane disagrees. Shane, the Case Western professor of entrepreneur studies who authored the book *The Illusion of Entrepreneurship,* published a quite controversial book more recently. In this book, *Born Entrepreneurs, Born Leaders: How Your Genes Affect Your Work Life,* published in 2010 by Oxford University Press, Shane argues that "genes affect nearly everything" (Shane, 2010, p. 1). That "everything" certainly includes entrepreneurial characteristics. The book "discusses how your genes influence your work interests, work values, decision making, risk taking, management style, approach to leadership, creativity, entrepreneurship, and work performance" (Shane, 2010, p. 3).

Shane's conclusions were primarily based on findings of studies of twins, which has long been the favored method of separating hereditary traits from environmental influences. By comparing the choices two sibling twins make in given situations, one can infer the source of the difference. There are two types of twins: identical twins, who share all of their DNA, and fraternal twins, who share half of their genetic composition. "If pairs of identical twins make more similar choices, such as starting a business, than pairs of fraternal twins, then genetics must affect the choices," writes Shane in a guest blog post on the *Entrepreneur* website in December 2011. Shane also uses data from molecular genetics research designed to study "the different versions of genes people have and see if entrepreneurs are statistically more likely to have one version over another" (Shane, 2011).

Shane concludes that DNA indeed influences people's job preferences, job satisfaction, and job performance. According to Shane, 75% of differences in job preference in creative arts can be explained by genetic differences, and for teaching, it is about 55% genetics. About 40% of salary differences can be attributed to genetic differences as well (Shane, 2010). When it comes to entrepreneurs, they are 40% born and 60% made (Mount, 2009).

One route that genes influence whether one becomes an entrepreneur is through personalities. "The same genes that affect whether we are extroverted, open to experience, disagreeable and sensation seeking also influence our decision to start our own business," Shane writes. "Furthermore, the same genes that influence the tendency to be open to experience also affect the tendency to identify new business opportunities" (Shane, 2011).

Sensation seeking, for example, is a personality trait believed to be related to entrepreneurship. Shane and his colleagues studied over 3,000 twins in the U.K. and found that "between 37 and 42 percent of the variance in the tendency of people to engage in entrepreneurship is accounted for by genetic factors . . . between 31 and 46 percent of this variance was mediated by the psychological trait of sensation seeking" (Nicolaou, Shane, Cherkas, & Spector, 2008, p. 16).

Shane's findings are not surprising or entirely new. Both popular beliefs and scientific evidence suggest biology plays a role in what we eventually become. Evolutionary psychologists have postulated that human behaviors, personalities, and values certainly are partly the result of the long process of human evolution that has encoded certain attributes in our genes to pass on from generation to generation (Barkow, Cosmides, & Tooby, 1992; Buss, 2004; Crawford & Krebs, 1998; Wright, 1994). We are not born a "blank slate" waiting to be scripted, as the MIT cognitive scientist Steven Pinker very well argues in his 2003 book *The Blank Slate: The Modern Denial of Human Nature* (Pinker, 2003). Evolution has granted all members of us *homo-sapiens* some common capacities.

And, for some reason, we are not born the same. We may have the same set of innate abilities, but the strengths of these abilities vary. Some are born extremely strong in music, others in math, still others in making things. These are the people we call geniuses or child prodigies. Mozart was a genius in music, Gauss in mathematics, and Picasso in art. Most of us are not geniuses, but we still have areas in which we are strong. The flip side of this coin is weaknesses. We are not equally strong in all domains. One may be great with words, but not as good at painting. Another may be talented in dancing, but have great difficulties with numbers (Gardner, 2006). We also differ in the affective domain. Some are more adventurous, willing to take risks, and tolerant of uncertainty; some seem to be more cautious and risk-averting.

But we must be careful because a simplistic interpretation of Shane's research and other suggestions of the biological basis of human behavior can lead to genetic determinism. Nature is only half of the story. Nurture plays an equally important role in the development of an individual, if not more. While nature provides the potential, the environment affects to what degree and which potentials are realized, as well as what talents are suppressed and thus not fully developed. Families, friends, and schools all affect how one turns out to be. A person may have a strong inclination for entrepreneurship, but if he is not given the opportunity to learn or in worse cases, if it is forbidden, the person's entrepreneurial talent cannot be developed. A child born with a more adventurous nature can be taught to be timid and cautious. Those who are born with a stronger propensity for "sensation seeking" can be discouraged by negative experiences and feedback. Similarly, those who may not have such a strong tendency can be encouraged and cultivated to become more entrepreneurial. This is why deliberate entrepreneurship education has shown an increase in people's intention to start businesses (Kent, 1990) and why Harvard Business School teaches an entrepreneurial manager course in its MBA curriculum (Hamermesh, Marshall, Roberts, & Stevenson, 2002).

The dynamics between nature and nurture also play a significant role in what ultimately a person can be or can do. Early experiences may accelerate or slow down the development of certain innate abilities. At the same time, those accelerated abilities gain more attention and change the environment to their favor, which will then further support their development and suppress the less developed ones. This is the Matthew Effect at work in psychological development: The richer gets richer and the poor poorer, just like the Master says, "For unto every one that hath shall be given, and he shall have abundance: but from him that hath not shall be taken away even that which he hath" (Matthew 25:29). Best-selling author Malcolm Gladwell illustrates the Matthew Effect with the story of Canadian hockey players: Those who showed stronger ability earlier received more attention and opportunities and became better players (Gladwell, 2008).

There exists tremendous disagreement among scientists and educators as to which of the above factors determine or play a more significant role in the development of human abilities. Some tend to attribute more to nature, while others more to nurture. Yet still others attribute it to something else. Richard Lewontin, a Harvard biologist, writes in his book *The Triple Helix*, "The organism is determined neither by its genes nor by its environment nor even by the interaction between them, but bears a significant mark of random process" (Lewontin, 2001, p. 38).

This means if and when there are opportunities to trigger, the expression of genetic potentials matter a great deal in the actual development of those potentials. Moreover, genetic potentials of entrepreneurial qualities are not a zero-sum game or binary. It is not one has it or does not have it. Rather, it is a continuum. One can have more or less, barring extreme cases. There may be entrepreneurial geniuses, and there may be some who are born with absolutely no entrepreneurial quality. But most of us should have the potential, although some may have more than others.

Therefore, based on available evidence, it is safe to say that entrepreneurs are both made and born or are neither born nor made. In other words, even if someone is born with the propensity for entrepreneurship, that potential cannot be materialized or at least reduced in an environment that does not trigger or discourages entrepreneurship. On the other hand, even if someone is not born with great potential for entrepreneurship, he could still become an entrepreneur in the right context, albeit not necessarily as great as Steve Jobs.

THE ENTREPRENEURIAL ACTIVITY GAP

Necessity vs. Opportunity

The discussion in the previous section leads to two assumptions. First, because genetic evolution takes a long time, and human beings have not had enough time for modern culture to alter their genes, it is generally accepted that human beings should not have any group differences (Ehrlich, 2000). In other words, the genetic pool of the Chinese, Koreans, Singaporeans, and Americans should be about the same. Individual genetic differences should be randomly and equally distributed within these pools. That is, if there is a certain percentage of people who are born with great propensity for innovation and entrepreneurial activities, the proportion should be similar, if not exactly the same, across different ethnic groups, geographical regions, or political institutions. Likewise, the share of born "non-entrepreneurs" should be about the same in each country. Second, as discussed before, most people are born with some tendency to become entrepreneurial and creative, and the distribution of such tendency should be about the same across countries as well. In other words, the genetic stock of entrepreneurs and entrepreneurial qualities should be similar around the world.

However, the Global Entrepreneurship Monitor (GEM) found significantly different levels of entrepreneurship activities in different parts of the world (Bosma et al., 2012; Kelley, Bosma, & Amorós, 2010). In Vanuatu, a tiny island country in the Pacific Ocean, the total early-stage entrepreneurship rate was 52.2%, meaning 52.2% of adults were engaged in starting a business in 2010. In Bolivia, the percentage was 38.6% and in Ghana, the eastern African country, the percentage was 33.9%. In contrast, in Italy, only 2.3% of adults were engaged in starting a business in 2010 and in Japan, 3.3% (Kelley et al., 2010). A 2011 Gallup Poll that surveys entrepreneurship intent in 83 countries found that in Sub-Sahara African countries 20% of adults plan to start a business in the next 12 months, while in the European Union only 3% had such plans (Badal & Srinivasan, 2011).

To identify patterns of entrepreneurship activities, GEM divides economies into three stages of entrepreneurship according to their overall economic situation: factor-driven, efficiency-driven, and innovation-driven. Factor-driven economies' primary activities are subsistence agriculture and extraction of natural resources. Examples of factor-driven economies are Sub-Sahara countries. In efficiency-driven economies, with increased industrialization and economy of scale, the activities shift away from necessity-driven entrepreneurship to that which improves efficiency of production, mainly manufacturing. Representatives of this category are China, Russia, Brazil, Latin American countries, and many former Eastern European countries. The innovation-driven economies are well developed already. Entrepreneurship in these countries is characterized by R&D, knowledge intensity, and an expanding service sector. The United States, Japan, and Western European countries fall into this category. The GEM study found a much higher level of entrepreneurial activities in the factor-driven economies than in the innovation-driven economies:

> Far more individuals in factor-driven economies (almost 43% on average) intend to start businesses over the next three years compared to the other economies. An average of just 23% of people in efficiency-driven economies expressed this intent, while even fewer (8%) of those in innovation-driven economies did. (Kelley et al., 2010, p. 22)

Why this gap in entrepreneurship activity then?

The answer is actually quite simple at the macrolevel. The high level of entrepreneurship in poor countries is a result of necessity, rather than opportunity. Most of the entrepreneurs in the poor countries are "necessity entrepreneurs" who are forced into self-employment because there are no better options. Starting a business is simply a way to make a living.

This is why GEM found that entrepreneurial activities are highest in the poorest countries. In developed countries, necessity entrepreneurs also exist but thanks to the availability of more opportunities and social support provided by government and/or family, not many people are pushed into such a situation that they have to start a business to make a living. In developed countries, more entrepreneurs are so-called "opportunity entrepreneurs." They are not forced to start a business. Instead, they choose to start businesses out of opportunity. The low entrepreneurship activities in developed countries means that not many people choose to start their own businesses. The GEM attributes the lack of opportunity entrepreneurs to the availability of stable jobs in developed countries:

> Many people appear to see fewer reasons for becoming entrepreneurs when they have stable job options. Surely, some will leave these jobs to become entrepreneurs. They may do so because they see opportunities, and have particular attitudes and beliefs to inspire them. Nonetheless, the motivation to take these paths may diminish when other seemingly more attractive options abound. (Kelley et al., 2010, p. 58)

Necessity-driven entrepreneurship is absolutely important and essential for developing countries. As a form of employment, necessity entrepreneurs can at least secure income for themselves. But "they are less likely to grow innovative businesses, reach for high growth and seek international markets" (Kelley et al., 2010, p. 58). It is the opportunity entrepreneurs who embody the entrepreneurial spirit that is needed in developed nations. And eventually when the developing countries further develop, opportunity entrepreneurship will become much more important as well. Furthermore, it is the opportunity entrepreneurs who will bring innovations that will drive economic prosperity and help address global problems in the future. "Societies also need opportunity entrepreneurs to ensure new ideas come into being through the energy of enterprising individuals" (Kelley et al., 2010, p. 58). Thus, it is opportunity entrepreneurship that is of great interest. However, as available data suggest, opportunity entrepreneurship is seriously missing in the world.

THE ENTREPRENEURIAL SPIRIT GAP

Poverty is indeed a powerful motivator, but the necessity vs. opportunity distinction does not explain all the entrepreneurship activity gaps among different countries. If necessity is the explanation behind the high entrepreneurship activity in developing countries, why is there such a big gap between Vanuatu (52.2%) and Egypt (7%), both "factor-driven economies?" And in Egypt, a nation that youth unemployment caused a revolution, it is definitely necessary to have more entrepreneurs to create jobs. As Clair Provost, a journalist of the U.K. newspaper *The Guardian,* observed in 2011: "Many Egyptian graduates are unable to find work that matches their education. Skills programmes that teach employability and entrepreneurship can help, but job creation is needed" (Provost, 2011). Why aren't there more entrepreneurs in Egypt than Vanuatu?

Similarly, why do some developed countries have higher entrepreneurship activities than others? Figures 3.1 and 3.2 show early-stage entrepreneurship activities in 2010 and 2011 for innovation-driven economies based on the GEM data. As shown in the figures, the early-stage entrepreneurship rate for Australia was 7.8 in 2010 and 10.5 in 2011. The rate for the United States was 7.6 in 2010 and 12.3 in 2011, but Japan had only 3.3 in 2010 and 5.2 in 2011 (Bosma et al., 2012; Kelley et al., 2010). In the Gallup survey, North America (U.S. and Canada) had 7% of adults who planned to start a business in the next 12 months, while in the European Union only 3% wanted to do so (Badal & Srinivasan, 2011). Apparently more people in the United States engage in entrepreneurship activities than in Japan. Are there more opportunities in the United States than in Japan? Or are there other factors at work?

Early Stage Enterpreneurship Activities in Innovation-Driven Economies 2010

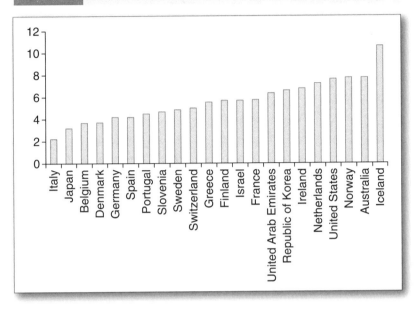

Figure 3.2 Early Stage Entrepreneurship Activities in Innovation-Driven Economies 2011

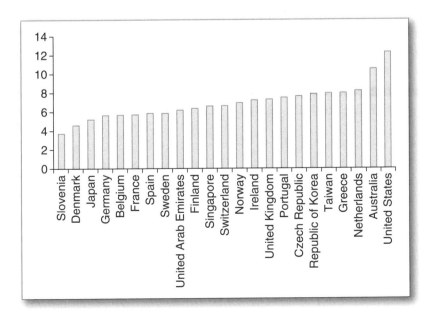

There certainly are other factors, in addition to necessity, that affect the level of entrepreneurship activities. For example, the rule of law, a healthy financing system, availability of capital, and general economic policy are important factors (Kelley et al., 2010; Schoof, 2006). Cultural factors such as social status of entrepreneurs and attitudes toward entrepreneurship also affect the level of entrepreneurship activities (Kelley et al., 2010; Schoof, 2006).

These factors may explain some of the differences across countries and regions. But there are also widely recognized gaps within a nation or region, which theoretically has the same economic, cultural, financial, and political context for everyone. Even under virtually identical conditions, why do some people choose to start a business, while others choose to start a revolution or protest against the government, and still others wait for government aid or keep looking for a job?

The answer goes back to the entrepreneurship spirit. It is apparent that there exists an entrepreneurship spirit gap among different countries and regions and among individuals. The gap among individuals may be partly explained by genetics, as Professor Scott Shane suggested (Shane, 2010), and still partly by experiences. The gaps among different countries are perhaps more due to experiences than genetics since as discussed earlier, the genetic stock of entrepreneurs should be evenly distributed across the human population.

CULTIVATING ENTREPRENEURS: ENTREPRENEURSHIP EDUCATION?

Designing and deploying experiences that help cultivate the entrepreneurship spirit has thus become essential in order to increase the level of entrepreneurship activities. One of the fastest-growing and most popular practices to develop entrepreneurs is entrepreneurship education. Governments, business leaders, and international organizations have issued urgent calls and made investment in entrepreneurship education programs (Fayolle & Klandt, 2006; Schoof, 2006; World

Economic Forum, 2012). Entrepreneurship courses and programs have been added to business schools and begun to enter the K–12 school curriculum. Academic journals and research centers have been established and professorships created. According to Donald F. Kuratko, the Jack M. Gill Chair of Entrepreneurship and executive director at The Johnson Center for Entrepreneurship & Innovation at Indiana University:

> Today, entrepreneurship education in U.S. has exploded to more than 2,200 courses at over 1,600 schools; 277 endowed positions; 44 refereed academic journals, mainstream management journals devoting more issues (some special issues) to entrepreneurship; and over 100 established and funded centers. The discipline's accumulated "wealth" has grown to exceed $440 million with over 75% of those funds accruing since 1987. (Kuratko, 2005, p. 583)

This reflects a typical response of human beings: If something is missing, we need to create it. In this case, if there are no entrepreneurs, we need to make some. And to make some is to instill the entrepreneurship spirit into our children from the outside through education.

Entrepreneurship education may have its place. But before we rush to add yet another component to the school curriculum and mandate all children take an entrepreneurship course, we need to question its effectiveness.

There are not many empirical studies available to prove the effectiveness of formal entrepreneurship education. The content, approaches, and programs undertaken vary a great deal, although they may all bear the name of entrepreneurship education. It is thus very difficult to make any sound judgment. For example, in a widely referenced article published in 1997 that reviewed 10 years of study on the effectiveness of entrepreneurship education, the authors found only preliminary evidence that "entrepreneurial attributes can be positively influenced by educational programs and that many entrepreneurship programs and courses are able to build awareness of entrepreneurship as a career option and to encourage favourable attitudes toward entrepreneurship" (Gorman, Hanlon, & King, 1997). This conclusion, however, is very questionable because the studies they examined themselves have serious methodological flaws. "Most of the studies in our review, aimed at assessing the impact of educational content or process, tended to be based on one particular course at one particular institution, making generalisation difficult at best. The absence of theoretically-derived sampling populations also poses a serious barrier to replication" (Gorman et al., 1997). In other words, most of the studies that came up with a positive answer have a conflict of interest—they wanted to prove they were effective.

There is also an inherent logical contradiction with entrepreneurship education. "Entrepreneurship education is the structured, formal conveyance of entrepreneurial knowledge, namely the concepts, skills and mentality individuals use during startups and development of growth-oriented ventures" (Holmgren & From, 2005, p. 385). However, the entrepreneurial spirit and qualities are about creativity, innovation, persistence, risk taking, and other fundamentally human spirits. There may be some entrepreneurial skills that can and should be taught formally, but can the other human spirits and qualities? Or worse yet, formal and structured programs may work counter to discourage creativity and innovation because that can imply conformity.

The entrepreneurial spirit is certainly the result of both biology and culture, but perhaps it cannot be taught formally. While it is tempting to provide formal programs to cultivate entrepreneurs, it is important to not automatically assume that people are empty vessels waiting for an injection of entrepreneurial skills and knowledge. Or, perhaps it is useful to adopt a different stance. Instead of assuming the entrepreneurial spirit as something that needs to be imparted, it may be more productive to accept the suggestion discussed earlier that people are born with the entrepreneurial potentials. What we need is to encourage and enable individuals to realize and strengthen that potential, or at least not to discourage and stifle it in the process of formal education. In this spirit, the World Economic Forum report forcefully argues:

> It is not enough to add entrepreneurship on the perimeter— it needs to be at the core of the way education operates. Educational institutions at all levels (primary, secondary and higher education) need to adopt 21st century methods and tools to develop the appropriate learning environment for encouraging creativity, innovation and the ability to think "out of the box" to solve problems. Embedding entrepreneurship and innovation, cross-disciplinary approaches and interactive teaching methods all require new models, frameworks and paradigms. It is time to rethink the old systems and fundamentally "reboot" the educational process. (World Economic Forum, 2011, p. 6)

"Rebooting" the educational process is precisely what we need to do to cultivate more entrepreneurs. Education can increase or reduce the stock of entrepreneurs and entrepreneurial qualities in at least two ways. First, it can eliminate the naturally born entrepreneurs, even the entrepreneurial geniuses, from the pool by pushing them out of the educational system, thus depriving them of the opportunity to practice entrepreneurship. On the other hand, education can bring up not so entrepreneurially talented individuals to a level that will make them great entrepreneurs. The second way education alters a society's entrepreneurial talents is by decreasing or increasing the level of entrepreneurial capability, such as self-confidence in individuals, by rewarding or punishing certain behaviors. As a result, the overall level of entrepreneurial qualities is decreased or increased.

In the next chapter, I discuss how education in general affects the entrepreneurial spirit negatively.

References

Badal, S., & Srinivasan, R. (2011). *Mentor support key to starting a business.* Washington, DC: Gallup Poll.

Barkow, J. H., Cosmides, L., & Tooby, J. (Eds.). (1992). *The adapted mind: Evolutionary psychology and the generation of culture.* New York, NY: Oxford University Press.

Bosma, N., Wennekers, S., & Amorós, J. E. (2012). *Global entrepreneurship monitor: 2011 extended report: Entrepreneurs and entrepreneurial employees across the globe.* London, England: Global Entrepreneurship Research Association.

Buss, D. M. (2004). *Evolutionary psychology: The new science of the mind.* New York, NY: Pearson.

Crawford, C., & Krebs, D. L. (Eds.). (1998). *Handbook of evolutionary psychology: Ideas, issues, and applications.* Mahwah, NJ: LEA.

Dees, J. G. (1998). *The meaning of "social entrepreneurship."* Durham, NC: Center for the Advancement of Social Entrepreneurship (Duke University).

Drucker, P. (1985). *Innovation and entrepreneurship.* New York, NY: Harper & Row.

Ehrlich, P. R. (2000). *Human natures: Genes, cultures, and the human prospect.* New York, NY: Penguin Books.

Fayolle, A., & Klandt, H. (Eds.). (2006). *International entrepreneurship education: Issues and newness.* Northampton, MA: Edward Elgar Publishing.

Florida, R. (2002). *The rise of the creative class and how it's transforming work, leisure, community & everyday life.* New York, NY: Basic Books.

Gardner, H. E. (2006). *Multiple intelligences: New horizons in theory and practice.* New York, NY: Basic Books.

Gladwell, M. (2008). *Outliers: The story of success.* New York, NY: Little Brown.

Gorman, G., Hanlon, D., & King, W. (1997). Some research perspectives on entrepreneurship education, enterprise education and education for small business management: A ten-year literature review. *International Small Business Journal, 15*(3), 56–77.

Hamermesh, R. G., Marshall, P. W., Roberts, M. J., & Stevenson, H. H. (2002, April 22). Entrepreneurship: It can be taught. Retrieved January 17, 2012, from http://hbswk.hbs.edu/item/2905.html

Harris, M., & Kinney, R. (Eds.). (2004). *Innovation and entrepreneurship in state and local government.* Lanham, MA: Lexington Books.

Holmgren, C., & From, J. (2005). Taylorism of the mind: Entrepreneurship education from a perspective of educational research. *European Educational Research Journal, 4*(4), 382–390.

Hughes, I. (2008, September 10). Southside Lansing businessman starts green taxi cab company. Retrieved January 17, 2012, from http://www.capitalgainsmedia.com/devnews/cab0235.aspx

Internal Revenue Service (IRS). (2011). SOI tax stats—Nonfarm sole proprietorship statistics. Retrieved January 14, 2012, from http://www.irs.gov/taxstats/indtaxstats/article/0,,id=134481,00.html

Kelley, D. J., Bosma, N., & Amorós, J. E. (2010). *Global entrepreneurship monitor.* London, England: Global Entrepreneurship Research Association.

Kent, C. A. (Ed.). (1990). *Entrepreneurship education: Current developments, future directions.* New York, NY: Quorum Books.

Kuratko, D. F. (2005). The emergence of entrepreneurship education: Development, trends, and challenges. *Entrepreneurship: Theory and Practice, 29*(5), 577–597.

Landes, D. S., Mokyr, J., & Baumol, W. J. (Eds.). (2010). *The invention of enterprise: Entrepreneurship from ancient Mesopotamia to modern times.* Princeton, NJ: Princeton University Press.

Lewontin, R. C. (2001). *The triple helix: Gene, organism, and environment.* Cambridge, MA: Harvard University Press.

Martin, R. L., & Osberg, S. (2007). Social entrepreneurship: The case for definition. *Stanford Social Innovation Review 2007, 29*–39.

Mintrom, M. (1997). Policy entrepreneurs and the diffusion of innovation. *American Journal of Political Science, 41*(3), 738–770.

Mount, I. (2009, December 9). Are entrepreneurs born or made? Scientists and academics battle out the nature-vs-nurture debate. Retrieved January 17, 2012, from http://money.cnn.com/2009/12/09/smallbusiness/entrepreneurs_born_not_made.fsb/

Nicolaou, N., Shane, S., Cherkas, L., & Spector, T. D. (2008). The influence of sensation seeking in the heritability of entrepreneurship. *Strategic Entrepreneurship Journal, 2*(1), 7–21.

Petroski, H. (1994). *The evolution of useful things: How everyday artifacts—from forks to pins to paper clips and zippers—came to be as they are.* New York, NY: Vintage Books.

Pink, D. H. (2002). *Free agent nation: The future of working for yourself.* New York, NY: Warner Books.

Pinker, S. (2003). *The blank slate: The modern denial of human nature.* New York, NY: Penguin.

Provost, C. (2011, August 3). Egypt: Tackling youth unemployment. *The Guardian.* Retrieved from http://www.guardian.co.uk/global-development/2011/aug/03/egypt-education-skills-gap

Rabbior, G. (1990). Elements of a successful entrepreneurship/economics/education program. In C. A. Kent (Ed.), *Entrepreneurship education: Current developments, future directions* (pp. 53–68). New York, NY: Quorum Books.

Schoof, U. (2006). *Stimulating youth entrepreneurship: Barriers and incentives to enterprise start-ups by young people.* Geneva, Switzerland: International Labor Organization.

Shane, S. A. (2010). *Born entrepreneurs, born leaders: How your genes affect your work life.* New York, NY: Oxford University Press.

Shane, S. A. (2011, December 6). Are you a born entrepreneur? Retrieved January 17, 2012, from http://www.entrepreneur.com/article/220804

Sobel, R. S. (Ed.). (2008). *The concise encyclopedia of economics* (2nd ed.). Indianapolis, IN: The Liberty Fund.

Swearingen, J. (2008, April 10). Great intrapreneurs in business history. Retrieved January 14, 2012, from http://www.cbsnews.com/8301-505125_162-51196888/great-intrapreneurs-in-business-history/

U.S. Census Bureau. (2011). 2009 Nonemployer statistics. Retrieved January 14, 2012, from http://censtats.census.gov/cgi-bin/nonemployer/nonsect.pl

World Economic Forum. (2011). *Unlocking entrepreneur capabilities to meet the global challenges of the 21st century: Final report on the entrepreneurship education work stream.* Geneva, Switzerland: World Economic Forum.

World Economic Forum. (2012). Education. Retrieved January 14, 2012, from http://www.weforum.org/issues/education

Wright, R. (1994). *The moral animal: The new science of evolutionary psychology.* New York, NY: Vintage Books.

Yunus, M., & Webber, K. (2010). *Building social business: The new kind of capitalism that serves humanity's most pressing needs.* Philadelphia, PA: Public Affairs.

Achievement Gap vs. Entrepreneurship Gap

The Myth of Education Giants

Education is a better safeguard of liberty than a standing army.

—Edward Everett

An educated people can be easily governed.

—Frederick the Great

C hina needs [Steve] Jobs," China's Premier Wen Jiabao told a group of business leaders in Jiangshu during his tour of one of the most developed provinces in China in December 2011. "We must have products like Apple's that can dominate the world's markets." Wen's comments reflect China's burning desire for innovative and entrepreneurial talents, but more important it reinforces Steve Job's iconic stature as the ultimate innovative entrepreneur that every government leader wishes to have in their society. The legend of Jobs and Apple, the company he cofounded that brought to the world transformative products such as the Apple II, Macintosh, iPod, iPhone, and iPad, has undoubtedly inspired numerous efforts in the world to reproduce their successes. China's Ningbo City of Zhejiang Province, for example, announced that it plans to spend 50 million *yuan* to cultivate innovative entrepreneurial talents just a few days after Jobs' passing in October 2011. The city government plans to produce 1,400 Jobses in five years, according to the *Ningbo Evening News,* a local paper of the city (Luo, Wu, & Yan, 2011).

Ningbo's plan was met with doubts and mockery. The overwhelming reactions to the plan in Chinese media and cyberspace were so negative that the government had to clarify that it never explicitly claimed to reproduce Steve Jobs. The news, however, added fuel to an already raging discussion about China's lack of entrepreneurs like Jobs, ignited by the news of his death. Wen's comments further intensified the discussion, inviting more online comments from ordinary citizens as well as the intellectual elites.

But China cannot have a Steve Jobs, at least according to one of the most influential Chinese-American technology gurus, who has dedicated himself to incubating young entrepreneurs in China. "The next Apple, the next Google will come, but probably not in China," said Kai-fu Lee, founder of Innovation Works, an investment company aimed to cultivate innovative entrepreneurship in China. Lee was former founding president of Google China and former vice president of Interactive Services of Microsoft after working at Apple as a research and development executive (Caijing, 2010). "At least not in the next 50 years or 100 years there will not be an Apple or Google in China," was Lee's controversial prediction in his speech at the World Economic Forum's Summer Davos in Tianjin, China, in September 2010. Lee migrated from Taiwan to the United States at 11 and received his undergraduate education at Columbia and earned a PhD from Carnegie Mellon University.

Lee's provocative statement prompted a round of emotional discussion in China. Some took it with anger and frustration. "How could a Chinese make such self-depreciating statement about his own country and people? . . . I suggest those who have worked for foreigners for a few years not to be so self-righteous as to make such blunt statement," one blogger angrily wrote (Mr. Zheng, 2010). Others took it as an opportunity for reflection and discussion. While many dis-agreed with Lee's prediction, most expressed support for his identification of the barrier to innovation in China: education.

> If China wants this [to have an Apple or Google], it must rebuild its education system. It is a pity for a country so large and a people so wise not to have produced compa-nies like Apple and Google. This is related to the whole philosophy of education. Chinese education teaches stu-dents how to calculate the area of a triangle. [The student] can tell you how to obtain the result but he cannot answer why he needs to calculate the area. How do we change this? Simply speaking, blow it up [the Chinese education system]. (Kang, 2010)

Lee's message was echoed in another round of heated dis-cussion ignited by the passing of Steve Jobs a year later. "Searching for Jobs," "Can China Produce Steve Jobs?" "Why Cannot China Have Jobs?" headlined blog posts and com-mentaries in traditional media. Education, again, was identi-fied as the culprit. One of the most reposted articles on blogs, online forums, and websites was titled "Had Steve Jobs Been Born in China." In this article, whose original author cannot be traced because of numerous reposts and modifications, the author or authors ponder what would have happened to Steve Jobs if he had been born in China:

> If Jobs had been born in China, he would have had a very low self-esteem because he was born out-of-wedlock. He would have been mocked by his classmates all the time. To defend his dignity, Jobs would have been involved in daily fights with his classmates. As a result, his parents would have been forced to transfer him to a different school. But thanks to his talents, he had good grades and passed the exam to a decent middle school.
>
> Jobs would not have had any interest in rote memori-zation of the textbooks in middle school and told his par-ents that he decided to quit school. His parents would

have beaten him to submission after having failed to convince him with words. Jobs would have had no choice but to go on. But because he had no interest in studying, his grades would have become so bad, and he did not do well on the exam, so he ended up in a third rate high school.

In high school, Jobs met Steve Wozniak. The pair had a great passion for electronic products. They won first prize in the national innovation contest. Nevertheless, because of his poor test scores in English, Chinese, and Chemistry, both Jobs and Wozniak ended in a no-name three-year college.

The hypothetical story of China's Jobs goes on to describe how Jobs would have been forced to drop out of college because he was too focused on his passion for invention and how his lack of a college degree would keep him out of a good job. Essentially, despite his talents and passion, this entrepreneurial genius would never have been able to give the world the iPod, iPhone, or iPad. The moral of the story is simple: Even if Steve Jobs had been born in China, he would not have become Steve Jobs, nor could he have created the miracles at Apple.

This speculation of the Chinese Steve Jobs is in no uncertain terms a harsh criticism of China's education system and a solemn lament over China's inability to cultivate innovative entrepreneurs. But China is supposed to have an excellent education system. Its stunning No. 1 showing on the most recent PISA in math, sciences, and reading have convinced many that it is an "education giant" (Tucker, 2011b). "Surpassing Shanghai" has been a goal of American educators, as suggested by the title of a recent book authored by a leading expert in the United States and published by Harvard Education Press (Tucker, 2011a).

Why is such an "excellent education system" held responsible for China's failure to produce a Steve Jobs? Why would the Chinese want to blow it up if it is as outstanding as held by international experts? Apparently there is a mismatch of understanding of educational excellence.

THE SINGAPORE PUZZLE: EDUCATION GIANT, ENTREPRENEURIAL DWARF

The mismatch goes beyond China. Around the same time that China's Premier Wen Jiabao said his country needs Steve Jobs, the iconic entrepreneur and the company he cofounded incited a round discussion about creativity and entrepreneurship in another Asian country. On December 14, 2011, Steve Wozniak, who founded Apple with Steve Jobs, said during an interview on the U.K. radio network BBC that a company like Apple could not emerge in structured countries like Singapore:

> When you're very structured almost like a religion . . . Uniforms, uniforms, uniforms . . . everybody is the same. Look at structured societies like Singapore where bad behavior isn't tolerated. You are extremely punished. Where are the creative people? Where are the great artists? Where are the great musicians? Where are the great singers? Where are the great writers? Where are the athletes? All the creative elements seem to disappear. (BBC, 2011)

Wozniak's comments quickly got the attention of Singaporeans, who have been working hard at promoting creativity and entrepreneurship (Mahtani & Holmes, 2011; Ong, 2012; Wee, 2011). As expected, there are some who disagreed with Wozniak's assessment, but the overall reaction is that he told the truth. Singaporean entrepreneur Willis Wee wrote:

> I'm not sure how much Wozniak knows about Singapore and its system. But as a Singaporean, who grew up in this tiny island, I have to agree with his words. . . . But with regards to Singapore, I believe most people here actually do think for themselves. Before I graduated from college, a lot of friends told me that they have aspirations to do this and that.

We're big thinkers and very ambitious. What's really lacking is the guts to do things. Only few have the balls to do what they really want. And unfortunately, most Singaporeans who aren't that courageous end up as Thank-God-Its-Friday laborers, or folks who are always looking forward to Friday and the paycheck. They are the people who complain about their lives the most, not the entrepreneurs and creative minds. (Wee, 2011)

Alexis Ong, a Singaporean journalist, wrote on CNN in January 2012, "At first glance, it made the small pseudo-patriot in me annoyed, but for the most part, the great and mighty Woz speaks the truth." Ong goes on to suggest that it is Singapore's education system that is to blame:

Wozniak's comments are really a scathing indictment of the Singapore education system, its strictly regimented curriculum and by-rote study techniques that sustain the city's "formal culture." He points out that everybody is "educated," but clearly the Singaporean education isn't the kind of education that gives rise to the people like Sergey Brin and Mark Zuckerberg. . . . This mindset is cultivated from youth. But in Singapore, where children are streamed into different academic tracks and under pressure to get into a reputable school before the age of 12, the push to conform is enormous. (Ong, 2012)

Singapore is supposed to have an excellent education system as well. Like China, Singapore has been a country of envy and admiration by outsiders for its consistent high performance in international tests. Since the early 1990s, Singapore has ranked in the top five in TIMSS. In the most recent PISA, Singapore took second place in math, fourth place in sciences, and fifth in reading, whereas China was first in all three areas. Singapore thus represents another case of contradiction between test scores and creative entrepreneurship.

THE INVERSE RELATIONSHIP BETWEEN TEST SCORES AND ENTREPRENEURSHIP ACTIVITIES

This contradiction also exists in other high-performing countries. Korea and Japan are two other Asian countries that have consistently produced outstanding scores in international tests. In the most recent PISA administered in 2009 in over 60 countries, Korea ranked fourth in math, sixth in sciences, and second in reading, while Japan was ninth in math, fifth in sciences, and eighth in reading. As impressive as their test scores, these countries have not traditionally shown a level of creativity and innovation-driven entrepreneurship that matched their test scores. According to the 2010 Global Entrepreneurship Monitor (GEM) report, out of the 22 innovation-driven (developed countries), which China is not part of and Singapore did not participate in the GEM study, Korea and Japan were at the bottom, taking 19th and 21st, respectively, in terms of "nascent entrepreneurship rate" or percentage of people actively seeking to establish businesses in the next three years. In terms of "total early entrepreneurship ownership rate," or percentage of individuals who started and are still managing a business, Korea ranked seventh and Japan 21st. The same pattern was found in the 2011 GEM report.

An even more telling figure is the proportion of opportunity entrepreneurship among the total early entrepreneurs. Less than half of all the early entrepreneurship activities in Korea and Japan were driven by opportunity and improvement; the rest were driven by necessity. In this category, Korea ranked 16th and Japan 18th.

The contradictory relationship between test scores and entrepreneurship activities is further affirmed by a correlational analysis of PISA performance and entrepreneurship activities of nations. Thirty-eight out of the 53 countries surveyed by the Global Entrepreneurship Monitor in 2010 also participated in the 2009 PISA. Thirty-nine countries out of the 54 economies surveyed by the GEM in 2011 participated in the

2009 PISA. Table 4.1 displays the correlation between PISA raw scores and new entrepreneurship activities in these countries.

| Table 4.1 | Correlations Between PISA Raw Scores and New Entrepreneurship Activities |

	Reading		Math		Sciences	
	2010	2011	2010	2011	2010	2011
Entrepreneurial Intentions	−.57**	−.68**	−.52**	−.68**	−.59**	−.70**
Nascent Entrepreneurship Rate	−.69**	−.72**	−.64**	−.72**	−.68**	−.72**
New Business Ownership Rate	−.37*	−.64**	−.37*	−.64**	−.39*	−.66**
Early-Stage Entrepreneurial Activity (TEA)	−.66**	−.76**	−.62**	−.77**	−.66**	−.77**
Discontinuation of Business	−.58**	−.53**	−.57**	−.54**	−.61**	−.56**

$** p < .01; * p < .05$

As Table 4.1 shows, PISA scores in all three areas—reading, math, and sciences—are negatively correlated with entrepreneurship indicators in almost every category at statistically significant levels. In other words, countries that have higher PISA scores have lower entrepreneurship activities. Specifically, those countries that show better performance on the PISA tend to have fewer people who intend to or plan to start businesses and fewer people who have started new businesses.

The inverse relationship between PISA scores, often perceived as the measure of a nation's education quality and its students' academic abilities, and entrepreneurship activities, an indicator of a nation's entrepreneurial actions, seems to affirm the contradiction exemplified by Singapore and China.

That is, the commonly used measures of educational quality have negative or no relationships with entrepreneurship.

Correlation does not mean causality. Thus we cannot say that lower entrepreneurship activity causes high test scores or vice versa. The negative relationship can happen in a number of ways. First, it could happen by accident. It could be just a fluke. There could be no relationships at all. Second, there is a relationship and it could be causal, meaning that one results in the other, but the direction is not determined. So we would not know if high test scores cause low entrepreneurship or if it is the other way around. Finally, there is a relationship but not causal. Instead, both of them are the results of the same causes. In other words, what resulted in the high test scores is what causes the low entrepreneurship activity.

COULD SCHOOLING HARM ENTREPRENEURSHIP?

The first interpretation, that is, there is no relationship between test scores and entrepreneurship, could be true but unlikely for a number of reasons in this case. First, the statistic significance is so strong that it indicates the chance of the relationship being entirely accidental is very low. Second, the statistically significant relations show up too often to render them accidental. All 30 pairs of correlations are statistically significant and all in the same direction. There are no positive relationships that have reached statistical significance. Third, we know that the differences in test scores across different countries are the result of education or education-related practices. If these factors affect a person's academic ability, it should have an impact on other qualities of the same person— cognitive, emotional, and psychological. And entrepreneurial qualities, as discussed in the previous chapter, are certainly cognitive, emotional, and psychological traits, so they should be affected.

Moreover, additional data suggest that entrepreneurship activity is related to schooling. For example, the Kauffman

Index of Entrepreneurial Activity produced by the Kauffman Foundation shows that during the period from 1996 to 2010, the group with less than high school education showed a consistently higher rate of entrepreneurial activity than all other groups (high school graduates, some college, and college graduates) in the United States (Fairlie, 2011). A Harris Poll conducted in 2010 for the Kauffman Foundation found that although there is no difference in the percentage of individuals who said they may start a business someday among three youth groups—8- to 12-year-olds, 13- to 17-year-olds, and 18- to 24-year-olds—a lot more 18- to 24-year-olds (29%) than the 8- to 12-year-olds (15%) said no. The 18- to 24-year-olds certainly have more schooling than the 8- to 12-years-olds (Harris Interactive, 2010).

It seems reasonable to believe that there is a relationship between schooling and entrepreneurship, but the question is the nature of the relationship. Could test scores directly reduce entrepreneurial activities or vice versa? Possibly, but highly unlikely. For test scores to directly reduce entrepreneurial activities, a country would have to use test scores as a gatekeeper to entrepreneurship. It would bar high-scoring people from entering entrepreneurial activities and force low scorers into entrepreneurship directly. I am not aware of any country that has such policy. Conversely, for entrepreneurial activities to directly affect test scores, it would mean the low-scoring people are the ones who engage in entrepreneurial activities, which is not the case since the PISA was taken by 15-year-olds who were in school at the time.

Thus a more logical interpretation of the inverse relationship between PISA scores and entrepreneurial activities is that there are some factors that help raise the PISA scores and lower entrepreneurial activities. This interpretation is supported by further analysis of the data. The Global Entrepreneurship Monitor report included data concerning entrepreneurial qualities, that is, personal factors that affect their potential engagement in entrepreneurial activities. These factors have been established to predict to what degree one may decide to start a business. They include personal perceptions of the availability of entrepreneurship opportunities, to what degree they have the capability to succeed in business, the degree of fear of failure, whether entrepreneurship is a good career choice, whether successful entrepreneurs enjoy high social status, and how much the media pay attention to entrepreneurship. Table 4.2 summarizes the correlations between these factors and the 2009 PISA results of 38 countries that participated in both PISA and GEM in 2010 and 39 countries that both participated in the 2009 PISA and 2011 GEM.

Table 4.2 Correlation Between PISA Raw Scores and Entrepreneurial Qualities (All Countries)

	Reading		Math		Sciences	
	2010	2011	2010	2011	2010	2011
Perceived Opportunities	−.35*	−.42**	−.33*	−.41**	−.38*	−.45**
Perceived Capabilities	−.60**	−71**	−.59**	−74**	−.61**	−.73**
Fear of Failure	.12	.25	.10	.28	.10	.29
Entrepreneurship as a Good Career Choice	−.50**	−.65**	−.45**	−.63**	−.53**	−.67**
High Status of Successful Entrepreneurs	−.08	.22	−.13	.28	−.09	.24
Media Attention for Entrepreneurship	−.22	−.18	−.18	−.11	−.21	−.15

$** p < .01; * p < .05$

The results show a clear pattern of negative correlations between countries' PISA performances and entrepreneurial qualities. In countries that have higher PISA scores in math, reading, and sciences, fewer people believe there are entrepreneurial opportunities, fewer people believe they have the capability to start and succeed in entrepreneurship, and fewer people believe entrepreneurship is a good career choice. There is no significant correlation between PISA scores and "fear of failure," the status of entrepreneurs, or media attention for entrepreneurship.

This finding can be interpreted in two different ways. First, in countries where fewer entrepreneurial opportunities exist, students have higher academic achievement. Likewise, in countries where people believe they are less capable of entrepreneurial activities, students have higher achievement. Similarly, in countries where entrepreneurship is not perceived as a good career choice, students have higher academic achievement. Taken together, this could mean that the excellent academic achievement in some countries may be the result of a lack of other options. Academic achievement is the only way to success, in other words. In contrast, in countries that present more options, students may not exert all their energy and resources on academics because they could pursue other choices.

The second interpretation is that efforts to pursue academic achievement may come at the cost of entrepreneurial qualities. That is, the educational practices and societal factors that help students to achieve academically may hamper entrepreneurial qualities, making them believe there are few entrepreneurial opportunities or they do not have the entrepreneurial capability. Standardized testing and a focus on rote memorization, for example, are perhaps the biggest enemies for the entrepreneurial capability.

A contrast between Finland and the East Asian countries illustrates this point. Although Finland's entrepreneurship activities do not rank as high as its PISA performance, the Finns possess a much higher level of perceived entrepreneurial capabilities than the East Asian countries. In the 2011 Global Entrepreneurship Monitor Survey, 37.3% of Finns reported having the capability for entrepreneurship, more than 20 percentage points higher than the Japanese (13.7%), 10 percentage points higher than the Koreans (26.7%) and

Singaporeans (24.1%), and nearly 10 points higher than the Taiwanese (28.6%). This difference may come from the different style of education in Finland and the East Asian countries. Unlike education systems in the high-performing education systems in East Asia that has a well-known reputation for authoritarian and standardized-testing-driven education that emphasizes rote memorization, Finnish students do not take standardized tests until the end of high school. Finnish schools are a standardized-testing-free zone, according to Pasi Sahlberg in his book *Finnish Lessons: What Can the World Learn From Educational Change in Finland?* (Sahlberg, 2011). As a result, students in Finland are not pushed toward rote memorization. Finnish education is certainly not nearly as authoritarian as its Asian counterparts. Most important, as education historian Diane Ravitch observed, "the central aim of Finnish education is the development of each child as a thinking, active, creative person, not the attainment of higher test scores, and the primary strategy of Finnish education is cooperation, not competition (Ravitch, 2012).

The reality is probably that both interpretations are correct. The lack of entrepreneurial opportunities and the perception of entrepreneurship not as a good career likely lead people to pursue academic excellence. On the way to pursue academic excellence, entrepreneurial capabilities are lost, which further leads to fewer people who believe there are good entrepreneurial opportunities.

Whichever interpretation one might have, the data suggest that high PISA scores may be the result of "forced excellence." More important, PISA scores have not been shown to positively affect entrepreneurship or other productive activities. So it may not be worth as much attention as have been given by policy makers, the media, and the public. On the other hand, entrepreneurship is directly related to economic prosperity and success. Thus it should be of little doubt that entrepreneurial capabilities may be a more worthwhile goal than test scores. If entrepreneurial qualities are a more worthwhile goal of education, we then need to worry about the possibility of education doing damage to them.

THE LOSS OF CONFIDENCE: ONE COST OF HIGH SCORES?

As discussed in Chapter 3, entrepreneurs share some common traits—the entrepreneurial spirit. One ingredient of the entrepreneurial spirit is confidence and creativity. Explicit and direct measures of the entrepreneurial spirit are not available, but the GEM data included one measure that is fairly close: "perceived entrepreneurial capabilities." On this measure, Japan took last place and Korea second from the bottom. The overall correlation coefficients are presented in Table 4.3. To get an even closer look at the relationship, Table 4.3 includes only innovation-driven countries, that is, the developed countries whose economic development level is more comparable.

The most obvious observation is that in developed countries, educational systems that produced high PISA scores have lower

Table 4.3	Correlation Between PISA Raw Scores and Entrepreneurial Qualities (Innovation-Driven Economies)					
	Reading		Math		Sciences	
	2010	2011	2010	2011	2010	2011
Perceived Opportunities	.10	.08	.08	.04	−.00	.01
Perceived Capabilities	−.50*	−66**	−.45*	−.74**	−.38	−.67**
Fear of Failure	−.39	−.05	−.57**	−.09	−.58**	−.15
Entrepreneurship as a Good Career Choice	−.24	−.36	−.17	−.16	−.37	−.40
High Status of Successful Entrepreneurs	.03	.03	−.01	.21	.12	.02
Media Attention for Entrepreneurship	.57**	.42	.39	.62**	.49*	.51*

** $p < .01$; * $p < .05$

perceived capabilities and higher anxiety about failure while the scores are not correlated with opportunities. "Perceived entrepreneurial capabilities" can be interpreted as people's confidence in their capability to succeed as entrepreneurs. This means that the higher PISA scores a country achieved, the less likely their people believe they have the capability to succeed in entrepreneurship and people are more afraid of failure.

A different study provides a possibly direct bridge between schooling and perceived entrepreneurial capabilities or self-confidence, lending support for the assumption that the pursuit of academic achievement may sacrifice entrepreneurial qualities. Tom Loveless, a researcher at the think tank Brookings Institute found that in the 2003 TIMSS data countries where students had lower self-confidence scored higher in mathematics (see Table 4.4). The top-performing countries—Singapore, Japan, Korea, and Hong Kong—had the lowest percentage of eighth graders who said "I usually do well in mathematics." With 4%, Japan ranked at the bottom. Above Japan, second from the bottom, is Korea with 6%. And Singapore had 18%, while the United States had 39%. The overall correlation between test scores and confidence in all 46 countries was –.64, statistically very significant (Loveless, 2006).

Table 4.4	Correlations Between TIMSS Math Score and Confidence and Enjoyment	
	Grade	**Correlation Coefficients**
Confidence	4	–0.58
	8	–0.64
Enjoyment	4	–0.67
	8	–0.75
Relevance	8	–0.52

NOTE: Pearson Correlation Coefficient representing the relationship between each nation's average score and percentage answering in each question's "high" category.

SOURCE: Loveless, 2006.

While confidence in math may not necessarily be the same as confidence in entrepreneurship, it does indicate how much a country's education system values confidence, happiness, and the general emotional well-being of students. And confidence is a key factor in entrepreneurship, as longtime entrepreneurship educator and executive director of the Canadian Foundation for Economic Education, Gary Rabbior, writes:

> There is no more important attribute of entrepreneurship than a sense of self-confidence, the belief in oneself and one's own ideas. Entrepreneurs are agents of change, and change is usually resisted. Entrepreneurs will continually confront roadblocks and resistance from individuals who do not support or believe in their ideas. . . . To confront and overcome the resistance they will encounter, it is imperative that entrepreneurs have a sense of self-confidence. (Rabbior, 1990, p. 61)

The lack of self-confidence has been viewed as a major stumbling block to developing entrepreneurship in many countries. For instance, when asked why in South Africa entrepreneurship is not growing as fast as the country needs, Judi Sandrock, chief entrepreneurship officer (CEO) of South Africa's Branson Centre of Entrepreneurship, said during an interview in 2010:

> I think it has a lot to do with confidence. . . . As South Africans, we tend to be low on confidence. Self-belief is standing in the way of success. What gets in people's way is themselves. That sense of ability and confidence is lacking. (Daniel, 2010)

But for people infatuated with test scores, confidence is not necessarily good; in fact, it may be a bad thing because it may be the cause of low test scores. Brookings Institute's Tom Loveless, for instance, concludes the following, based on his correlational analysis of self-confidence and test scores on TIMSS:

The evidence does suggest, however, that the American infatuation with the happiness factor in education may be misplaced. The international evidence makes at least a prima facie case that self-confidence, liking the subject, and relevance are not essential for mastering mathematics at high levels. (Loveless, 2006, p. 18)

Regardless of the differences in opinion about the value of confidence, it is obvious that nations' test scores in international tests do not go the same way as their entrepreneurship activities, perceived entrepreneurial capabilities, and students' self-confidence. In other words, superior test scores do not result in more creative entrepreneurs. On the contrary, it may hamper the development of entrepreneurial and creative activities, as suggested by Alexis Ong about Singapore and Kai-fu Lee about China.

This difference in opinion about the value of confidence is a good explanation of the differences in views about education. While those who ascribe high value to test scores admire and envy China, Singapore, Finland, Korea, and other countries that produce great test takers, others who want more innovators and entrepreneurs are unhappy with these systems' inability to produce another Steve Jobs and Apple. The latter wants an education system that does not stifle entrepreneurship at worst, and at best promotes entrepreneurship and creativity.

The loss of confidence as a result of pursuing test scores is only one of the many ways that education could damage the entrepreneurial spirit and hamper a nation's entrepreneurial activities. The traditional paradigm of education reduces the stock of entrepreneurship in many more forceful manners, because the goal of the traditional paradigm is about finding instead of creating jobs.

Although the presently dominant paradigm all over the world is the employment-seeking one, different countries vary in their execution. As a result, countries that execute it well have better academic achievement, better performance on international tests, and at the same time lower entrepreneurial capabilities. In the next chapter, I use China and the United States as case studies to further illustrate how the variation in execution of the traditional paradigm produces different outcomes in academic achievement and entrepreneurial capabilities, and I will explore the process by which a nation loses its capacity for innovation and entrepreneurship.

References

BBC (Producer). (2011). Steve Wozniak: "Think for yourself." Retrieved from http://news.bbc.co.uk/today/hi/today/newsid _9661000/9661755.stm

Caijing. (2010). Li Kaifu: Xiayige pingguo buhui chuxian zai zhongguo (Kai-fu Lee: The next Apple will not be invented in China). Retrieved January 3, 2012, from http://www.caijing.com .cn/2011–09–16/110862857.html

Daniel, J. (2010, October 6). Entrepreneurship drought: "South Africans low on confidence." Retrieved January 21, 2012, from http://memeburn.com/2010/10/branson-center-of-entre preneurship-appoints-new-ceo/

Fairlie, R. W. (2011). *Kauffman Index of Entrepreneurial Activity: 1996– 2010.* Kansas City, KS: Kauffman Foundation.

Harris Interactive. (2010). *YouthPulse^{SM} 2010: Kauffman Foundation Custom Report.* Kansas City, KS: Kauffman Foundation.

Kang, G. (2010, March 16). Li Kaifu daodi tang de shi chuangxin haishi jiaoyu (Was Kai-fu Lee talking about innovation or education?). Retrieved from http://blog.sina.com.cn/s/blog_53742 bef0100m8df.html

Loveless, T. (2006). *How well are American students learning?* Washington, DC: Brookings Institute (Brown Center).

Luo, X., Wu, X., & Yan, J. (2011, October 11). Ningbo chizi wuqianwan peiyang chuangxin lingjun bajian rencai (Ningbo plans to spend 50 million to cultivate innovate talents). *Ningbo Wanbao (Ningbo Evening News).* Retrieved from http://news.sciencenet .cn/htmlnews/2011/10/253650.shtm

Mahtani, S., & Holmes, S. (2011, January 20). Wozniak: Apple couldn't emerge in Singapore. Retrieved from http://blogs.wsj .com/searealtime/2011/12/15/wozniak-apple-couldnt-emerge -in-singapore/

Mr. Zheng. (2010, September 16). Li Kaifu zai 2010 xiaji dawosi luntan shang de jianghua jiduan le xie (Kai-fu Lee's speech at the 2010 Summer Davos too extreme). Retrieved January 16, 2012, from http://212313.com/article/detail_2303_47_47.html

Ong, A. (2012, January 10). Singapore needs to encourage "bad behavior." Retrieved January 20, 2012, from http://www.cnngo.com/singapore/life/tell-me-about-it/alexis-ong-singapore-needs-encourage-bad-behavior-718985

Rabbior, G. (1990). Elements of a successful entrepreneurship/economics/education program. In C. A. Kent (Ed.), *Entrepreneurship education: Current developments, future directions* (pp. 53–68). New York, NY: Quorum Books.

Ravitch, D. (2012, March 8). Schools we can envy. *The New York Review of Books.* Retrieved from http://www.nybooks.com/articles/archives/2012/mar/08/schools-we-can-envy/?pagination=false

Sahlberg, P. (2011). *Finnish lessons: What can the world learn from educational change in Finland?* New York, NY: Teachers College Press.

Tucker, M. S. (Ed.). (2011a). *Surpassing Shanghai: An agenda for American education built on the world's leading systems.* Boston, MA: Harvard Education Press.

Tucker, M. S. (2011b). *Standing on the shoulders of Giants: An American agenda for education reform.* Washington, DC: National Center Education and the Economy.

Wee, W. (2011, December 15). Apple co-founder Steve Wozniak questions Singapore's creativity. Retrieved January 20, 2012, from http://www.penn-olson.com/2011/12/15/wozniak-questions-singapore-creativity/

5

China vs.
the United States

How the Best Education Stifles
the Entrepreneurial Spirit

All medicine is poisonous.

—Chinese Proverb

*The aim of public education is not to spread enlighten-
ment at all; it is simply to reduce as many individuals as
possible to the same safe level, to breed a standard citizenry, to put down dissent and originality.*

—H. L. Mencken

We have a wake-up call now about America's kids,"
a worried Diane Sawyer, anchor of ABC World
News, announced on December 7, 2010. Three weeks earlier,
Sawyer took her viewers to China to show "the ambition and
energy of 1.3 billion people competing for the American
dream." "Today the new international reading, math, and science scores were released and Chinese students left American
teens in the dust in all three categories," continues Sawyer.
"We keep thinking all day of this scene we saw during our
journey in China." Then we are shown a classroom of
tired Chinese children rubbing their eyes and their heads.
"These are third-grade students pausing to massage their

heads for relief because they said they study so hard that they need to relax" (Sawyer, 2010).

"In fact these numbers are stunning for the entire world. Shanghai stunner, you could call it," said David Muir, an ABC reporter who traveled to China with Sawyer, who came on to further explain the significance of these scores, citing U.S. Secretary Arne Duncan who said this is a wake-up call for America and President Obama, calling this "a modern day Sputnik Moment to catch up." The rest of the three-and-a-half-minute news clip features stunning graphics representing how far behind American students performed after Shanghai and other Asian countries and Europe's Finland and footage of President John F. Kennedy talking about the Soviet's "Sputnik," the first man-made satellite to orbit the Earth, launched in 1957 (Sawyer, 2010).

"In our travels to China it was everywhere, that laser focus on education," Muir's voice continued over a scene of a class of two-year-old Chinese children. "This public school in Shanghai where the children are two years old. By three they are in school from 8 until 4, already learning phrases in English." Muir then added that on average Chinese students attend school 41 more days a year than American students, and with extra lessons on the weekend, Chinese students receive 30% more hours of instruction (Sawyer, 2010).

Sawyer and Muir add to a large group of policy makers, educational researchers, and the media in the United States who have been "stunned" by the No. 1 showing of students from Shanghai, the most developed city in China. They also repeated what has often been praised as China's education advantage: a laser focus on education, hard-working students, and more instructional time.

Ironically, what Sawyer and others praise has been denounced by the Chinese government, parents, and educators for a long time (Jiaoyubu [Ministry of Education], 1964; Zhonggong Zhongyang [Central Committee of the Chinese Communist Party] & Guowuyuan (State Council), 1999; Zhonggong Zhongyang [Central Committee of the Chinese Communist Party] & Guowuyuan [The State Council], 1993;

Zhonggong Zhongyang Bangongting [Office of the Central Committee of the Chinese Communist Party] & Guowuyuan Bangongting [Office of the State Council], 2000). The Chinese Ministry of Education, the central government branch responsible for all educational institutions, has repeatedly over the last few decades issued regulations that forbid schools from offering extra lessons to students. "Reducing student academic burden," that is, reducing the amount of time devoted to academic studies, has been a consistent theme in the numerous reform efforts China has undertaken since the early 1990s. China has also struggled hard to shorten the school day and school year.

As recent as January 2012, the Chinese Ministry of Education issued another order to all provincial-level education departments demanding that kindergartens[1] not provide formal instruction or cover content that should be taught in elementary school. The Ministry of Education requires that:

> Kindergartens must follow the physical and psychological development principles and remove elementary school level content and instruction . . . the majority of the daily activities should be play . . . kindergartens are strictly forbidden from teaching elementary-school-level content, offering any kind of intensive training activities under the disguise of interest class, talented and gifted class, or experimental class, and assigning homework. (Jiaoyubu [Ministry of Education], 2012)

Provincial-level education authorities have made even more specific requirements based on the Ministry of Education's order. For example, Jiangsu Province's *Regulations for Pre-school Education*, in effect as of March 2012, imposes severe punishment including a fine and/or revocation of its license if any preschool (kindergartens) offers "formal organized instruction on Chinese pinyin or characters, any practice on written

---

[1]In China, kindergartens refer to educational institutions before formal schooling and typically cover the ages of three to six.

mathematics, or reading and writing in any foreign language" (Jiangsu Provincial People's Congress, 2012).

And extra instructions have been banned for a number of years, but apparently the numerous orders have not been effective. On February 2, 2012, a story broke out and quickly spread across the Chinese media. Over 400 students of Yutian Secondary School in Shenyang, the capital city of China's Liaoning Province, were bused to another city for two weeks of extra instruction. The students were to be housed in a dorm and receive instruction before the formal school term started. The school had to provide the instruction offsite to evade inspections by the city government because it is strictly forbidden for any school to offer instruction during the winter break. Fearing for their children's safety and health, parents tipped the media and the extra instruction was stopped. The school and its administrators would face serious consequences (H. Gao, 2012). The story led to more reporting of schools offering instructions in other Chinese cities and local governments cracking down on them.

THE EXCELLENT EDUCATION THAT HURTS: THE CASE OF CHINA

The Chinese apparently don't appreciate Diane Sawyer's and other outsiders' assessment of Chinese education. Furthermore, they would be very glad to be rid of what Sawyer praised because they have seen the tremendous damage it has caused. They have long realized that what gives them the enviable academic accomplishment is precisely what has led to the shortage of creative and entrepreneurial titans like Steve Jobs.

Open Secrets of China's Academic Excellence: Focus, Hard Work, and Testing

It is no doubt that the Chinese have a laser focus on education, but education here is defined as the pursuit of academics or whatever the government counts as important in its high-stakes testing program, namely the *gaokao,* the college entrance exam in China that has been used as the sole measure to admit college students. Because attending college has been virtually the only way for upward social mobility, everything in China's education system is about ultimately achieving excellent scores on this test.

The focus on academic achievement is the continuation of a long Chinese tradition that puts book knowledge above all others. The modern day *gaokao* is the reincarnation of the thousand-year-old *keju,* a Chinese invention that used tests to select government officials. Although in the beginning the *keju* included a broader set of subjects, it eventually evolved into a test of memorization and interpretation of the Confucian classics (Zhao, 2009). The *keju* has ingrained in the Chinese psyche that book knowledge is the only way to gain social and economic status—the only way to enter the ruling class. For a long time, *dushuren* (literally, the book-reading people) was used to refer to the educated, and in the less Westernized parts of China *dushu* (reading books) is still used to refer to "attending school." The phrase *wanban jie xiapin, wei you dushu gao,* roughly translated into English as *everything is of low value, only book-reading is of high value,* remains the motto for many Chinese today.

Thus in a Chinese student's life, nothing is more important than preparing for the *gaokao.* And the preparation starts early, before kindergarten. Through various early childhood education programs, Chinese parents who can afford the costs work hard to make sure that their children master the knowledge and skills needed to pass tests so they can be admitted to elite kindergartens. A study in 2011 shows that the annual market value of China's early childhood education is estimated to be about 50 billion RMB—the total spending of the 80 million children ages zero to three (Wu, 2011). The majority of the early childhood programs are operated privately and are expensive. While some may include elements of play, what truly convinces parents to open their wallets are bilingual education (English and Chinese), math education, and other sorts of cognitive skill training.

At the age of four, children begin to enter kindergarten, which mostly serves as a place to prepare for passing tests to elementary schools. Despite the repeated callings from the government and numerous regulations that elementary schools should enroll students without any tests, the practice continues in China. The fact that as recent as 2012, the Ministry of Education issued yet another rule to ban kindergartens from preparing students to take tests shows that elementary schools still use tests to admit students. Chinese language, mathematics, and English are the subjects that most schools test and thus kindergartens teach them.

Elementary schools essentially prepare children for passing tests to middle school, middle school for high school, and high school for the ultimate battle: the *gaokao*. Along the way, parents, students, and schools all work hard to maintain a laser focus on what truly matters: excellent performance on the college entrance exam at the end of 12th grade.

Parents make significant investment in their children's education. They spend enormous amounts on securing a good school and extra lessons for their children. The average education spending per household in 2011 was 23,000RMB (about $4,000), but the majority (74%) of Chinese household income in China was below 40,000RMB, with 36% below 10,000RMB, according to the *2011 China Family Education Spending White Book* (MarketProbe & Sina Education, 2011). These numbers are remarkable considering that the Chinese education system is primarily public. The private spending mostly goes to tutoring and other extra education programs. The same study found that 73% of primary school students' parents pay particular attention to tutoring and training outside school and 43% of parents pay special attention to subjects that are tested in these extra education programs, while the other half wanted something that strikes a balance between preparing for tests and developing the children's overall abilities. "Over 80% of parents send their children to tutorial school" (Organisation for Economic Co-operation and Development [OECD], 2011, p. 92).

Parents also make sure that their children are focused only on academic studies. In general, Chinese children are freed from household chores and not allowed to engage in anything except academic study. More important, the children do not have time for anything else. Chinese students spend nearly 10 hours studying in primary grades, 11 hours in middle school, and 12.5 hours in high school per day, according to a study by the Hangzhou Education Science Publishing House (Jingri Zaobao, 2011).

Schools make sure that students are fully occupied with academic studies as well. Although in theory schools are only allowed to offer six instructional hours a day, five days a week, and 40 weeks a year, according to the Ministry of Education (Jiaoyubu [Ministry of Education], 2001), in practice, schools find ways to squeeze in more. Some schools offer classes over the weekend and during the 11-week summer and winter holidays. To extend the school day, schools assign an extraordinary amount of homework. "Homework is an essential part of their learning activities and in a way governs their lives at home after school. Parents expect students to do homework every evening and are prepared to devote their family lives to student study. . . . Homework is such a burden to students that many local authorities in China have stipulated a maximum amount of homework (measured in hours) that schools are allowed to assign," observes a report by OECD (OECD, 2011, p. 92).

There is little doubt that Chinese students are among the most devoted students in the world. "Compared with other societies, young people in Shanghai may be much more immersed in learning in the broadest sense of the term" (OECD, 2011, p. 93). It is thus not surprising at all that they have the highest academic achievement, indicated by test scores.

What Happened to the Creative and Entrepreneurially Talented?

However, this laser focus on education is widely recognized in China as problematic. Even OECD, the organization that administers the PISA, which catapulted China to the world's education leader status, admits:

[W]hat they (Shanghai students) learn and how they learn are subjects of constant debate. Critics see young people as being "fed" learning because they are seldom left on their own to learn in a way of their choice. They have little direct encounters with nature, for example, and little experience with society either. While they have learned a lot, they may not have learned how to learn. (OECD, 2011, p. 93)

The loudest criticism, though, is that this laser focus on education is responsible for China's failure to produce creative and entrepreneurial talents, as Dr. Kai-fu Lee charged in his 2010 Summer Davos speech (Caijing, 2010).

Although there may be many different contributing factors, China's education has been identified as a primary one because, first of all, there is no reason to believe the Chinese lack the creative or entrepreneurial genes. In fact, if the distribution of born entrepreneurs and creative talents are randomly and equally distributed among all human beings, and there is no reason not to believe that, China, with a population of 1.3 billion, should have a larger stock of the entrepreneurial and creative genes than the United States—in other words, it should have more genetic prototypes of Steve Jobs. But China has not seen truly innovative entrepreneurs of the stature of Steve Jobs. Second, China has made significant investment in research and development, as well as cultivating innovation and entrepreneurship. Yet, recent data show that in 2010, with 20% of the world's population, 9% of the world's GDP, and 12% of the world's R&D expenditure, China had only 1% of the patent filings with or patents granted by any of the leading patent offices outside China. In addition, 50% of the China-origin patents were granted to subsidiaries of foreign multinationals (Gupta & Wang, 2011).

Naturally, education is believed to be the culprit. But how does education reduce creative and entrepreneurial potentials?

First, the laser focus on education means nothing outside academic excellence is of value. If it does not help with getting good scores, it is not important. As a result, children are discouraged from pursuing anything else but study. Even the extra lessons provided in arts, music, sports, engineering, and other things are tied to the tests because winning prizes or passing certain levels of tests can be converted into *gaokao* scores.[2] Extracurricular activities are typically limited and only pursued rigorously when they have direct connection to admissions tests. Moreover, the heavy class load does not permit much extra time to explore other possibilities for most students anyway. As a result, there are few opportunities and programs for students to explore their own interests and talents in China. With an absence of opportunity for exploration and experimentation, the creative and entrepreneurial potential remains dormant at the best, and withers at the worst. Lady Gaga could not have become Lady Gaga if she did not have any access to music, for example. Hence, the lack of opportunities to try out different talents and interests than the tested subjects as a result of exclusive focus on education, that is, schooling, in essence deprives the creative and entrepreneurially talented the chance and resources to discover their potential, let alone developing them.

Second, some creative and entrepreneurial talents are sorted out because they do not fit the academic requirement. The formal school experience in China, as described in the previous section, serves more like a selection mechanism than an education institution. It in essence selects those who are talented in taking tests to move on and up the social ladder. Those who are entrepreneurially talented and creative, but not good at taking tests or uninterested in academics, are sorted out of the system often and early, denied access to resources and prestige. If they are lucky, persistent, and truly

---

[2]In order to encourage a diversity of talents and creativity beyond the traditional academics, China has been experimenting with the idea of converting accomplishments in nonacademic areas into *gaokao* scores. For example, a national championship in sport may be worth 10 points, so does a gold medal in an international robotics contest. The practice is also used for equity purposes. Ethnic minorities may receive 10 bonus points.

talented, they may emerge eventually, but the chances are slim in a society obsessed with credentials and degrees.

Worse yet, the most entrepreneurially talented and creative suffers the most because they are more likely to have an unbalanced genetic predisposition for things other than the academics. They are the potentially great musicians, artists, sportsmen, entrepreneurs, and scientists who are just not good at taking tests and studying the school subjects. They have so much potential in one area that it is difficult for them to have the interest, the patience, or ability to do well in traditional academics. As a result of their poor performance in academics or their unwillingness to play the academic game, they are put into lower-quality schools or classes (tracks), kicked out of schools, or they may simply choose to drop out.

Third, for the majority of people, who are all born with some level of natural curiosity, capacity for creativity, and potential for entrepreneurship, the focused education works to remove curiosity, stifle creativity, and suppress entrepreneurial impulses, while teaching the ability to excel in tests. Generally speaking, most tests reward the ability to find answers instead of asking questions. In other words, most of the tests are an assessment of one's ability to memorize answers and give them back in the format demanded by the test makers. Some tests even penalize wrong answers to discourage guessing. But asking questions, challenging the status quo, and risk taking are the hallmarks of entrepreneurial and creative ventures, which are in direct conflict with the spirit of standardized tests. Not surprisingly, those who survived and thrived in a test-taking culture like China's have learned to conform and suppress their creativity and entrepreneurial impulses.

Fourth, when children spend all their time studying, they cannot have much time socializing or engaging in team activities that may provide the opportunity to learn to fail, to interact with others, to develop one's identity, to understand one's interests, and to develop social skills—all important qualities of entrepreneurship. Thus in China, few students have developed the independent living skills to manage their own life, let alone starting businesses.

Fifth, when children follow a strictly prescribed path, there is little chance of a detour. While the Chinese students certainly work hard, they are simply working to complete the prescribed tasks in the prescribed manner. They have no opportunity to make their own mistakes, to undertake tasks out of their own interest, or to deviate from the prescribed path. In the end, they will have learned what the government, the school, and their parents want them to learn, but nothing out of their own passions. In fact, they are taught to ignore their interests and passions.

Finally, when children are judged by a single criterion, they are constantly asked to compare with their peers. They are ranked all the time and in public. They are rewarded or punished accordingly. The result is most children will be worse than the few top performers in the class, school, or city. Thus the majority of children learn to internalize a sense of inferiority and eventually lose self-confidence. And confidence, as discussed before, is key to entrepreneurship.

The Chinese Ministry of Education best summarizes the ways that Chinese education harms creativity and entrepreneurial qualities. In a 1997 policy document, the Chinese Ministry of Education (then the Chinese National Education Commission) forcefully laid out the damages of China's education:

> "Test-oriented education" refers to the factual existence in our nation's education of the tendency to simply prepare for tests, aim for high test scores, and blindly pursue admission rates [to colleges or higher-level schools] while ignoring the real needs of the student and societal development. It pays attention to only a minority of the student population and neglects the majority; it emphasizes knowledge transmission but neglects moral, physical, aesthetic, and labor education, as well as the cultivation of applied abilities and psychological and emotional

development; it relies on rote memorization and mechanical drills as the primary approach, which makes learning uninteresting, hinders students from learning actively, prevents them from taking initiatives, and heavily burdens them with [an] excessive amount of course work; it uses test scores as the primary or only criterion to evaluate students, hurting their motivation and enthusiasm, squelching their creativity, and impeding their overall development. (Guojia Jiaowei [National Education Commission], 1997)

Journey to the West: China's Admiration of American Education

China has not been happy with its education, despite all the praises from the outside. China has been working toward transforming its education for decades now because of its desire to produce a creative and entrepreneurial workforce. In its quest for a better education that could produce great creative entrepreneurs like Steve Jobs, China has turned its attention to the United States, the country that produced most Nobel laureates, dominated in the number of modern-day innovations, and seen the birth of the largest collection of influential entrepreneurs. While the Americans have been lamenting on its education, the Chinese have been working hard at emulating it. What has been condemned in the U.S. education system seems to be precisely what the Chinese wish to have.

"No uniform textbooks, no standardized tests, no ranking of students, this is American education in the eyes of a Chinese journalist," opens *Encountering American Education* (G. Gao, 2003), a story written by a journalism professor and now dean of the College of Journalism of one of China's top universities, Renmin University. The story has been a popular read in China for parents, educators, and even children themselves since its publication in 2003. It was listed as the No. 2 most popular item in the category of reportage in 2003. The story has been posted and reposted numerous times on the

Internet and attracted discussions and admiration. In this story, the author, Gang Gao, recounts his 10-year-old son's experience in American schools when he was a visiting scholar at Arizona State University in the 1990s. The following sentences, recited back to the author by a young girl who carved them in her desk, best summarize his observations of American education:

> American classrooms don't impart a massive amount of knowledge into their children, but they try every way to draw children's eyes to the boundless ocean of knowledge outside the school; They do not force their children to memorize all the formulae and theorems, but they work tirelessly to teach children how to think and ways to seek answers to new questions; They never rank students according to test scores, but they try every way to affirm children's efforts, praise their thoughts, and protect and encourage children's desire and effort.[3]

Echoing similar observations of American education, *Quality Education in America*, authored by Quanyu Huang, a Chinese native who now teaches at Miami University in Ohio after earning his doctoral degree in higher education in the United States, tells of the author's son's education experiences in the United States. The book became an instant best seller in China. And the author has since written more about American education for the Chinese market.

Among other things, the book praises American education's respect for the child, tolerating individual differences, and not attempting to impart abstract prescribed knowledge in the child. An often-referenced story in this book is the author's description of his son's "research" experiences as an elementary school student. His second-grade son was asked to conduct research and complete a paper that must be at least two pages and addresses three questions. After reading over 10 books, his son finished his research report about blue

---

[3]http://www.360doc.com/content/07/1114/10/50242_820904.shtml

whales. The final product included a cover page with title and author and the report had four parts: introduction, what do blue whales eat, how do blue whales eat, and what makes blue whales unique.

This type of activity is common in American schools but a huge surprise that stuns many Chinese educators and parents. Gang Gao told a similar story in *Encountering American Education*. His son was asked to write a research paper about human culture. Stories like this fascinate Chinese parents and educators because they are lacking in Chinese schools, where students are to receive knowledge rather than creating their own. Research is only reserved for experts. These stories are told to reflect a different philosophy of education, one that is believed to result in independent and critical thinking, curiosity and habits of inquiry, and the ability and confidence to assume responsibilities.

Respect for individual differences and recognition for individual contributions are other aspects of American education that are often praised by Chinese observers of American education. Xigui Li, principal of a prestigious school in Beijing, wrote about his encounters with American education while visiting Columbia University's Teachers College in 2007. In his *36 Days: My American Education Trip*, Mr. Li recounts his interactions with American teachers, professors, and school leaders. Among many other interesting interactions, he tells one in which he was surprised to find that his host professor invited classroom teachers as *experts* to discussions. Classroom teachers are not considered *zhuanjia* (expert) in China. He was also surprised to see portraits of ordinary staff members hanging by the statue of John Dewey, which he had thought to be the pictures of presidents of Teachers College. These observations suggest to Mr. Li that in the United States everyone can be an expert and is accorded such status. He writes:

When a society allows and encourages everyone, regardless of his class and occupation, to become an expert in their own way, it is certain that human potentials can be maximally realized, and consequently there is fertile soil for cultivating individuality. And more importantly, only in these soils can we cultivate children who can express their individuality and dare to follow their own ambitions and only then can they truly become "themselves."[4]

What the Chinese find valuable in American education is a decentralized, autonomous system that does not have standards, uses multiple criteria for judging the value of talents, and celebrates individual differences. However, what the Chinese enthusiastically embrace is just what the Americans have been as enthusiastically trying to be rid of. Over the past few decades, America has been on the journey to centralize its education system, standardize its curriculum, and impose uniform practices. From Clinton's Goals 2000 in the 1990s to Bush's No Child Left Behind in the first decade of the 21st century, and now Obama's Race to the Top, America education has been reformed. As the Common Core standards movement accomplishes its goal, America will have lost what the Chinese envy and admire.

A SAUSAGE MACHINE THAT ALSO MAKES BACON

The Case of American Education

The American education reformers view the aspects of its education admired by the Chinese as an indication of a broken and obsolete system that is considered responsible for the lackluster academic performance[5] and the persistent achievement gap. The lack of uniformity in terms of textbooks, curriculum, and assessment across all schools in the nation is considered the cause of the uneven academic achievement

---

[4]http://news.cersp.com/HQSY/lists/200704/659_3.html

[5]The United States has a long history of poor ranking in international tests. In the First International Mathematics Study (FIMS) conducted in the 1960s, American 12th graders ranked at the bottom of 12 participating countries.

among different ethnic and income groups. The some 15,000 locally elected school governance bodies that oversee education in their communities are considered discriminatory, inefficient, and fragmented. The attention to individual differences is viewed as a lack of rigor and low expectations of students. The professional autonomy teachers and school leaders have are viewed as protection for poor teaching.

Nevertheless, as President Barack Obama stated in his 2011 State of the Union address:

> America still has the largest, most prosperous economy in the world. No workers—no workers are more productive than ours. No country has more successful companies, or grants more patents to inventors and entrepreneurs. We're the home to the world's best colleges and universities, where more students come to study than any place on Earth. (Obama, 2011)

Plenty of evidence backs the president's assessment (Zhao, 2009). The U.S. economy is three times as large as the second largest economy in the world, China, which has four times the population. America boasts the largest collection of global enterprises that have come up with products and services consumed worldwide. And the United States is still viewed as *the* hotbed of innovation and entrepreneurship.

How can such a broken, obsolete, and inefficient system accomplish all of these? Why does the United States remain the world's innovation hub despite its long history of poor standing in international education assessments? Furthermore, American schools do not have courses to teach creativity or entrepreneurship. American children do not attend creativity or entrepreneurship training camps either. Where did all the creative entrepreneurs come from?

The short answer is that American education has not been as good as the Chinese at killing creativity and the entrepreneurial spirit. In the most fundamental ways, American education operates under the same paradigm as the Chinese. Both have the same goals—to teach children the skills and knowledge they need for career and college. Both have the same apparatus—an adult teaches to a group of children grouped by age in a physical location. Both have a formal curriculum that covers similar subjects—math, English language arts, sciences (biology, chemistry, and physics), social studies (geography, history, and civics), physical education, music, and art. In a nutshell, both American education and Chinese education are designed to turn a group of children into products with similar specifications indicated by how much they have mastered the curriculum, that is, what the adult decides they should know and be able to do, regardless of their backgrounds, interests, and differences.

The process is not much different from sausage making. Ingredients go in and sausage comes out. While education in both China and America attempts to make sausage, compared to the Chinese sausage making machine, the American one is not as good. So it does not make very good sausages, but somehow it also makes bacon by accident. In other words, the creative and entrepreneurial talents America has enjoyed are like bacon from a sausage machine—not necessarily intended but a much appreciated byproduct. And of course, it comes at the cost of not so great sausages.

The features of American education that have been much criticized by American education reformers for ruining the sausage are what allow the bacon to emerge. First, the lack of a laser focus on education or rather schooling means American children are not pressured to spend all their time on studying the prescribed curriculum. They thus have more access to and can spend more time on nonschool activities—music, art, sports, carpentry, glass-blowing, debate, and many other activities of their liking—that may not have much to do with academics or college readiness. As a result, American children have more opportunities to explore what they may be good at. But at the same time, they are not spending as much energy on the school subjects or what is tested. Naturally they won't be as good as those who spend more time on these subjects.

Second, the lack of a uniform national curriculum and a national high-stakes test creates more autonomy at the local level. It gives teachers and schools the freedom to develop programs and activities that are potentially more relevant to their students, or at least not to force their students to conform to one set of knowledge and skills. It also creates a culture in school that all talents can be valuable through a diversity of in school programs—sports teams, talent shows, orchestra, choir, debate teams, and so on. However, the lack of a uniform curriculum also means vast variations in what is offered and expected in different classrooms and schools across the nation. As a result, students in the nation have very different educational experiences depending on which school they attend and which teachers they have. A uniform curriculum does not guarantee equality, but it provides the basis to offer every student similar education experiences. Hence if education is about producing similar talents, as it is believed today, the lack of a uniform curriculum is at least partially responsible for the achievement gap, that is, gaps in test scores in a limited number of subjects, in the United States.

Third, the "play time" American students have, that is time spent hanging out with friends, playing video games, managing lemonade stands, working at a gas station, and selling Girl Scout cookies, may not do much in helping with their mastering the academic content, but it helps them learn to socialize, manage relationships, and be responsible and independent. Again, the play time is distraction from studying the school subjects. If the school subject is the only learning that matters, time spent on play is certainly wasted and contributes to the low academic performance in America.

Fourth, the lack of rigor or "being tough on students" in school work means lack of direct competition among students for the first place on tests all the time. This is what Brookings Institute researcher Tom Loveless calls "the happiness factor"—teachers paying attention to enjoyment of their class. As a result, students are not constantly beaten down and told they are not good enough, hence preserving confidence.

However, the happiness factor also means a less demanding and less rigorous school experience. Students are not as pressured to master what is taught and may not devote as much energy to the school subjects. Consequently, they do not do as well as others, such as the Chinese students, in these subjects.

Finally, the general availability of out-of-school events and institutions such as sports events, museums, art galleries, and public libraries in the United States means that the time children can have to make use of them may distract them from studying but are invaluable for the development of creative and entrepreneurial qualities. These resources also provide more choices and options for students. They could inspire students to pursue different life and career paths, which at the same time discourages them from believing academic excellence as the only path for success.

Vivek Wadhwa, vice president of academics and innovation at Singularity University, fellow at Stanford Law School, and director of research at Pratt School of Engineering at Duke University, wrote in *Business Week* in 2011:

Meanwhile, the perception is that American children live a relatively easy life and coast their way through school. They don't do any more homework than they have to; they spend an extraordinary amount of time playing games, socializing on the Internet, text-messaging each other; they work part time to pay for their schooling and social habits. And they party. A lot. These stereotypes worry many Americans. They believe the American education system puts the country at a great disadvantage. But this is far from true.

The independence and social skills American children develop give them a huge advantage when they join the workforce. They learn to experiment, challenge norms, and take risks. They can think for themselves, and they can innovate. This is why America remains the world leader in innovation. (Wadhwa, 2011)

In other words, the strengths of American education are not so much in its deliberate design to cultivate creative and entrepreneurial talents as in its "poor" execution as a designed schooling system. That is, if education is defined as a system to transmit predefined content and knowledge, American education is an ineffective system because it has so many holes that allows students to pursue activities and interests that are not necessarily conducive to the mastery of the pre-scribed target of learning. But these other activities and inter-ests provide the room for creative and entrepreneurial talents to grow.

NO FREE LUNCH

The Side Effects of Education

It seems that the Chinese and Americans have engaged in a contest of mutual admiration of each other's education, a rare occurrence between the two rivals. Behind the mutual admi-ration of each other's education is a seemingly paradoxical dichotomy. The Chinese education seems to be able to pro-duce outstanding test scores, interpreted by many as aca-demic excellence, but it has apparently been unable to result in a creative and entrepreneurial workforce. In contrast, the American education has been perceived to possess the magic potion that produces more creative and entrepreneurial peo-ple, yet it is the same American system that produces medio-cre test scores, the highest high school dropout rates in developed countries, and a persistently large achievement gap between the poor and the wealthy.

This is akin to the side effects of medicine. All medicine has side effects. When it cures, it can harm the body as well. Put it another way, there is no free lunch. Everything comes at a cost. Education cannot escape this simple and obvious law of nature for a number of reasons. First, time is a constant. When one spends it on one thing, it cannot be spent on others. Thus when all time is spent on studying and preparing for exams, it cannot be spent on visiting museums. By the same token, when time is spent on activities not necessarily related to academic subjects, less time is available for studying the school subjects and preparing for exams. Second, certain human qualities may be antithetical to each other. When one is taught to conform, it will be difficult for him to be creative. When one is punished for making mistakes, it will be hard for her to take risks. When one is told to be wrong or inadequate all the time, it will be difficult for her to maintain confidence. In contrast, when students are allowed freedom to explore, they may question what they are asked to learn and may decide not to comply. Finally, resources are finite as well. When a school or society devotes all of its resources to certain things, it does not have them for others. For example, when all resources are devoted to teaching math and language, schools will have to cut out other programs. When more money is spent on testing students, less will be available for actually helping them grow.

These side effects are rarely mentioned in education, but they are what can explain the conundrum of the discrepancy between test scores and entrepreneurship. They explain why countries that have higher ranks in the PISA have lower entrepreneurial qualities. They also explain why Singapore wants to abolish its first-rate education and why China cannot have a Steve Jobs unless it abandons its educational tradition. A well-organized, tightly controlled, and well-executed education system can transmit the prescribed content much more effectively than a system that is less organized, loosely monitored, and less unified. In the meantime, a less organized system has more room for individual exploration and experimentation and allows exceptions. The question is then what matters in the future. Do we want individuals who are good at taking tests or individuals who are creative and entrepreneurial? The answer I believe is the latter, as the previous several chapters discussed.

Thus the side effect phenomenon suggests that before we jump at teaching creativity and entrepreneurship, we should start by not stifling them in schools. We should be very careful when we try to fix the "broken sausage" machine by imposing uniform standards, increasing pressure on teachers and students, and narrowing the curriculum. We must be aware of the potential damages, because as the Singaporean journalist Alexis Ong wrote in response to Steve Wozniak's comments on Singapore's inability to cultivate an Apple computer: "Bottom line: creativity isn't something that can be enforced, taught or bought" (Ong, 2012).

Furthermore, even when the "sausage" machine is fixed to perfection, it makes sausage while the society needs something different. American education is far from perfect. In fact, it is very problematic. But the problem is not that it does not make perfect sausage, but rather it does not make the bacon or prepare the entrepreneurial and creative talents by design. So the entrepreneurial and creative talents exist largely as a result of "accidents" or fortunate oversight. Even the best schools do not prepare students for what is needed in the new era (Wagner, 2008). To prepare the talents we need, we cannot count on accidents or side effects; we must work toward a paradigm shift. The remaining chapters of this book discuss the new paradigm we need.

References

Caijing. (2010). Li Kaifu: Xiayige pingguo buhui chuxian zai zhongguo (Kai-fu Lee: The next Apple will not be invented in China). Retrieved January 3, 2012, from http://www.caijing.com .cn/2011–09–16/110862857.html

Gao, G. (2003). Encountering American education. *Beijing Wenxue,* 6–35.

Gao, H. (2012, February 2). Shenyang Yutian zhongxue yidi buke bei jingji jiaoting (Shenyang Yutian secondary school stopped from offering extra lessons in another location). Retrieved February 6, 2012, from http://news.ifeng.com/mainland/detail_2012_02/ 04/12288319_0.shtml

Guojia Jiaowei (National Education Commission). (1997). *Guanyu dangqian jiji tuijin zhongxiaoxue shishi shuzhi jiaoyu de ruogan yijian (Several suggestions for the promotion of quality education in secondary and elementary schools)*. Retrieved from http://xhongcom .diy.myrice.com/page1/fagui/newpage8.htm

Gupta, A. K., & Wang, H. (2011, July 28). Chinese innovation is a paper tiger. Retrieved December 15, 2011, from http://online.wsj .com/article/SB10001424053111904800304576472034085730262 .html

Jiangsu Provincial People's Congress (2012). *Jiangsu regulations for pre-school education*. Retrieved from http://www.ec.js.edu.cn/art/ 2012/2/23/art_5944_65502.html

Jiaoyubu (Ministry of Education). (1964). Guanyu kefu zhongxiao xuesheng fudang guozhong xianxiang he tigao jiaoxue zhiliang de baogao (Report about how to overcome the problem of student burden and improving quality of teaching). Retrieved December 15, 2006, from http://news.xinhuanet.com/ ziliao/2005–02/01/content_2533971.htm

Jiaoyubu (Ministry of Education). (2001). *Yiwu jiaoyu kecheng shezhi fang'an (Curriculum framework for compulsory education)*. Retrieved from http://www.edu.cn/ke_cheng_775/20060323/t20060323 _109425.shtml

Jiaoyubu (Ministry of Education). (2012). *Jiaoyubu guanyu guifan youeryuan baoyu jiaoyu gongzuo fangzhi he jiuzheng "xiaoxuehua" xianxiang de tongzhi (Ministry of Education executive order on preventing and correcting the phenomenon of turning kindergartens into primary schools)*. Retrieved from http://www.jyb.cn/info/jyzck/ 201201/t20120112_474065.html

Jingri Zaobao. (2011, December 8). Diaocha: Zhongxiaoxue xuexi shijian yuechao chengren gongzuo shijian (Study: Study time of primary and secondary students far exceeds working time of adults). Retrieved February 4, 2012, from http://chuzhong.eol .cn/news_9136/20111208/t20111208_716949.shtml

MarketProbe, & Sina Education. (2011). *2011 zhongguo jiating jiaoyu xiaofei baipishu fabu* (2011 China family education spending white book released). Beijing, China: Sina.

Obama, B. (2011, January 25). Remarks by the president in State of the Union Address. Retrieved July 30, 2011, from http://www .whitehouse.gov/the-press-office/2011/01/25/remarks-president -state-union-address

Ong, A. (2012, January 10). Singapore needs to encourage "bad behavior." Retrieved January 20, 2012, from http://www.cnngo

.com/singapore/life/tell-me-about-it/alexis-ong-singapore
-needs-encourage-bad-behavior-718985

Organisation for Economic Co-operation and Development (OECD). (2011). *Strong performers and successful reformers in education: Lessons from PISA for the United States.* Paris, France: Author.

Sawyer, D. (Producer). (2010). China beats U.S. in reading, math and science. Retrieved from http://abcnews.go.com/Politics/china -debuts-top-international-education-rankings/story?id=12336108# .TyuwMmNU2Fe

Wadhwa, V. (2011, January 12). U.S. schools are still ahead—way ahead. *Businessweek.*

Wagner, T. (2008). *The global achievement gap: Why even our best schools don't teach the new survival skills our children need—and what we can do about it.* New York, NY: Basic Books.

Wu, J. (2011, December 20). Zaojiao shichang zongzhi 500 yi, zhuanjia jianyi chutai hanye guifan (Early childhood education market value reaches 50 billion, experts suggest regulations). *Zhongguo Jiaoyubao (Chinese Education Newspaper).* Retrieved from http:// news.xinhuanet.com/edu/2011-12/20/c_122448958.htm

Zhao, Y. (2009). *Catching up or leading the way: American education in the age of globalization.* Alexandria, VA: ASCD.

Zhonggong Zhongyang (Central Committee of the Chinese Communist Party) & Guowuyuan (The State Council). (1993). *Zhongguo jiaoyu gaige fazhan gangyao (Framework for education reform and development in China).* Retrieved May 10, 2012, from http://development.yangtzeu.edu.cn/jyfg/jyglzh/law_12 _1202.htm

Zhonggong Zhongyang (Central Committee of the Chinese Communist Party) & Guowuyuan (State Council). (1999). Guanyu shenhua jiaoyu tizhi gaige quanmian tuijin suzhi jiaoyu de jueding (Decision to further educational systemic reform and promote quality-oriented education). Retrieved May 10, 2012, from http://www.china.com.cn/chinese/zhuanti/tyzcfg/885952 .htm

Zhonggong Zhongyang Bangongting (Office of the Central Committee of the Chinese Communist Party) & Guowuyuan Bangongting (Office of the State Council). (2000). *Guanyu shiying xinxingshi jingyibu jiaqiang he gaijing zhongxiaoxue deyu gongzuo de jianyi (Suggestions for further enhancing and improving moral education in secondary and primary schools to meet the challenges of the new era).* Beijing, China: Author.

From Accident to Design

A Paradigm Shift

All the time you are in school, you learn through experience how to live in a dictatorship.

—Grace Llewellyn

Schools have not necessarily much to do with education ... they are mainly institutions of control where certain basic habits must be inculcated in the young. Education is quite different and has little place in school.

—Winston Churchill

I understand why the top students in America study physics, chemistry, calculus and classic literature. The kids in this brainy group are the future professors, scientists, thinkers and engineers who will propel civilization forward. But why do we make B students sit through these same classes? That's like trying to train your cat to do your taxes—a waste of time and money. Wouldn't it make more sense to teach B students something useful, like entrepreneurship?

This is from Scott Adams, creator of the well-known cartoon strip *Dilbert*. Adams made the plea on behalf of those

B students, who are unwilling or unable to follow the pre-scribed education path, in his article titled "How to Get a Real Education" in the *Wall Street Journal* (Adams, 2011). "I speak from experience because I majored in entrepreneurship at Hartwick College in Oneonta, N.Y.," Adams writes jokingly, because "technically, my major was economics. But the unsung advantage of attending a small college is that you can mold your experience any way you want."

Adams molded his college experience into one about busi-ness. Adams joined the management of The Coffee House, a student-run and college-subsidized small business on campus as the Minister of Finance to make a difference in this "money losing mess." On this job, he spotted the problems with the accounting system and proposed to his professor that he would "build and operate a proper accounting system for the business" for three credits. He did it. He also helped the busi-ness by firing one of his best friends from the bartending job and turned him into the group leader. His "friend lacked both the will and the potential to master the bartending arts," but "he was tall, good-looking and so gifted at b.s. that he'd be the perfect leader." So the group voted to fire the worst bartender and hired him as the Commissioner. "He went on to do a ter-rific job," Adams added.

Adams was lucky to have the opportunity and flexibility to mold his experiences, thanks to the small college he attended. His bartender-turned-into-group-leader friend was also lucky to have his leadership capacity recognized. But Adams's experience is not the norm of all education today. His case was an exception.

So was Bill Gate's experience at Lakeside School in Seattle. He was first fortunate to be in such a school that could raise enough funds to buy computing time, so he had the opportu-nity to be exposed to computers in eighth grade—not a com-mon treat for all children in the 1970s. He was also lucky to be excused from math class so he could pursue his interest in computers. Actually, he was excused for many other things that most other schools would not excuse their students. The school practically turned a blind eye when Gates and his friends missed classes and turned their homework in late because they were programming the computer all day and night. I'm not sure what his parents or teachers were thinking, but thankfully they did not try to make him a good student. Had he been strictly forced to be a typical good student in a prep school, Microsoft may not exist and "Windows" would likely still be referring to glass-covered holes in a wall instead of a computer operating system.

So was Steve Jobs's experience. Not necessarily a good student to begin with, Jobs was fortunate to have a fourth-grade teacher who saw beyond his bad behaviors as a student and channeled his energy to reading. He was also fortunate to have a father who believed in him. Instead of making him conform to the school, to scold his son for his bad school behaviors, the senior Jobs transferred him to a different school.

Throughout history, stories of exceptional individuals abound. For example, many well-known and ultrasuccessful entrepreneurs and innovators are some sorts of dropouts: Bill Gates (Microsoft), Steve Jobs (Apple), Michael Dell (Dell Computers), Larry Ellison (Oracle), and Mark Zuckerberg (Facebook); technically, even Larry Page and Sergey Brin (Google) were dropouts—they did not complete their doctoral programs. Joichi Ito, a serial entrepreneur and college dropout, was recently appointed the director of MIT Media Lab, one of the world's most prestigious computing science laboratories, housed at one of the world's most prestigious universities filled with PhDs. Ito dropped out of college twice. He first attended Tufts and studied computer science but found it "drudge work." Then he tried the University of Chicago to study physics but dropped out again because it was simply stultifying (Markoff, 2011). But MIT may be one of a handful of institutions that have the courage to hire a college dropout to lead a group of people with advanced degrees.

These individuals made it for one reason or another. But there are many more who did not make it. There may have been numerous Steve Jobses, Bill Gateses, and Joichi Itos who have been taught to conform, rendered bad students, forced to quit school, or told to give up before they even had a chance to try out their entrepreneurial and creative interests because, as discussed in the previous chapter, the paradigm that has dominated education has been aiming to produce standardized "sausages," not creative, nonconforming entrepreneurs.

THE DOMINANT PARADIGM

Preparing Employees

At present, the dominant education paradigm is not concerned with preparing entrepreneurs, as the previous chapter discussed. Rather, this paradigm aims to prepare individuals to find gainful employment in the current economy and to fit into the existing society. It was designed to produce workers for the mass-production economy that came with the Industrial Revolution. The mass-production economy needed a large workforce with similar skills and knowledge, but at very basic levels. There was no need for the majority of individuals to be inventors or entrepreneurs. The few great inventors and entrepreneurs could occur by accident as long as the society permitted them to thrive.

Prescribing Learning

To educate the masses with similar basic knowledge and skills requires a common curriculum, or a prescription of the skills, knowledge, talents, and abilities that must be taught in schools so as to prepare children to function well in society. Since schools cannot possibly teach everything, the task to define what to teach is basically an exercise of making choices about what to include and what to exclude. This exercise has always been contentious and controversial because not all agree on what is considered important and necessary for all sorts of reasons. For example, about 150 years ago, the British philosopher Herbert Spencer posed the question "what knowledge is of most worth" in an essay to argue for replacing what was taught in schools at that time—Latin, Greek, and grammar—with modern sciences because they would be of more value for citizens living in a society transformed by technology (Spencer, 1911). His suggestion was not without resistance from the establishment at the time. In the United States, the Committee of Ten of the National Education Association (NEA) made an historical attempt to prescribe what American secondary schools should teach in their report published in 1894 (National Education Association of the United States [Committee on Secondary School Studies], 1894). But the prescription by the Committee of Ten was replaced by recommendations of another NEA committee only a few decades later. In 1918, the Commission on the Reorganization of Secondary Education produced *Cardinal Principles of Secondary Education* (National Education Association of the United States [Commission on the Reorganization of Secondary Education], 1918). The *Cardinal Principles* took a practical approach to curriculum very much like that of Herbert Spencer and thus moved away from the Committee of Ten, which prescribed much more academically rigorous and intellectually challenging subjects. For that change, many have launched criticism against the *Cardinal Principles* for being anti-intellectual and dumbing down American children. The current push for the Common Core standards is yet another example of national attempts to prescribe what students should learn to be ready for college and career.

Regardless of their disagreement, they all attempt to prescribe what students should learn. And once the prescription is completed, the resulting definition governs students' learning experiences. It dictates what students are exposed to in the form of textbooks, classroom instructions, assessments, and homework.

Making It Work: Executing the Curriculum

Governments, educational authorities, parents, and educators are responsible for ensuring that students master the curriculum. Curriculum standards, textbooks, and supplemental materials are developed to make sure the prescribed content is prominent in the children's school life. Teachers are trained to dispense the prescribed content effectively. Tests are administered to assess to what degree students have acquired the prescribed content. And then children are sorted based on the extent to which they master the prescribed curriculum into different tracks at the end of their basic education—some going to vocational school, some going to community colleges, some to four-year colleges, and a few to prestigious universities. The different tracks correspond to different careers that offer varying returns in terms of social status and economic resources. The type of school and the number of years attended thus have a direct correlation with the jobs people can have and how much money they make.

A Master Plan for Success

This paradigm puts out a clear path toward life's success, often defined externally by society, for example, a good college, a decent job, or a handsome income. It has a set of clearly defined learning objectives and multiple regular checkpoints (i.e., tests) to ensure that the objectives are met. If a child meets the objectives, she is rewarded and recognized, with good grades, good test scores, and then a spot in a good college; this in turn gives her access to better jobs, a better income, and presumably a better life. Otherwise, the child may be given a bad grade, retained for one more year, or given remedial lessons.

This education paradigm essentially resembles a benevolent dictator who says if you follow his commands, HE will reward you. For a short period of time, it operated this way in China. Up until the early 1990s, Chinese college graduates were assigned jobs by the government. The students who mastered the prescribed content well enough to pass the college entrance exam were guaranteed a job for life.

Figure 6.1 The Employment-Oriented Education Paradigm

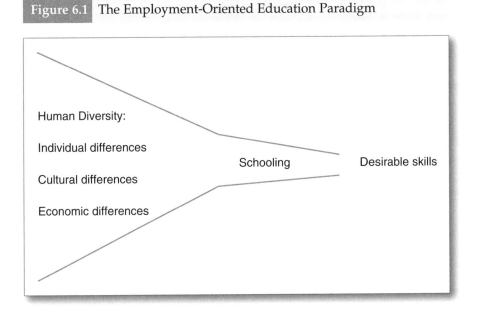

In essence, the traditional paradigm or the employment-oriented paradigm is about reducing human diversity into a few desirable skills, as illustrated in Figure 6.1. When executed well, this paradigm is effective in producing people with similar skills and conformity, indicated by test scores or academic performance. Virtually all schools in today's world operate under this paradigm. The difference lies in their level of success in executing the plan. Countries that do well have better academic performance than those who do not. Meanwhile, a well-educated, employment-oriented education in the process of forcing conformity and imposing uniformity is also very successful in weeding out those unwilling or unable to conform. They become outcasts and dropouts, and are rendered to lower-status, lower paying jobs, or even no jobs. While most of them are not rewarded with high social status or high income, a few of those outcasts do become successful, and if they do, extremely successful. Think of Albert Einstein, Cher, Lady Gaga, Steve Jobs, and Bill Gates.

The extent to which the approach is executed explains the differences in educational achievement. China's stunning test scores come as a result of a well-executed, employment-oriented education, at the cost of creativity and imagination; meanwhile, American education, which has traditionally executed the approach with much less control, standards, and precision for the lack of a national common curriculum, has produced more creative talents. In other words, America's success in creativity is the outcome of its ineffectiveness in forcing conformity and standardization. It has more room for outcasts to survive, and such room results in lower performance on single measures such as test scores.

A Necessity That No Longer Works

This paradigm has been necessary and has worked well so far for many people. It is necessary because for a long period of time, human societies remained local, lacked much interaction with others, and were slow to change. In those societies, maintaining order and preparing a labor force with similar skills and knowledge to support the local economy were of paramount importance. Most likely, the local economy was homogenous, requiring a massive number of people with similar skills and knowledge. There was not much need for outcasts or individuals with extraordinary or "abnormal" abilities.

This paradigm worked well also because a group of smart people could predict relatively easily what the future will be like based on past experiences and thus determine what knowledge and skills were needed. This also worked fine in a society where the predominant economical mode was mass production and standardization, which required many people with similar skills and knowledge. It also worked well in a society where knowledge was not easily accessible and where a few experts monopolized all the skills.

But such a society no longer exists, at least in much of developed world today, as discussed in Chapter 2.

Globalization has made all societies open to outside influences. Jobs can be easily sent to other countries. People cross national boundaries in vast numbers. Ideas travel around the globe at light speed. Technological changes continue to accelerate. All evidence suggests that Alvin Toffler was right: We have entered the *Third Wave* society, where the Industrial Era creed of standardization is no more.

As a result, it has become increasingly difficult to predict the future, to know what jobs will be available in a given society due to outsourcing or replacement by technology, and to even know where and for whom our children will be working. It is, as has been recognized by many, no longer possible to prescribe the knowledge and skills children may need for future careers and employment. The idea of "career ready" is but a fancy dream, when one does not know what careers will exist when a child leaves school. Furthermore, teachers or schools are no longer the only, or even primary, sources of knowledge or opportunities to develop skills. More important, the opportunities for different types of talents and skills to be deemed valuable have dramatically expanded. Consider the large number of scientists, comedians, painters, musicians, and even chefs for TV shows—they were useless for most of human history up until now.

All these changes require a paradigm shift—from one that prepares employees to one that cultivates innovative entrepreneurs so creative entrepreneurs are not simply an accidental outcome but the result of deliberate design.

THE ALTERNATIVE PARADIGM

Following the Child

There is another paradigm of education. This paradigm does not presuppose or predefine what knowledge or skills are worthwhile. In this paradigm the "curriculum" is one that follows the child. It begins with the children: what they are interested in, what excites them, what they are capable of, and how they learn. This paradigm does not assume all children are the same; therefore, it does not impose artificial standards or age-based, grade-level expectations. It helps children move forward from where they are. Furthermore, it does not believe children are simply empty vessels ready to be filled with knowledge, but rather it assumes that each child is a purposeful agent who actively interacts with the outside world.

The great American educator and philosopher John Dewey summarizes the differences between the two paradigms almost 80 years ago in his *Education and Experience:*

> To imposition from above is opposed expression and cultivation of individuality; to external discipline is opposed free activity; to learning from texts and teachers, learning through experience; to acquisition of isolated skills and techniques by drill, is opposed acquisition of them as means of attaining ends which make direct vital appeal; to preparation for a more or less remote future is opposed making the most of the opportunities of present life; to static aims and materials is opposed acquaintance with a changing world. (Dewey, 1938/1998, pp. 5–6)

Enhancing and Expanding Human Talents: Follow the Child

As illustrated by Figure 6.2, education following this paradigm aims to guide, support, and celebrate individual students rather than reducing human diversity into a few employable skills. It is designed to enhance and expand human talents and exceptionality instead of standardizing them. Outcasts are the new normal in this paradigm. Great creative people are not accidents, but they are deliberately cultivated and supported.

Figure 6.2   Entrepreneur-Oriented Education Paradigm

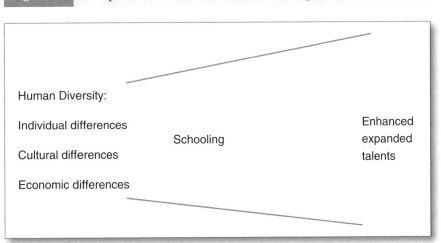

It would be a mistake to say that this new paradigm denies the importance of common and essential knowledge and skills; they are required of all citizens in order for a society or community to function. By promoting child-centered learning, this paradigm places the responsibility of learning on the child, instead of external agencies. By following the children's passion and interest, this paradigm capitalizes on their intrinsic motivation and natural curiosity to learn. When a child has a reason to learn, the basics will be sought after, rather than imposed upon. If they are true basics, they are hard to avoid.

This new paradigm also recognizes the arrival of the era of globalization. Children will no longer live in isolated societies, and thus their context of learning and living should not be confined to a physical location anymore. They must become citizens of their local community, the nation, and also the world. Hence the new paradigm asks that the education we need make the global society as the default context of learning.

An Old Idea That Gets a New Life

The core spirit of this alternative paradigm of education is not new. The idea that education should be centered on the

child—not on externally defined knowledge, skills, or rules—
has been around for centuries. The French philosopher Jean-
Jacques Rousseau advocated for following the nature of
children and criticized the imposition of knowledge on children more than 200 years ago: "I hate books; they only teach
us to talk about things we know nothing about." In the pref-
ace of one of his masterpieces, *Emile: Or, On Education,*
Rousseau wrote:

> We know nothing of childhood, and with our mistaken
> notions the further we advance the further we go astray.
> The wisest writers devote themselves to what a man
> ought to know without asking what a child is capable of
> learning. They are always looking for the man in the child
> without considering what he is before he becomes a man.
> (Rousseau, 2011)

Rousseau never implemented his educational plan out-
lined in his *Emile,* some of which was impractical or extreme
anyway. But the Swiss education reformer Johann Heinrich
Pestalozzi worked to implement a child-centered education,
for he wished "to wrest education from the outworn order of
doddering old teaching hacks as well as from the new-
fangled order of cheap, artificial teaching tricks, and entrust
it to the eternal powers of nature herself" (in Silber, 1965,
p. 134). Pestalozzi's student Friedrich Froebel, the German
educator who invented kindergarten, popularized the notion
that children are creative and unique in their own ways. In
his famous *The Education of Man,* first published in 1826, he
wrote:

> The purpose of education is to encourage and guide man
> as a conscious, thinking and perceiving being in such a
> way that he becomes a pure and perfect representation of
> that divine inner law through his own personal choice;
> education must show him the ways and meanings of
> attaining that goal. (Froebel, 2005, p. 2)

In the ensuing two centuries, the movement toward more child-centered education has garnered more support and grown exponentially. There has been growth in the general recognition of human rights, respect for individuals, and protection of freedom, which has resulted in increasing acceptance and recognition of children's rights as individuals.

How Children Learn

Scientific research has also generated more evidence that supports a more child-centered educational approach. Starting with works of the Swiss developmental psychologist Jean Piaget and the Russian psychologist Lev Vygotsky, the last century saw a "constructivism" revolution in learning theory, which significantly altered the traditional view of the learner and the learning process. Constructivist psychologists have brought abundant evidence to show that children are unique learners with unique needs and backgrounds and actively construct knowledge based on their previous experiences instead of passively receiving it (Glasersfeld, 1989). Furthermore, cognitive scientists such as Steven Pinker of Harvard University have brought evidence to support that human beings are not born a "blank slate" waiting to be carved by experiences and teachers. Children have certain innate propensities for developing and learning that must be respected. Psychologists such as Howard Gardner of Harvard University (Gardner, 1983) and Robert Sternberg, formerly of Yale University (Sternberg, 1985), have challenged the traditional narrow view of human intelligence and postulated that human beings are talented in different areas, further supporting the proposition that each child is unique and must be treated differently.

While disagreements regarding the specifics exist today, it is generally agreed among cognitive scientists and educational researchers that children (for example, see Bransford, Brown, & Cocking, 2000):

- Are born with curiosity and the ability to learn
- Are not born with exactly the same capacities for learning the same things
- Come to school with different levels of cognitive, emotional, physical, and social development due to a combination of nature and nurture
- Come to school with different needs, interests, and abilities
- Are active learners with unique needs
- Should bear the responsibility of learning
- Learn best when intrinsically motivated
- Are motivated when respected, encouraged, and exposed to opportunities that capture their interest, build on their previous experience, and are recognized for their accomplishment

Thus, education must be designed around the child and be child centered. Good education should aim to meet each child's unique needs, capitalize on each child's strengths, and grant the child autonomy so he or she can take the responsibility for learning.

Grand Experiments

Many great educators have also pioneered child-centered education. From John Dewey's founding of the University of Chicago Lab Schools in 1896 to Maria Montessori's opening of the first *Casa dei Bambini* or Children's House in 1907, various models of child-centered education began to grow. The last century also saw the addition and spread of Waldorf education, with the first Waldorf School founded in 1919 in Stuttgart, Germany. Shortly after World War II, parents around Reggio Emilia in Italy began to pilot yet another child-centered education approach that has spread across the world: The Reggio Emilia approach believes that children must have control over the direction of their learning and must be provided endless ways and opportunities to express themselves. Reggio schools adopt the "emergent curriculum." The curriculum emerges from mutual interests and passion of the child and teacher through discussion and coplanning.

There are more. In 1921, Alexander Sutherland Neill founded the Summerhill School in Germany and later settled in England. The Summerhill School operates with the philosophy that school should be made to fit the child, instead of making the child fit the school, because children learn best when freed from coercion. In 1968 the Sudbury Valley School was established in Massachusetts, in the United States. Following a similar philosophy as the Summerhill School, the Sudbury Valley School offers no prescribed curriculum and allows students to decide what to do with their time in a democratic environment. Not far from the Sudbury Valley School is the Albany Free School, founded in 1969 in Albany, New York. The Albany Free School follows a similar democratic education philosophy and pedagogy.

ONE STEP FORWARD, TWO STEPS BACKWARD

The Incomplete Shift

Nevertheless, the child-centered education paradigm remains on the fringe. The Progressive Education movement started by John Dewey is now practically a historical relic. The Montessori model, despite its worldwide interest, is practiced in only about 20,000 schools worldwide, many of which are private, independent, and small entities. The total number of Waldorf schools globally is below 5,000. And the Reggio approach has only been practiced in a small number, mostly private, preschools and kindergartens. The number of *democratic education* institutions is even smaller. By and large, the world's public education system has been barely touched by these child-centered education approaches. The vast majority of children in the world today still attend schools that attempt to instill in them predefined knowledge and skills in a lock-step fashion.

Worse yet, we are moving backwards. As discussed in Chapter 1, the world is moving toward more curriculum standardization as a way to fix the traditional paradigm. From the No Child Left Behind Act to the Race to the Top program and the Common Core State Standards Initiative, America has put a tremendous amount of political and financial resources into prescribing what children should learn, to ensure that they have mastered prescribed content through high-stakes testing. Globally, PISA and other international assessments are luring countries to import international curriculum and practices to further homogenize what children will learn. Nations that had a slightly more enlightened education system are moving backwards, and nations that wish to move forward are struggling because of their heavy historical baggage.

In other words, education today is becoming more authoritarian and dictatorial as authorities around the world bring more resources to ensure children learn what is prescribed. Instead of creating an education for the future, we are busy "perfecting a 19th century system," as Daniel Pink once told me.

EVOLUTIONARY HANGOVERS AND THE CHALLENGES OF CHANGE

The reasons for a paradigm shift in education are compelling, but why is today's education besieged by the traditional paradigm? Why do school systems around the globe continue to focus on producing good tests takers at a time when the world needs more creative and innovative talents to meet the unprecedented challenges and take advantage of the vast opportunities presented by technological changes and globalization? Why do schools continue to force students to prepare for jobs that may not even exist when they graduate, when old industries are rapidly replaced by new ones? Why do schools continue to push a nationalistic Cold War–style curriculum to make them "globally competitive" at a time when students need to learn to collaborate globally in this interconnected and interdependent village? Why are schools asked to cram more of the same when children have become increasingly disengaged and disinterested with the outdated Industrial Age curriculum and pedagogy? And why are schools asked to homogenize the curriculum and narrow children's educational experiences when human diversity should be celebrated and tapped into as assets?

Why is the traditional paradigm so powerful, after all? Why are well-intentioned, smart people pursuing something that will eventually lead to the opposite of what they want? (I am assuming innocence and good intention in all, despite the fact that there are many who believe in a conspiracy theory that the evil and greedy corporate world played a role.)

Evolutionary Hangovers

Evolutionary hangovers may be one answer. The Stanford biologist Paul Ehrlich describes these in his 2000 book *Human Natures: Genes, Cultures, and the Human Prospect* as "structures or behaviors that once were adaptive but whose positive influence on reproductive performance has declined or disappeared" (Ehrlich, 2000, p. 34). Evolutionary hangovers come into existence because "natural selection has no foresight" and genetic evolution takes a long time. Thus when the environment changes, what was useful in the past may no longer be of any utility in the new environment. Vestigial organs in our body (e.g., the appendix) are an example.

The appendix and some other evolutionary hangovers may be benign, but some can be harmful. Our love for sweets and fatty food, for example, used to give us an adaptive advantage in our long evolutionary history when sugar and fat were difficult to come by. But in modern society when sugar and fat are in abundant supply, this evolutionary advantage has become the primary culprit for obesity and other health hazards. Evolutionary hangovers are very powerful because they are inherently part of us. They are instinctual. It takes tremendous and conscious efforts to reject their commands.

The traditional paradigm of education itself has become a hangover of cultural evolution. It used to work and may still work in some areas for some people, but it does not work for the future. It is, however, very difficult to abandon the traditional educational paradigm for something new, not only because we have been used to it and there are complex social and economic institutions closely tied with its operations, but also because it has features that hold tremendous appeal to the human nature: our naturally evolved desire for orderliness, control, competitive advantage, and short-term or immediate tangible results.

Appeals of the Traditional Paradigm

With a prescribed standardized curriculum, the traditional paradigm gives a sense of orderliness and control. We know what is being taught and since the curriculum comes from a body of experts and authorities, it is believed to be valuable. Adding to its regular assessment, we then know how well children are progressing and how teachers and schools are doing. We can also use the assessment results to judge the value of children, teachers, and schools. This is particularly appealing for officials who are charged with the responsibility for delivering high-quality education with public funds: They can present to the public nicely arranged diagrams, charts, and tables of what their tax dollars are buying.

The traditional paradigm also appeals to parents because it puts forth a clear path toward success, which is often defined externally by society. It has clearly defined learning objectives and thus multiple checkpoints (i.e., tests) to ensure that the objectives are met. If a child meets the objectives, she is rewarded and recognized, with grades, good test scores, and then a spot in a good college; this in turn gives her access to better jobs, a better income, and presumably a better life. In other words, one can see the entire racecourse and knows what is required to run the course and jump the hurdles. As long as she can complete the course, the reward at the end is hers. Everyone knows the game and its rules; as long as you play and play it well, you will see the rewards.

The commanding power of this paradigm lies not only with its presentation of a master plan for life's success, but also with its provision of ways to know how well the plan is being executed at any time. And it is simple, too. Is the child getting all As? Does the child read at his grade level? Is she meeting or exceeding state expectations in math? How many points has she scored on the SAT or ACT? Where does he stand compared to his peers in the school or against national norms?

Furthermore, the traditional paradigm satisfies the needs to compete and compare with others because it reduces education to a few simple measured outcomes, that is, test scores. Stephen Jay Gould, the late Harvard paleontologist and science historian known for his contributions to the public understanding of evolution, brilliantly debunks the myth of biological determinism in human mentality and the reduction of human intellectual capacity to simplistic measures such IQ test in the book *The Mismeasure of Men*. He points out that the philosophic fallacy of *reification*, or "our tendency to convert abstract concepts into entities," is responsible for the wide acceptance of IQ tests or other measures such as the size of the skull as indicators of human intelligence. "We recognize the importance of mentality in our lives and wish to characterize it. . . . We therefore give the word 'intelligence' to this wondrously complex and multifaceted set of human capabilities. This shorthand symbol is then reified and intelligence achieves its dubious status as a unitary thing" (Gould, 1996, p. 56). Our desire to rank things is also at play. Human beings have a "propensity for ordering complex variation as a gradual ascending scale . . . but ranking requires a criterion for assigning all individuals to their proper status in the single series. And what better criterion than an objective number?" (Gould, 1996, p. 56).

By reducing education to simple indicators—grades and test scores in a limited number of subjects—and making them common across schools, states, or nations, the traditional paradigm gives parents, governments, and the public the ability to quickly size up where their children, students, and schools stand against others. This is one of the reasons why the PISA scores, although merely measures of 15-year-olds in three areas, have been considered as an indication of national education quality and economic competitiveness.

The other reason that prevents us from making the drastic shift is our inability to perceive large and distant changes. University of California–Los Angeles professor and Pulitzer Prize winner Jared Diamond analyzes the fate of a great number of once-great societies that failed in his 2005 book *Collapse: How Societies Choose to Fail or Succeed* (Diamond, 2005). He found that the society's inability to perceive or unwillingness to accept large and distant changes—and thus work to come up with the right response—is among one of the chief reasons that societies fail. This inability also leads human beings to look for short-term outcomes and seek immediate gratification. The few years prior to the most recent financial crisis triggered by subprime mortgage practices saw a widespread euphoria in the society because all short-term economic measures looked so good: people were buying houses, bankers generated huge profits, mortgage lenders received huge bonuses, and consumers were confident. But we know the story now; dangers were brewing and the storm was gathering—unfortunately all warning signs were ignored. History is replete with examples of this sort. The British historian Arnold Toynbee warns: "Civilizations die from suicide, not by murder."

We are facing significant changes, as this book has documented so far. These changes require a paradigm shift instead of fixing the traditional model. After all, perfecting the horse wagon won't get us to the moon. We need to build an entirely different vehicle. In the next few chapters, I discuss the elements of a framework of education under the new child-centered paradigm that aims to cultivate creative entrepreneurs.

References

Adams, S. (2011). How to get a real education. *The Wall Street Journal.* Retrieved from http://online.wsj.com/article/SB100014240527 4870410160457624714338349656.html

Bransford, J. D., Brown, A. L., & Cocking, R. R. (Eds.). (2000). *How people learn: Brain, mind, experience, and school.* Washington, DC: The National Academies Press.

Dewey, J. (1998). *Education and experience: The 60th anniversary edition.* Bloomington, IN: Kappa Delta Pi. (Original work published 1938)

Diamond, J. M. (2005). *Collapse: How societies choose to fail or succeed.* New York, NY: Viking.

Ehrlich, P. R. (2000). *Human natures: Genes, cultures, and the human prospect.* New York, NY: Penguin Books.

Froebel, F. (2005). *The education of man* (W. N. Hailmann, Trans.). New York, NY: Dover Publications.

Gardner, H. (1983). *Frames of mind: The theory of multiple intelligences.* New York, NY: Basic Books.

Glasersfeld, E. (1989). Cognition, construction of knowledge, and teaching. *Synthese, 80*(1), 121–140.

Gould, S. J. (1996). *The mismeasure of man.* New York, NY: Norton.

Markoff, J. (2011, April 26). M.I.T. Media Lab Names a New Director. *The New York Times,* B1. Retrieved from http://www.nytimes .com/2011/04/26/science/26lab.html

National Education Association of the United States (Commission on the Reorganization of Secondary Education). (1918). *Cardinal principles of secondary education: A report of the Commission on the Reorganization of Secondary Education.* Washington, DC: Department of the Interior, Bureau of Education.

National Education Association of the United States (Committee on Secondary School Studies). (1894). *Report of the committee of ten on secondary school studies: With the reports of the conferences arranged by the committee.* New York, NY: American Book Company.

Rousseau, J.-J. (2011). Emile, or on education. Available from http:// www.gutenberg.org/catalog/world/readfile?fk_files=2232329

Silber, K. (1965). *Pestalozzi: The man and his works.* London, England: Routledge and Kegan Paul.

Spencer, H. (1911). Essays on education and kindred subjects. Available from http://www.gutenberg.org/files/16510/16510-h/ 16510-h.htm

Sternberg, R. J. (1985). *Beyond IQ: A triarchic theory of human intelligence.* New York, NY: Cambridge University Press.

7

Freedom to Learn

Student Autonomy and Leadership

The teacher is not in the school to impose certain ideas or to form certain habits in the child, but is there as a member of the community to select the influences which shall affect the child and to assist him in properly responding to these influences.

—John Dewey

Children have to be educated, but they have also to be left to educate themselves.

—Ernest Dimnet

Summerhill is not providing an adequate education for its pupils," wrote Her Majesty's Inspector of School (HMI) Neville Grenyer in a report to the British Office for Standards in Education, *Children's Services and Skills (Ofsted) in 1999* (Grenyer, 1999). "Whether the pupils make sufficient progress and achieve the standards of which they are capable is left to each child's inclination," the report continues, "Consequently, for the great majority of the pupils, their curriculum is fragmented, disjointed, narrow and likely adversely to affect their future options." Grenyer complains that: "The school has drifted into confusing educational freedom with the negative right not to be taught. As a result, many pupils have been allowed to mistake the pursuit of idleness for the exercise of personal liberty." The report concluded, "The school fails to meet the requirements for registration under the Education Act 1996 in the following respects: the instruction is not efficient or suitable; the welfare of boarders is not adequately safeguarded and promoted; the school does not provide suitable accommodation."

The school was ordered to change or face closure in six months by then U.K.'s Secretary of State for Education and Employment David Blunkett (Smithers, 2000). The school did not accept the recommendations and took the government to court. After three days of hearing at the high court in London, Summerhill School reached an agreement with Ofsted, which withdrew its complaints against the school and agreed to exempt the school from annual inspections. And the Department of Education and Employment was ordered to pay the legal fees, which could be nearly $200,000 (Smithers, 2000).

A few years later in 2007, Her Majesty's Inspector Judith Matharu and three additional inspectors conducted another inspection of Summerhill. The inspectors issued a glowing report:

This is a good school with some outstanding features. It provides a consistently good standard of education and gives good value for money. Achievement is good and standards are above average overall and improving. The school is taking robust and effective action to raise standards at Key Stage 4 and is well placed to continue this improvement. Staff and students are rightly proud of their school. Relationships in the school are very good and almost all students enjoy their education. This supportive and safe atmosphere leads to very high levels of attendance. Students' personal development is outstanding. They display excellent behaviour and very positive attitudes towards their learning. Students appreciate the strong contributions they are encouraged to make to many aspects of school life. Consistently good and challenging teaching enables students to achieve high standards in their work. Lessons are usually lively and stimulating, providing appropriate challenge for all abilities. (Matharu, 2008, p. 4)

Many may think this is a great story of school improvement, from bad to great. But in reality, the school did not change, according to Zoe Readhead, head of Summerhill and daughter of its founder, A. S. Neill. "Summerhill has been running continuously since 1921 and has not changed fundamentally since it started," states its website (Summerhill School, 2004). Thus, it is the government that has turned around, not the school. "The government has refused to acknowledge the individual philosophy of the school, such as that children can learn just as well out of the classroom. We feel vindicated," Readhead was quoted saying in a report published by the British newspaper *The Guardian* (Shepherd, 2007).

The battle between Summerhill and the British government is a battle between the two educational paradigms discussed in Chapter 6. At the heart of the battle is the fundamental issue of who should be in control of children's learning. The government wanted to make sure that children learn what the government prescribed in ways the government defined as proper, and demonstrate their learning through assessments endorsed by the government. But Summerhill wanted freedom—freedom for the children to decide what to learn, how to learn, and if they wanted to be assessed. Thus Summerhill's vindication is the triumph of a philosophy, an educational paradigm that believes children, not an outside agency, should be in control of their learning.

Summerhill School is a small, independent boarding school in Suffolk, Britain. Founded by the Scottish educator Alexander Sutherland Neill in 1921 with five pupils, the school has about 100 students aged from 5 to 18. Despite its small student population, the school has been one of the most famous and controversial schools in the world since its establishment. The court battle between Summerhill and the government has made it even more famous, inspiring a TV drama produced by BBC.

Summerhill was established to provide a different kind of education, which is considered radical by many even today. Its underpinning principle is Neill's notion that "the function of the child is to live his own life—not the life that his anxious parents think he should live, nor a life according to the purpose of the educator who thinks he knows best" (Summerhill School, 2004). True to this notion, the school follows the child instead of the other way around. It allows children the maximum freedom to live and learn, only within the confinement of rules made by themselves and other members of the community through a democratic process. Featured on the school website are five statements that capture the school's spirit:

Imagine a school . . .

Where kids have freedom to be themselves . . .

Where success is not defined by academic achievement but the child's own definition of success . . .

Where the whole school deals democratically with issues, with each individual having an equal right to be heard . . .

Where you can play all day if you want to . . .

And there is time and space to sit and dream . . .

The freedom children enjoy in the school is tremendous, to the degree that most adults would find unbelievable, even outrageous. For example, students are not obliged to attend any class. If a child feels like staying in a tree all day, all week, or all year, he can do so without adult interference. In fact, one child attended the school for 13 years without attending any class and he became an expert toolmaker and precision instrument maker, according to a 1949 inspection report (Neill,

1960). "We do what we want to do," Chae-Eun Park, 16, from South Korea, told a reporter of the British newspaper *The Independent* in 2008 (Stanford, 2008).

And indeed, the children do what they want to do, as *The Independent* reporter observed during his visit:

> Although it is midday and lessons are running when the Guardian visits, many pupils are not in class. A teenage girl is engrossed in a novel, and three friends are adding up the scores of their table tennis tournament. There is busy project work going on in the woodwork room, with music playing loudly. (Stanford, 2008)

What was happening in class was diverse and student driven. In one class, a teacher was working with a 10-year-old to decide which period she would like to study in history. Another boy was investigating fighter bombers on the computer, while two girls from Japan were working on translating a novel. "In the adjoining book-lined snug, another girl is lying on the sofa, reading. A classmate is asleep on the beanbag, Roald Dahl's *Danny the Champion of the World* open on his lap" (Stanford, 2008).

And the adults, the teachers, were used to the level of freedom granted to students. A reporter of the British newspaper *The Guardian* observed:

> It is halfway through mid-morning science class and there is still only one seat occupied—that of the teacher, David Riebold. "It's my first no-show in a while," Riebold says wistfully, looking at the test tubes he has laid out. "Ah well, there's always lesson preparation to do." Skipping class is no big deal at Summerhill, Britain's most progressive school, where pupils set the rules and can miss lessons to play or pursue their own interests. (Shepherd, 2007)

It goes without saying that the school does not follow the British national curriculum or forces students to take exams, but the students can choose to take the General Certificate of Secondary Education, commonly known as the GCSE, the British national qualification exams for secondary school graduates, just like they choose to study anything else.

While the students have the freedom to spend their time however they want, reading, climbing trees, sleeping, or attending class, they cannot do things that can cause any harm or disruption to others or damage to the community. Hence rules are made and enforced, but the rules are created and enforced through a democratic process. All members of the Summerhill community, adults and children alike, have equal rights in determining what rules should be developed at school meetings. The meetings are held on Monday, Wednesday, and Fridays from 1:45 to 2:30 each week. The school meetings serve as both the legislative and judicial body. School laws are made and changed at these meetings by majority vote. Those who broke the laws are brought to justice at these meetings as well, usually in the form of a fine, determined by the majority.

These meetings are not compulsory. Everyone and anyone within the community can attend. Students and staff have equal votes, which means the influence of students is greater than the staff, since there are more students than staff. The rules, once made, apply to both children and staff.

Although Summerhill does not require students to take the GCSE or intends to prepare students for college, it has produced good test results and college graduates. Today even the British government recognizes it as a good school. And over the past 90 years, Summerhill has produced artists, musicians, dancers, actors, photographers, professors, hedge fund analysts, and other professionals (Riding, 1999; Shepherd, 2007). More important, it has a group of graduates who love their experiences at the school, which should be a much better criterion for judging a school's success than what has been applied conventionally, such as college attendance rates, test scores, or successful professionals.

It is not Summerhill's intention to prepare entrepreneurial and creative talents. In fact, Summerhill has no stated goals to prepare students for anything other than themselves. The school was founded to provide an alternative education environment for children to be themselves "at a time when the rights of individuals were less respected than they are today. Children were beaten in most homes at some time or another and discipline was the key work in child rearing" (Summerhill School, 2004). For over 90 years, the school has shown that children can "learn to be self-confident, tolerant and considerate when they are given space to be themselves" (Summerhill School, 2004).

While Summerhill and other "free schools" didn't and still don't purport to prepare entrepreneurs, their approach to education exemplifies the first principle of a new education paradigm needed for cultivating entrepreneurial and creative talents. The Summerhill spirit needs to move from the fringe to the core, from alternative to the mainstream because it embodies part of the answer to the urgent challenges education faces today, as this book has covered so far.

ENGAGEMENT

Shifting the Responsibility to the Learner

Giving children the space to learn and allowing children to do what they want to appear to be an irresponsible action on the part of the school and adults, as Ofsted accused Summerhill of "confusing educational freedom with the negative right not to be taught," thus resulting in mistaking "the pursuit of idleness for the exercise of personal liberty." But in reality, it is allowing children to pursue their own interests and take responsibility for their own learning. Only when children learn what they want to learn and begin to take the responsibility for learning and living can they stay truly engaged. When they are forced to learn something they don't see as relevant, no matter how important adults believe it will be for their future, children may simply go through the motions at best, and become disengaged and drop out at worst.

Student engagement or lack thereof has been a persistent plague of traditional education. Although students have high aspirations, they often find schooling boring and become disengaged. In the United States, for example, about a quarter of high school students in the class of 2008 dropped out or did not complete high school on time despite more than 91% expecting to attain at least a high school diploma and over 87% wanting to go to college. Students are simply bored. According to a longitudinal survey of over 350,000 high school students in 40 states in the United States, only 2% reported never being bored in school. Two out of three (66%) students reported being bored at least every day in class in high school. The top two sources of boredom are "material wasn't interesting" (81%) and the lack of relevance (42%). Over 50% of high school students surveyed skipped class in 2009 and one in five students considered dropping out because "I didn't like the school" (50%), "I didn't see the value in the work I was being asked to do" (42%), or "I didn't like the teachers" (39%) (Yazzie-Mintz, 2010). Where they are forced to study for cultural and family reasons, they may be doing the job of learning, but they do not necessarily enjoy and instead experience significant psychological damages. The negative correlation between enjoyment and confidence and TIMSS math performance noted by Tom Loveless (Loveless, 2006) is a telling example, so is the tremendous psychological pressures of Asian American students observed by contributors to the book *Model Minority Myth Revisited: An Interdisciplinary Approach to Demystifying Asian American Educational Experiences* (Li & Wang, 2008).

But at Summerhill, "the children are full of life and zest" and "of boredom and apathy there was no sign" observed Her Majesty's Inspectors in 1949 (Neill, 1960). And in the 2008 report, the British government found students at Summerhill:

act responsibly and with great maturity, and have positive attitudes towards learning. As a result, they thoroughly enjoy the learning experiences offered by the school. . . .

Attendance is well above average. Students' good progress and high standards in basic skills prepare them well
for their future lives. (Matharu, 2008, p. 5)

Furthermore, in terms of academic achievement, despite
the complete freedom granted to students, Summerhill students' achievement is above the national average. Again the
2007 inspectors reported:

Standards are consistently above average. From above
average attainment on entry, students achieve standards
at the end of Year 9 that are well above the national average. In 2007, Key Stage 3 test results were well above
average in all subjects. In particular, results in English
significantly improved from 2006 and placed the school
at the first percentile of schools nationally. Students make
good progress in all subjects at Key Stage 3 and sometimes excellent progress, as in English in 2007. Standards
at the end of Key Stage 4 are also above the national average, although the gap between the school's results and
national performance has closed over the past three
years. The percentage of students gaining an A*- C grade
GCSE in English and mathematics has been well above
the national average for the past three years. (Matharu,
2008, p. 5)

INITIATIVE AND CREATIVITY

Cultivating the Entrepreneurial Spirit

Moreover, allowing students the freedom to choose what to
do in school helps children learn to take initiatives, a necessary quality of the entrepreneurial spirit. When children are
given the freedom, they have to take the initiative to decide
what to do. And when they do what they want to do, they
have commitment. In contrast, when asked to follow a
prescribed routine, they simply follow directions. The more

prescribed the work, the less opportunity children have to exercise their own will. And the more prescribed, the less risk is involved. As a result, children simply become followers who learn to conform, to find the correct answers expected by adults.

Similarly, granting children the freedom to do what they want to do rather than forcing them to follow directions, to complete what has been prescribed, or to comply with external expectations helps to preserve creativity, another quality of entrepreneurs. Traditional schools have been generally found to be either insignificant or suppressive of creativity. Boston College psychology professor John Dacey and his coauthor Kathleen Lennon wrote in their book *Understanding Creativity: The Interplay of Biological, Psychological, and Social Factors:*

> Most young children are naturally curious and highly imaginative . . . after children have attended school for a while, they become more cautious and less innovative. . . . Unfortunately it is necessary to conclude from the investigations of many scholars, that our schools are the major culprits. Teachers, peers, and the educational system as a whole all diminish children's urge to expressive their creative possibilities. (Dacey & Lennon, 1998, p. 69)

This happens because traditional schools demand conformity and obedience. They are held accountable for passing as much of the prescribed content to children as possible. Thus their primary goal is to ensure that children comply with externally defined standards. Excessive focus on external indicators of success such as grades and test scores can pressure children, sending the message that academic success is important, not for personal reasons, but to please others (Ablard, 1997). As a result, children lose interest. Research has shown that parents of talented children pay little attention to external standards (Ablard & Parker, 1997). And the Summerhill experience shows that when schools do not pay attention to external standards, children become more confident and creative.

STRENGTH AND EXCEPTIONAL TALENT

Pursuing One's Passion

Finally, giving children the freedom to do what they want enables them to discover and pursue their strengths and preserves exceptional talents who may not meet externally defined standards. Creative entrepreneurs are passionate individuals who capitalize on their strengths rather than spending time making up for their weaknesses. Driven by passion and given the freedom, they can construct their resources to enhance what they are good at instead of wasting efforts to become like others. As discussed earlier, successful entrepreneurs need to offer something unique, something different from what is already in existence. That uniqueness does not come from standardized experiences. Instead, it comes from the freedom to be individuals.

The traditional education paradigm reduces the possibility of cultivating uniqueness by forcing children into the same sausage maker, in the hope to produce standardized products. Here is a telling example. Fifteen-year-old Yang Yue is a ninth grader in a middle school near Chongqing, China. He spent the last year writing a historical novel that is already 600,000 Chinese characters long. He has become quite a popular writer among his classmates, who would pay to read it. According to his teachers and some experts, the novel is full of imagination and the fact that a 15-year-old has the perseverance and concentration to complete such a huge task is commendable. But in order for him to prepare for the impending high school entrance exam, Yang Yue was told by his parents and teachers to stop writing. "He needs to concentrate on his studies because as a student, his primary duty is still studying," said a psychology professor of China's Southwest University (Fu, 2012).

THE ENVIRONMENT

Constraints and Affordances

Giving children the freedom does not mean that adults in the school have nothing to do or have given up their educational responsibilities; neither does it mean that adults exercise no influence on children. Quite the contrary, this new paradigm presents even more challenges to school leaders and teachers because their primary responsibilities have shifted from instilling the prescribed content in students following well-established procedures in a structured fashion to developing an educational environment that affords children the opportunity to live a meaningful and engaging educational life. This environment also imposes constraints on children so as to discourage them from undertaking undesirable activities and developing unwanted habits.

To meet the needs of educating the whole child, a sound education environment should have at least three interconnected elements: a safe, healthy, aesthetically appealing, and inviting physical environment; an engaging, friendly, and supportive social-emotional environment; and a rich, stimulating, and diverse cognitive environment. The physical environment is the physical space where children conduct their education. It is the campus and the buildings of a school. The social-emotional environment is the culture of the school. It is the values, the rules that govern social interactions, and the infrastructure that deploys human resources to support student education experiences in the school. The cognitive environment is the brains and hearts of the staff, the teaching and learning activities, and other resources that children can engage with cognitively.

These environments do not appear to be much different from what would be considered necessary for traditional education, but there are a number of characteristics that distinguish them from a traditional school environment. The traditional school is about efficiently and effectively transmitting prescribed content and thus is built to standard-ize and dictate, while the new paradigm is about expanding and enhancing what children are interested in and want to be good at and thus is built to accommodate and support. The characteristics that separate the two lie in three areas: diversity, structure and organization, and agency.

Diversity

Research has long provided evidence to show that the richness and complexity of the environment have significant impact on brain development and learning in both lab animals and humans. Since the late Canadian psychologist Donald Hebb reported that the lab rats he allowed to explore his home as his children's pets for some weeks showed better problem-solving ability than rats that had remained in the lab throughout the 1940s (Hebb, 1949), scientists from multiple disciplines have continued to study the quality of the environment on brain development and cognitive functions. While the specifics may vary, the typical method is to place rats or other animals in complex or impoverished environments and then compare their brain plasticity or ability to run through mazes. A complex environment is typically a cage filled with a variety of objects such as swings, wooden blocks, plastic tunnels, and mirrors, while an impoverished environment is a plain cage. Some other studies have also explored the impact of social interactions by comparing rats housed in a cage with those housed individually. The findings have been very consistent: Animals exposed to complex environments outperform those in impoverished environments. They perform better in cognitive tasks (Hebb, 1947) and have more synapses per neuron and brain plasticity (Beckett et al., 2006; Briones, Klintsova, & Greenough, 2004; Rampon et al., 2000; Renner & Rosenzweig, 1987; Rosenzweig & Bennett, 1996; Sirevaag & Greenough, 1987).

Impoverished environments can have detrimental and lasting effects on the cognitive, social, and physical development, as the horrendous case of the infamous Romanian orphanages under Communist rule has illustrated. In the 1980s, tens of thousands of children were placed in orphanages in Romania. These orphanages provided extremely poor conditions for children as young as one month after birth. For example, child–caregiver ratios were 10:1 for infants and 20:1 for children over three years of age, and infants spent up to 20 hours per day in their cribs unattended (Chugani et al., 2001). After the collapse of the Communist regime, some of the children were removed from the orphanages and adopted by families in the United Kingdom and the United States. Studies of these children revealed severe social, cognitive, and physical deficits (Kaler & Freeman, 1994). Brain research also found the Romanian orphans showed significantly decreased metabolism in the brain, suggesting brain damage (Chugani et al., 2001).

It is unlikely that any modern school would be providing an environment as appallingly poor as the infamous Romanian orphanages, but it is possible that an excessive focus on one type of learning could reduce the diversity of the education environment and place unnecessary stress on children. For example, the narrowing of curriculum and reduction in time devoted to recess, lunch, and other nonacademic activities resulted from NCLB is effectively a way to reduce the richness of the education environment. Depriving children of the opportunities to be exposed to arts, music, field trips, and sports in order to focus on the prescribed and assessed curriculum leads to an impoverished education.

It is thus very important not to fall into the trap of doing harm with the intention to do good. It is understandably difficult for schools to resist the political pressure to continue to offer a broad and rich curriculum in the age of standardization and test-based accountability, especially for those schools that have been identified by government as not meeting the standards. But schools should resist and explore different ways to ensure a rich environment for their students. Summerhill resisted, for example. Roosevelt Elementary School, a public school in Bellingham, Washington, in a way resisted as well. It has expanded its arts offerings despite the fact that it has not produced the standardized test scores to meet the NCLB-mandated Adequate Yearly Progress or AYP. With over 60% of students receiving free or reduced-price lunch and a high percentage of minority students, the school has been a "failing school" under NCLB; but unlike many such schools, Roosevelt did not narrow its curriculum to math and reading. Instead it worked to garner resources to increase arts opportunities for all students by 25%. The school emphasizes creativity and critical thinking, with opportunities to share student work publicly. "The parents love our approach and students are more engaged," Steve Morse, the principal, told me during an interview. The parents and staff I talked with agreed with him.

A rich environment is not only necessary for children's cognitive, social, and physical development, but it is also key to individual students to try out different activities and discover their passion and strengths. Moreover, it provides the variation needed for every child to have something to do and enjoy. Since children come with different backgrounds, interests, and strengths, an environment with limited choices cannot possibly meet the needs of all children in a school.

When applied to the physical aspect of the environment, a diverse environment means that to the extent possible schools should have flexible space—for group as well as individual work, for large meetings as well as individual pursuit, and for instructor-led activities as well as student-initiated independent activities. It also means facilities for the musicians and the athletes, for the artists and the dancers, for the mathematicians and the anthropologists, for the fashion designers and the carpenters, and for the debaters and the social leaders. In other words, the school designed to prepare entrepreneurs cannot just have the one-size-fits-all classrooms designed for lectures.

Likewise, the school designed to cultivate creative entrepreneurs cannot have just one type of cognitive activities either. The most common cognitive activities offered by the traditional school are teacher-led classes designed to impart the prescribed curriculum. It should first provide more variations of classes in terms of formats. Some can be the traditional 45- or 50-minute classes that last a semester or term, but others can be short lectures on special topics, field trips to a museum, or long workshops with specialists. Second, it should include more variations in terms of content, going way beyond the prescribed curriculum, if there is any. Third, the school should provide opportunities that go beyond the school, such as activities that involve interaction with experts within a local community or professionals from afar online.

One of the most important elements of a rich environment is the availability of a diverse group of adult talents—the staff and others who can serve as role models, counselors, critics, friends, collaborators, assistants, and teachers. In the traditional paradigm, the teaching staff members are selected to teach the curriculum based on their content knowledge and skills to transmit knowledge, but in the new environment, we need adults to be passionate and talented in working with students as a community member. The more diverse their talents, the richer the intellectual environment is in the school.

In addition, schools should expand the teaching staff to include talents from outside the school. For example, the Community High School in Ann Arbor, Michigan, offers Community Resource Classes (CRs), "a contracted learning experience taught by an 'expert' member of the community" (Community High School, 2012). Students can develop their own courses with experts they find from home or the community. With approval, CRs are awarded high school credit and meet graduation requirements.

Structure and Organization

In a typical traditional school, the environment is well structured, governed by "the grammar of schooling." In a seminal piece, Stanford professors David Tyack and William Tobin coined the term "the grammar of schooling" to refer to "the regular structures and rules that organize the work of instruction.

Here we have in mind, for example, standardized organizational practices in dividing time and space, classifying students, allocating them to classrooms, and splintering knowledge into "subjects" (Tyack & Tobin, 1994, p. 454). Following this grammar, schools have a neat way to organize students into groups of children of the same age and impart in them what has been prescribed for each group with an adult in a classroom designed for this purpose. What happens in each classroom is governed by content standards developed for each subject. There can be few exceptions: Students cannot easily skip a class, choose to study something else not prescribed, or move to a different class.

The new paradigm requires a different structure and organization that are characterized by flexibility. An environment can be rich and composed of diverse resources, but it can be rigid. To support the development of individual talents, entrepreneurship, and creativity, it is not sufficient that the school environment provides a variety of diverse resources. How these resources are structured and organized is very important. The school environment must be flexible enough to enable students to make use of these resources.

A flexible environment allows and enables personalization. Children should have the freedom to self-select when and how to make use of available resources. While it may be desirable to mandate certain things sometimes in a school, it would be a mistake to mandate all children to do the same thing all the time or mandate a plan that consumes all of a child's time in school. But freedom is not sufficient; there should be an infrastructure designed to assist children to personalize their learning experiences, because children may not be aware of or understand what is available and how they may be meaningful. In other words, children should be provided with opportunities to have different experiences and consult with adults about the consequences of different experiences. In a school under the new paradigm, different students construct personalized pathways instead of following a predetermined path.

Agency

The biggest difference between a rich environment in the traditional paradigm and the new paradigm is the degree to which the children actively participate in constructing the environment. Traditionally the children play little or no role in the making of the physical, social, or cognitive aspects of the environment. They are subjects of a kingdom built by adults, rather than citizens of a democratic society who help to shape the society. In contrast, the child-centered paradigm that believes the school should fit the child must involve children in the making of the environment.

The notion that students should become partners of their educational experiences has gained popularity in recent years through the "personalized learning" movement (Fielding, 2004; A. Hargreaves, 2009; A. Hargreaves & Shirley, 2009; D. Hargreaves, 2004). The U.K. University of Sussex professor Michael Fielding observed in a 2006 article:

> There is a "new wave" of what many now call "student voice" ranging over a huge vista of activities encouraging the involvement of young people which echoes the energy, if not the aspirations, of the 1960s and 1970s. These range from the familiar engagement with social and interpersonal matters (e.g. prefects, buddying, mentoring, coaching, and traditional school councils), through more innovative, often student-led developments (e.g. school ambassadors, student-led learning walks, lead learners, student leaders, students as co-researchers and lead researchers, and more radical forms of student council), to a burgeoning range of ways in which professional perceptions about the suitability and performance of staff are significantly informed by student perspectives and judgements (e.g. students as observers, students on staff appointment panels, students as governors/school board members, student focus groups and surveys, and students as key informants in the processes of external inspection and accountability). (Fielding, 2006, p. 299)

Student voice goes beyond token representations of students on school committees. It requires a deep reconsideration of the role of students in the school, not as a place that transmits knowledge, but as a community of learners. Cambridge University professor David Hargreaves, a leading expert in personalizing learning, puts "student voice" as one of the gateways to personalizing learning and suggests:

> The idea of community most neatly captures what student voice is about. It is not simply about introducing new structures, such as student councils, or about providing other occasional opportunities for students to speak their mind or have their say. It is about forming more open and trustful relationships between staff and students. This works when the same applies to relationships between students, between staff and students, among the staff, and between school leaders and their professional colleagues. (D. Hargreaves, 2004, p. 7)

Research has shown that student voice has a positive effect on the school culture, increased student engagement, and overall improvement in children's well-being. Penn State University Education professor Dana Mitra documented the evolution of a student voice initiative in a U.S. high school in her 2008 book *Student Voice in School Reform: Building Youth-Adult Partnerships That Strengthen Schools and Empower Youth* (Mitra, 2008). Through observations and interviews, she found that students bring unique perspectives and knowledge that can help improve the school environment and academic quality. Students can point out structural and cultural obstacles in the school that may be overlooked by adult administrators and teachers. Thus students should be considered "capable and valuable members of a school community who can help initiate and implement educational change," Mitra said in an interview (Savrock, 2008). More relevant to our purpose to cultivate creative entrepreneurs, student voice helps improve confidence and self-esteem and other crucial competencies for responsible and creative entrepreneurs and citizens "including tolerance, getting along with others, respectfully and effectively questioning authority, and public speaking" (Savrock, 2008).

Students should be considered an integral part of school leadership in the new education paradigm. They should be entitled to participating genuinely in all decision making regarding the school environment and actively shaping the school culture from curriculum to pedagogy, from facilities to teaching staff, and from school governance policies to rules and regulations. For example, at Summerhill students certainly play a major role in defining the educational environment. They shape the social environment through their meetings devoted to defining rules and regulations for the whole community. They also shape their own educational experiences by making choices of activities to partake. At High Tech High in San Diego, for instance, students are given the opportunity to interview prospective teachers as a way to shape their cognitive environment.

SUMMARY

Freedom to learn and authentic student leadership constitute the first fundamental principle of the new education paradigm we need for the 21st century. As illustrated by the case of Summerhill, through freedom to learn and student leadership, students develop the foundational competencies that will help them become confident, creative, passionate, and responsible individuals and citizens. These are all necessary components of the entrepreneurial spirit.

To ensure students have the freedom to learn and are truly considered valuable members of a community of learners, schools must have an environment that:

- Provides a broad spectrum of experiences
- Allows flexibility and exceptions
- Enables personalization of educational experiences
- Involves student as decision makers

However, freedom to learn and authentic leadership are necessary but are not sufficient to cultivate entrepreneurs. They can produce excellent students but to produce entrepreneurs, we must also help students develop an entrepreneurial orientation and the entrepreneurial skills. In the next chapter, I discuss the principles and strategies to develop entrepreneurial orientation and skills through making authentic products and services for a global audience.

References

Ablard, K. E. (1997). Parents' conceptions of academic success: Internal and external standards. *The Journal of Secondary Gifted Education, 8*(2), 57–64.

Ablard, K. E., & Parker, W. D. (1997). Parents' achievement goals and perfectionism in their academically talented children. *Journal of Youth and Adolescence, 26*(651–667).

Beckett, C., Maughan, B., Rutter, M., Castle, J., Colvert, E., Groothues, C., et al. (2006). Do the effects of early severe deprivation on cognition persist into early adolescence? Findings from the English and Romanian adoptees study. *Child Development, 77*(3), 696–711.

Briones, T. L., Klintsova, A. Y., & Greenough, W. T. (2004). Stability of synaptic plasticity in the adult rat visual cortex induced by complex environment exposure. *Brain Research, 108*(1), 130–135.

Chugani, H. T., Behen, M. E., Muzik, O., Juhasz, C., Nagy, F., & Chugani, D. C. (2001). Local brain functional activity following early deprivation: A study of postinstitutionalized Romanian orphans. *NeuroImage, 14*(1290–1301).

Community High School. (2012). CR at a glance. Retrieved March 19, 2012, from http://www.aaps.k12.mi.us/community.cr/cr_at_a_glance

Dacey, J. S., & Lennon, K. H. (1998). *Understanding creativity: The interplay of biological, psychological, and social factors.* San Francisco, CA: Jossey-Bass.

Fielding, M. (2004). "New wave" student voice and the renewal of civic society. *London Review of Education, 2*(3), 197–217.

Fielding, M. (2006). Leadership, radical student engagement and the necessity of person-centred education. *International Journal of Leadership in Education, 9*(4), 299–313.

Fu, D. (2012, March 10). Chusan nansheng xie 60 wan zi chuanyue xiaoshuo zhouhong (Ninth grader becomes popular with a history novel of 600,000 characters). Retrieved March 14, 2012, from http://edu.sina.com.cn/zxx/2012-03-10/1535330553.shtml

Grenyer, N. (1999). *Summerhill School*. London, England: Ofsted.

Hargreaves, A. (2009). The fourth way of change: Towards an age of inspiration and sustainability. In A. Hargreaves (Ed.), *Change wars* (pp. 11–43). Bloomington, IN: Solution Tree.

Hargreaves, A., & Shirley, D. L. (2009). *The fourth way: The inspiring future for educational ehange*. Thousand Oaks, CA: Corwin.

Hargreaves, D. (2004). *Personalising learning—2: Student voice and assessment for learning*. London, England: Specialist Schools Trust.

Hebb, D. O. (1947). The effects of early experience on problem solving at maturity. *American Psychologist, 2*(306–307).

Hebb, D. O. (1949). *The organization of behavior: A neuropsychological theory*. New York, NY: Wiley.

Kaler, S. R., & Freeman, B. J. (1994). Analysis of environmental deprivation: Cognitive and social development in Romanian orphans. *Journal of Child Psychology and Psychiatry, 35*(4), 769–781.

Li, G., & Wang, L. (Eds.). (2008). *Model minority myth revisited: An interdisciplinary approach to demystifying Asian American educational experiences*. Charlotte, NC: IAP.

Loveless, T. (2006). *How well are American students learning?* Washington, DC: Brookings Institute (Brown Center).

Matharu, J. (2008). *Summerhill School inspection report*. London, England: Ofsted.

Mitra, D. L. (2008). *Student voice in school reform: Building youth-adult partnerships that strengthen schools and empower youth*. Albany, NY: State University of New York Press.

Neill, A. S. (1960). *Summerhill: A radical approach to child rearing*. Oxford, UK: Hart Publishing.

Rampon, C., Jiang, C. H., Dong, H., Tang, Y.-P., Lockhart, D. J., Schultz, P. G., et al. (2000). Effects of environmental enrichment on gene expression in the brain. *Proceedings of the National Academy of Sciences, 97*(23), 12880–12884.

Renner, M. J., & Rosenzweig, M. R. (1987). *Enriched and impoverished environments: Effects on brain and behavior*. New York, NY: Springer.

Riding, A. (1999, November 07). Summerhill revisited. *The New York Times.* Retrieved from http://www.nytimes.com/1999/11/07/education/summerhill-revisited.html?pagewanted=all&src=pm

Rosenzweig, M. R., & Bennett, E. L. (1996). Psychobiology of plasticity: Effects of training and experience on brain and behavior. *Behavioural Brain Research, 78,* 57–65.

Savrock, J. (2008). Student voice is an integral component of school reform. Retrieved March 18, 2012, from http://www.ed.psu.edu/educ/news/news-items-folder/mitra-student-voice

Shepherd, J. (2007, December 1). So, kids, anyone for double physics? (But no worries if you don't fancy it): Official approval at last for school where almost anything goes. *The Guardian.* Retrieved from http://www.guardian.co.uk/uk/2007/dec/01/ofsted.schools

Sirevaag, A. M., & Greenough, W. T. (1987). Differential rearing effects on rat visual cortex synapses: III. Neuronal and glial nuclei, boutons, dendrites, and capillaries. *Brain Research, 424*(2), 320–332.

Smithers, R. (2000, March 24). Radical boarding school escapes closure threat. *The Guardian.* Retrieved from http://www.guardian.co.uk/uk/2000/mar/24/schools.news1

Stanford, P. (2008, January 24). Summerhill: Inside England's most controversial private school. *The Independent.* Retrieved from http://www.independent.co.uk/news/education/schools/summerhill-inside-englands-most-controversial-private-school-772976.html

Summerhill School. (2004). Summerhill: The early days. Retrieved March 5, 2012, from http://www.summerhillschool.co.uk/pages/history.html

Tyack, D., & Tobin, W. (1994). The "grammar" of schooling: Why has it been so hard to change? *American Educational Research Journal, 31*(3), 453–479.

Yazzie-Mintz, E. (2010). *Charting the path from engagement to achievement: A report on the 2009 High School Survey of Student Engagement.* Bloomington, IN: Center for Evaluation & Education Policy, Center on Education.

Product-Oriented Learning

Works That Matter

A man who carries a cat by the tail learns something he can learn in no other way.

—Mark Twain

All genuine education comes about through experience does not mean that all experiences are genuinely or equally educative.

—John Dewey

always look forward to meeting with Larry Rosenstock. As the founding principal of High Tech High (HTH) in San Diego, Larry is one of the most brilliant and action-oriented education leaders I have ever met. Meeting with Larry is like reading a great book that is full of surprises, insights, and challenges. He tells fascinating stories of education's past, emits contagious enthusiasm about its future, and presents penetrating analysis of its present. He is charismatic, energetic, and generous.

The highlights of meetings with Larry have been the gifts he gives me. Every time we met, he gave me a book written by High Tech High students. The books themselves are of professional quality and sold to the public on the self-publishing services blurb[1] and lulu.[2] I have found these books to be more interesting than many written by adult professional authors. *Economics Illustrated* (Wise & Robin, 2010), for example, is a book authored by 10th graders at High Tech High. The book contains students' artistic illustrations of economic terms accompanied by explanations of each term and an article about a contemporary issue illuminated through an understanding of the term. I learned a lot about economics from this book, because it explains the concepts in plain language.

For example, "warm glow," a concept used to explain "impure altruism," is defined in the online Handbook of Economics "as an increase in utility resulting from the act of giving in addition to utility generated by increase in the total supply of the public good" (Experimental Economics Center, 2006). But Nora Johnson, a High Tech High student, offers an explanation that is much easier for me to understand:

> Someone who does something out of "warm glow" does the deed for the sole purpose of feeling good about himself. Even if there's someone else to volunteer to help or to donate to a cause, he wants to be the one to feel the warm and fuzzy feeling of goodness. (Johnson, 2010, p. 43)

Nora provides four examples to further illustrate the idea. One of the examples:

> Example 4: At the grocery store, next to the change dispenser, there is often a donation jar for a specific organization. People want to put their change into the donation jar. After making their donation, they feel a "warm glow." (Johnson, 2010, p. 43)

"The scientific components are as good as any I've seen, while the poems and personal reflections on nature, science

---

[1]http://www.blurb.com

[2]http://www.lulu.com

and place help to bring the San Diego Bay area alive. Taken together, they capture the essence of not just a region, but of the deep connections between nature, science and humanity" was praise given by Thomas Hayden, senior writer of *US News & World Report* to another High Tech High book created by 11th graders, *Perspectives of San Diego Bay: A Field Guide* (The Students of High Tech High, 2006). And Jane Goodall was moved to write a foreword for it after seeing the students presenting at a conference where she was delivering a keynote speech.

The books are just part of the gifts. The other part is Larry's proud recount of how the books were made, which inevitably includes the creative, multitalented, and hardworking teachers and students at High Tech High. I have followed the story of High Tech High since its establishment in 2000 and have had the opportunity to visit one of its campuses and interact with its students and staff. I must say that Larry has every reason to be proud: happy, confident, and responsible students engaged in real-world projects led by creative, inspiring, and knowledgeable teachers. "The episode reflects not only the confidence and abilities of one good student but also the entire attitude High Tech High," commented Grace Rubenstein in an *Edutopia* article about the school in 2008 (Rubenstein, 2008). The episode was her encounter with a high school student who confidently volunteered to help her create the soundtrack for an audio slide.

Books are not the only things students make at High Tech High. They make documentary films, video games, art exhibits, posters, music, audio fictions, photographs, identity masks, and many other imaginable and unimaginable products. They use traditional media and materials such as wood, plastic, words, and text as well as contemporary digital media. Making things is the central theme of the school. Everywhere you go, the students are making something or preparing to make something. And the school is full of things the students have made. "When you walk into High Tech High you feel like you're in a workplace," Bob Pearlman wrote in *TECHNOS* about the school shortly after it was opened.

> The main section of the school, the Great Room, houses the student workstation suites where upper-school grades 11 and 12 students work on self-directed projects one-half of every day. Artwork and glass walls are everywhere. So is wiring, neatly routed in visible overhead cable trays and conduits. Classrooms, which HTH calls seminar rooms, feature flexible furniture and Smart Boards. Not a lot of teachers are presenting in this environment. Mostly it's the students who present their work and ideas. (Pearlman, 2002, p. 13)

A school of and for makers is what Larry, a maker himself, had always wanted to create for all students. When he went to law school at Boston University in the 1970s, Larry would skip classes to teach woodworking to kids with psychological problems. He continued to teach carpentry classes after getting his degree. From there he went on to help make the law that directed federal funding for vocational education toward classic academics (Murphy, 2004). Then he made High Tech High based on the work he did for the New Urban High School Project supported by the U.S. Department of Education, which aimed "to find six urban high schools that were using school-to-work strategies as a lever for whole-school change" (The Big Picture Company, 1998, p. 8). Since 2000, he has made 10 more schools under the High Tech High umbrella. As of 2011, High Tech High is a family of five high schools, four middle schools, and two elementary schools. He has also made a graduate school of education that offers masters degrees to teachers and school leaders.

As a school of and for makers, High Tech High is nothing like traditional schools. "It has scrapped a lot of what's arbitrary and outdated about traditional schooling—classroom design, divisions between subjects, independence (read: isolation) from the community, and assessments that only one teacher ever sees," *Edutopia*'s Grace Rubenstein writes.

> Instead, the textbook-free school fosters personalized project learning with pervasive connections to the community. Any visitor can see the evidence in the students' engagement and the eye-popping projects that adorn almost every corner and wall—many of which the teens have exhibited to local businesspeople, not just teachers. As the school's name implies, technology enables many of the projects students create. And teachers routinely craft lessons that blend subjects, reflecting how interwoven they truly are. (Rubenstein, 2008)

Unlike traditional college prep schools, High Tech High does not drill students on tests. It does not even offer Advanced Placement (AP) courses. Unlike typical wealthy suburb schools, High Tech High students are admitted using a lottery system based on ZIP codes. In fact, High Tech High has made every effort to recruit students from all neighborhoods and communities. Unlike some elite urban schools, HTH does not use any type of entrance exam to select students. Unlike expensive private schools, HTH is a public school and students pay no tuition or fees. But 100% of its graduates have been admitted to college, with 80% to four-year institutions. About 35% of them are first-generation college students (High Tech High, 2012).

In pursuing its mission "to prepare students—all kinds of students—to be savvy, creative, quick-thinking adults and professionals in a modern world" (Rubenstein, 2008), High Tech High exemplifies the second cornerstone of the new paradigm of education that cultivates creative entrepreneurs: *making things for real audiences.* It complements the first cornerstone, that is, *student autonomy and leadership* exemplified by A. S. Neill's Summerhill School. Summerhill illustrates the *what* of education and High Tech High exemplifies the *how*.

LEARNING BY MAKING

Constructionism and Project-Based Learning

Learning by doing is not a new concept. It can be traced all the way back to John Dewey, who forcefully argued for the importance of experiences in education (Dewey, 1938/1998). Seymour Papert, inventor of the computer programming language *Logo* and a visionary pioneer in using technology to support student learning by doing, coined the term *constructionism* to advocate *learning by making* over 20 years ago in his co-authored book *Constructionism* (Harel & Papert, 1991). A more commonly known name for the educational approach of learning by doing is project-based learning or problem-based learning (PBL).

PBL has been practiced in various ways in education and has become increasingly common with the advent of digital technologies in recent years. PBL has been said to have many benefits, compared with traditional instructional approaches, including "building deep content understanding, raising academic achievement, and encouraging student motivation to learn" (Buck Institute for Education, 2009). While the approach High Tech High uses may be generically labeled as *project-based learning* (PBL) because it has all the characteristics of PBL, it would be a big mistake to equate HTH with a traditional school that simply applies PBL in its classrooms. HTH's approach is PBL and a lot more. PBL is implemented within a larger context within High Tech High, which follows four design principles distilled from the findings of the New Urban High School Project (The Big Picture Company, 1998): personalization, adult world connection, common intellectual mission, and teacher as designer.[3] These design principles result in an environment that maximizes the effectiveness of PBL as a pedagogical approach. In other words, although PBL, as a generic instructional approach, may have benefits, it

---

[3]For detailed information on High Tech High's design principles, visit its website: http://www.hightechhigh.org/about/design-principles.php.

requires a lot more to achieve the outcomes of High Tech High and is ultimately what this book is about: *creative global entrepreneurs.*

THE GOOD, THE BAD, AND THE UGLY

Many Faces of Project-Based Learning

My two children have been involved in numerous PBL experiences throughout their school years. They have grown pumpkins and lilies. They have made posters and PowerPoint slides. They have created ceramic plates and books. They have demonstrated their models of the ecosystem of tree frogs at science fairs and presented their findings of a foreign country at parent evenings. Over the years, the products they brought home were proudly displayed on the refrigerator or carefully curated on shelves and in special boxes by my wife. But frankly speaking, if they had not been made by my own children, I probably would not have done so because they were not *that* good or useful beyond the sentimental value. They are definitely not as good as some of the products made by High Tech High students. The only useful thing my son has made in school is a plant (a lily) in third grade as a birthday present for his mother; for my daughter, it is a Chinese painting we proudly hang on the wall of my office, but she made that in a private class.

I don't know exactly what and how much they have learned from these projects. But I know they did not treat the products any different from doing any other homework, except they were more trouble for my wife and me. As good parents and to show our support, we chauffeured them to shop for materials and to attend project meetings with classmates, we dug deep into our storage room for things that could be used, and we fulfilled many of their last-minute requests for construction paper or colored pencils. As someone who believes in project-based learning and learning by doing, I had always tried to take every project as an opportunity to engage my children, to ask them questions so they can expand on their reading, to provide feedback so they can revise their products, and to challenge them to be creative. But more often than not, they would tell me: "Dad, we don't need that. The teacher only wants . . ." Then they turned in the products or made a presentation, and they got a grade. They were happy to get an A, but they were not extremely bothered by a B either.

My children's PBL experiences seem to be quite different from those of High Tech High students. They both can be called project-based learning since the simplest definition of PBL is that "PBL is a model that organizes learning around projects" (Thomas, 2000, p. 1). This definition was given by John Thomas in his extensive review of research on project-based learning commissioned by the Autodesk Foundation in 2000 (Thomas, 2000). While there were many attempts to define the essential features of PBL, there is not one single universally accepted model. "This diversity of defining features coupled with the lack of a universally accepted model or theory of Project-Based Learning has resulted in a great variety of PBL research and development activities" (Thomas, 2000, p. 2). It is thus no surprise that PBL comes in different flavors.

The differences in flavors largely result from the inclusion or exclusion of certain ingredients and the quantity of the ingredients when included. John Thomas's extensive review found a list of ingredients that have been put into PBL from different sources:

> According to the definitions found in PBL handbooks for teachers, projects are complex tasks, based on challenging questions or problems, that involve students in design, problem-solving, decision making, or investigative activities; give students the opportunity to work relatively autonomously over extended periods of time; and culminate in realistic products or presentations. Other defining features found in the literature include authentic content,

authentic assessment, teacher facilitation but not direction, explicit educational goals, cooperative learning, reflection, and incorporation of adult skills. To these features, particular models of PBL add a number of unique features. Definitions of "project-based instruction" include features relating to the use of an authentic ("driving") question, a community of inquiry, and the use of cognitive (technology-based) tools; and "Expeditionary Learning" adds features of comprehensive school improvement, community service, and multidisciplinary themes. (Thomas, 2000, p. 1)

Out of this long list, "project-based learning in practice can assume a variety of forms depending upon the pedagogical, political or ethical reasons for its adoption" (Helle, Tynjala, & Olkinuora, 2006, pp. 288–289) by including and thus excluding certain features and varying the importance of some features. For example, John Mergendoller, a well-known researcher of PBL and executive director of the Buck Institute for Education, a nonprofit organization dedicated to promote PBL, emphasizes the process of engaging "students in a series of complex tasks that include planning and design, problem solving, decision making, creating artifacts, and communicating results" (Mergendoller, Markham, Ravitz, & Larmer, 2006, p. 483). A group of researchers from Finland stresses the importance of problem, products, and student control based on their review of the literature on PBL (Helle et al., 2006, p. 288). "The most distinctive feature of project-based learning is problem orientation, that is, the idea that a problem or question serves to drive learning activities," according to Laura Helle of University of Turku, Finland, and colleagues. The second distinctive feature is "constructing a concrete artifact," followed by the third feature: learner control of the learning process. Contextualization and multiple forms of representation are the remaining features.

The Buck Institute for Education (BIE) appears to emphasize "academic content" and "21st century skills." As a result, the learner control element and the product or artifact element is not as important in its definition:

> While allowing for some degree of student "voice and choice," rigorous projects are carefully planned, managed, and assessed to help students learn key academic content, practice 21st century skills (such as collaboration, communication & critical thinking), and create high-quality, authentic products & presentations. (Buck Institute for Education, 2012)

This is further evidenced in the order of the essential features of "rigorous, meaningful and effective Project Based Learning" listed by BIE. The first is PBL must intend to teach significant content. In the words of BIE: "Goals for student learning are explicitly derived from content standards and key concepts at the heart of academic disciplines." The second feature is that it must require "critical thinking, problem solving, collaboration, and various forms of communication" or what are commonly referred to as 21st century skills. "Allowing some degree of student voice and choice" is sixth out of a total of eight features and "involving a public audience" is the last feature (Buck Institute for Education, 2012).

In contrast, PBL at High Tech High tends to value the artifact more than the content. A 2012 publication jointly produced by High Tech High and England-based Learning Futures Project entitled *Work That Matters: The Teachers' Guide to Project-based Learning* defines PBL as "students designing, planning, and carrying out an extended project that produces a publicly-exhibited output such as a product, publication, or presentation" (Patton & Robin, 2012, p. 13). The three "keys to successful projects" listed in this publication are exhibition, multiple drafts, and critique—all relevant to producing an outstanding artifact.

The variations primarily occur on three dimensions. The first dimension has to do with the expected outcome or goal of the PBL experience, which can be used to either teach certain content or produce an outstanding product. In other

Table 8.1   Features of Three Different PBL Models

	Expected Outcome	Control	Setting
Academic Model	Academic content	Teacher-led	Primarily a single classroom
Mixed Model	Product within constraints of academic requirements	Teacher-student collaboration	Single or multiple classes, community
Entrepreneurship Model	Product	Student-led	School and community

words, the project can vary from being driven completely by a product to wholly prescribed content or curriculum. Second, a PBL experience can vary from being completely controlled by the teacher to one that is completely controlled by the students. The third dimension has to do with the setting, which can vary from an individual classroom or single discipline to cross classes or disciplines. Combinations of these variations then result in three different models of PBL, each serving different purposes. Table 8.1 summarizes the primary differences between three possible variations that I have named: Academic, Mixed, and Entrepreneurship.

The Academic Model

The *academic model* is the traditional flavor of PBL, with the intention to teach content and skills. In this model, PBL is used as a more effective way to teach prescribed content and skills. Consequently, the prescribed content and skills drive the project. The outcome is better understanding of the content or enhanced ability to apply the skills. The resulting products, if any, are only byproducts, of little consequence. In some cases, the products are used as incentives or motivational devices. But rarely are the products meant for an authentic audience, someone other than the teacher, the students, or their parents. This model can be used interchangeably with problem-based learning, another PBL, since the product is of no significance. Effectiveness of this model is often assessed by how well the students master the content or acquire the skills.

In this model, because the goal is to teach prescribed content, the teacher has much more, if not complete, control of what is to be taught, what project to implement, how the project is conducted, and how the product is evaluated. Students may have limited choices from a menu devised by the teacher, that is, "some degree of voice and choice." And typically, this model is used by an individual teacher in a single classroom.

This model is the most frequently used in schools today. My children's PBL experiences are of this flavor. Virtually all research studies on PBL to date are concerned with this model and thus the central question they attempted to answer is whether and to what degree PBL is more effective in imparting the content or developing the skills than other methods, such as lectures. This is well evidenced by the many review studies of research on PBL (Helle et al., 2006; Strobel & Barneveld, 2009; Thomas, 2000; Walker & Leary, 2009).

The Mixed Model

The *mixed model* values the artifacts—the books, the videos, the posters, and audio fictions, but at the same time, it also values prescribed academic content. The end products must be of high quality and are usually consumed by an authentic audience beyond the school. It is "work that matters." This is perhaps why High Tech High's teacher's guide considers *exhibition* as the first key to project success and it places emphasis on multiple drafts and critique (Patton & Robin, 2012). They are steps to ensure both high-quality products and sustained, deep learning.

Externally prescribed content and skills, such as the state-mandated academic standards, are not ignored, but they are not starting points. The content and skills are not allowed to define, constrain, or guide the projects. *"Do what you love* and *Let the project drive the curriculum,"* High Tech High teacher Angela Guerrero wrote in an article entitled "Where Do Projects Come From":

> These are the mantras of my wise teaching partner, Rod Buenviaje. Rod would listen patiently as I voiced my concerns about my inability to come up with what felt like meaningful projects. At the end of each conversation, he would repeat these mantras. I would nod in agreement and stare blankly out the window. I could never fully comprehend what he meant. After viewing Antin's exhibition, however, the mantras made sense. I was doing something I loved. I was passionate about it. I wanted the kids to see it. I wanted to teach it. It turned into a project that would guide the curriculum. (Guerrero, 2009)

To ensure certain content and skills are taught, this model puts the teacher or a group of teachers in control of the process. While they could solicit student input, the teachers generally decide what project to launch, what products to create, and how the project is to be carried out. Students are given varying degrees of freedom within the prescribed project to be creative and specialize in certain areas within the large project. Students are also involved in providing peer reviews of products.

This model typically requires multiple teachers or classrooms because the project is multidisciplinary, requiring expertise from a variety of areas. The setting can be in a traditional classroom, but more likely a combination of the classroom, facilities specifically designed for certain types of projects such as an art studio, a digital media lab or a garden, and settings outside the school such as museums or community businesses.

The mixed model of project-based learning does not happen very often in today's schools because it requires transformation at the school level. PBL is not used as a classroom instructional enhancement over traditional methods, but a strategy to transform the whole school environment. It is both the cause for and result of using PBL as a lever for whole-school change, a nice combination of vocational technical education and traditional academics, something Larry Rosenstock has been pursuing. The goal of this model is less about transmitting knowledge and more about developing skills that have a real-world connection. For this purpose, the Buck Institute for Education argues:

> If we are serious about reaching 21st Century educational goals, PBL must be at the center of 21st Century instruction. The project contains and frames the curriculum, which differs from the short "project" or activity added onto traditional instruction. PBL is, "The Main Course, not Dessert." (Buck Institute for Education, 2012)

This model lies in the middle of a spectrum, from the more traditional academic model to the entrepreneurial model (discussed below). The purpose is both the project and the academic content, as reflected in the High Tech High and Learning Future's guide for assessment, which suggests three questions for final assessment:

- Does the product meet or exceed the criteria we set at the start of the project?
- Has the student developed the skills required for the execution of this project?
- Has the student learned the curriculum content required for this project? (Patton & Robin, 2012)

The Entrepreneurial Model

The *entrepreneurial model* of project-based learning builds on the mixed model, with a few significant changes. Because it aims to cultivate the entrepreneurial spirit and skills, the entrepreneurial model places more emphasis on the artifacts: the end products or services. They must not only be of high quality but also have appeal to an external audience: customers. The product or service must meet an authentic need of the customer, who is willing to put in resources (time, energy, or money) for the product or service. In other words, the PBL experiences are to help students create something others are willing to consume while learning the knowledge and skills that are essential to make the products of high quality and appealing to customers.

In the entrepreneurial model, the students are in more control of the project. They propose and initiate the project. They need to convince the teacher to approve the project and, if needed, convince their peers to become partners. And for that they need to create a business plan, complete with documentations and analyses of targeted audience and needs, a feasibility analysis, and marketing strategies. The teacher, in this model, serves as the "venture capitalist," who helps decide if the project is needed and feasible; the consultant, who provides suggestions and resources on demand; the motivator, who encourages at times of disappointment; the focus group, which provides feedback and critique on prototypes; and the partner, who provides complementary expertise and skills. The teacher or other adults could bring opportunities, help identify needs, make connections to potential customers, or make suggestions for potential projects because of the expertise and social capital—but ultimately, it is the students who should decide what products to make. In the mixed model, projects are often group-based, that is, a group (an entire class, for example) of students work on the same project. In the entrepreneurial model, projects can be group-based, but they can also be individually initiated.

The setting for the entrepreneurial model of PBL can be individual classes, but more often than not it requires a platform and culture at the school level for a number of reasons. First, in order to create high-quality products, students will most likely need large chunks of time beyond what a typical class period can offer. Second, the students will also need to have access to expertise beyond what one individual teacher could have. In some cases, such expertise may reside outside the school. Third, the knowledge and skills required to create authentic products would not fit nicely with one single school subject. Fourth, students will need some platform or venue to have access to potential customers. Finally, some students may be engaging in a project or service that are exceptionally time consuming, which would necessitate making special arrangement in terms of school scheduling.

To summarize, the entrepreneurial model of PBL is intended to celebrate individual talents, creativity, and the entrepreneurial spirit. The focus is on the product, not the project. To create and market a product would certainly result in learning, but what is learned may not fit government-sanctioned standards or curriculum. Moreover, to create and market a product is more than carrying out a project. It adds two more stages to a typical project-based learning experience: the proposal stage, when the students initiate a project or conceive a product, and the marketing and maintenance stage, when the students need to spend time "selling and maintaining" the product. Thus, I would like to call this model *product-oriented learning* to distinguish it from conventional project-based learning.

THE PROCESS OF PRODUCT-ORIENTED LEARNING

Creating Works That Matter

Entrepreneurship is about inventing a solution to an existing problem or creating a product or service to meet a need. Thus the entrepreneurial model of PBL or product-oriented learning makes the creation and marketing of products the center of the learning experience. It is about creating works that matter—matter to the students and to potential customers, not necessarily to the prescribed standards or curriculum.

The works do not have to be one end product, like a piece of art, a book, or a video. They can also be a service or program. For example, students could offer tutoring services, online or face-to-face, or a service to help others improve their math or writing.

The product-oriented learning experiences mimic a typical entrepreneurial activity that includes the following essential steps.

Identify Needs

Alertness is an essential element of entrepreneurship. "Alertness leads individuals to make discoveries that are valuable in the satisfaction of human wants," Tony Fa-lai Yu, an economics professor, wrote in his article "Entrepreneurial Alertness and Discovery" published in *The Review of Austrian Economics* in 2001, "The role of entrepreneurs lies in their alertness to hitherto unnoticed opportunities" (Yu, 2001, p. 48). Opportunities can be both unrecognized opportunities that exist in the current situation, a theory advanced by the economist Israel M. Kirzner, or opportunities to create something new that disrupts the current situation, an entrepreneurship theory proposed by the economist Joseph Schumpeter (Kirzner, 1999).

Thus in our attempt to cultivate entrepreneurs, it is essential to help students develop a habit of looking for and the ability to seek opportunities. Opportunities lie in unmet needs and dissatisfaction with the current condition. To develop the habit of discovering opportunities is to cultivate curiosity, unorthodox thinking, and an attitude to challenge the status quo. It is also to cultivate the ability to be empathetic about other people's conditions. Moreover, it is about seeing problems as opportunities and assuming responsibilities for proposing solutions to problems rather than complaining or waiting for someone else to come up with a solution.

To start a product-oriented learning experience, the teacher could ask students to make a list of things they are

unhappy with in the school, or a condition they are not satisfied with, or an unmet need someone else may have. The
teacher could also present a set of unsatisfying conditions,
unsolved problems, or unmet needs in different communities. The specific situation can vary, but the overarching idea
is to provide context in which children can find an entrepreneurial opportunity.

Come Up With an Idea

While some students may have an idea right away, many
would need to conduct extensive research and work on the
need for a while before they can come up with a possible
product or service to meet the need. Thus the second essential
element is to engage students in the creative and research process that would result in a possible product or service.

Ideas can come from different sources. Students could
consult with experts, examine the problem in depth, discuss
with peers, or study comparable examples. To stimulate idea
creation, the teacher could organize brainstorm sessions,
field trips, or expert presentations. The teacher should not
assume the entire responsibility for coming up with the idea.
In fact, the student should always bear the responsibility for
coming up with the idea. The teacher only serves to facilitate
the process, create the context, provide resources, and make
suggestions.

Assess Strengths and Resources

Once a need is identified and a solution is suggested, entrepreneurs need to assess whether they have the capacity and
resources to meet the need. This is essentially a process of
identifying one's strengths. But the strength does not mean
what the student can do at the moment by himself or herself.
Rather it is what he or she can learn to do and with the help
of others. It is also to determine if the need or problem is
beyond the capacity and resources available to the student.

Understanding one's weaknesses and strengths is key to entrepreneurial success. As previously discussed in this book, we cannot expect all students to have the same abilities. It is thus an important step to provide the opportunity for students to learn how to identify and further enhance their strengths, while avoiding their weaknesses. It is also important to help students understand that they do not have to be equally good at everything, because what is missing in them could be "outsourced" to others, that is, partners. Hence, identifying one's strengths and weaknesses is also to learn about the strengths and weaknesses of others.

Convince Someone

All entrepreneurs need to convince others of the value of their products or services, be it an investor, a partner, or someone who may work for them. Thus the product-oriented learning experience should include the requirement for students to convince others that the needs they identified are significant, the products they proposed are of value and feasible, and someone will "buy" what they produce. To do so, they may need to develop a business plan and make a public presentation in or outside the school to "sell" their ideas.

The stage of convincing someone may go beyond one single session because if the students fail to convince, they will need to revise their ideas and plans. The idea of "multiple drafts, critique, and peer review," suggested by the High Tech High teacher's guide, is applicable at this stage as well as at the stage of product making.

Make the Product/Service

Once the proposed idea is accepted, students move on to the product making stage, which is similar to the project enactment stage in traditional project-based learning. At this stage, students work on their products as proposed, individually or in teams. To help improve the quality of the final product, the same process of "multiple drafts and critique" should be used. It is also desirable to seek the involvement of professionals as reviewers and mentors and to apply professional standards to all products and services.

Market the Product

Once the product is made, the students need to market it to its intended audience. Learning to market their products can help students better understand what is required to be an entrepreneur as well as the real needs of the world. The results may be a huge success or a complete failure. Either way, the experience can help students develop essential entrepreneurial competences—reflection, resilience, confidence, communication, and perseverance.

Marketing is also the stage that students learn marketing skills and marketing tools. Depending on the specific product and intended customers, students need to engage in marketing activities using a variety of media and venues. They could use social media such as Twitter and Facebook, traditional media such as posters, or visiting the customers face-to-face.

Realizing that most teachers may not have the expertise in marketing, it may become necessary to engage professionals or those in the community with marketing experiences as mentors at this stage. There are also abundant resources and information on the Internet that students can consult. It is also possible that there may be some marketing geniuses among the students who could further develop their marketing talents as specialists.

Post-Product Management and Maintenance

The product-oriented learning cycle does not end with marketing. In some cases, they have to manage the sales and maintenance of the product. They may also need to upgrade the products, in cases of software (e.g., a computer game). Or they may have to manage an online store that sells their products and maintain communication with users.

SUMMARY

The Maker Movement in the School

Tim Carmody at *Wired* magazine called 2011 *The Year the Maker Movement Broke* (Carmody, 2011). PBS Newshour aired a special program entitled *Can DIY Movement Fix a Crisis in U.S. Science Education* in 2011 (PBS Newshour, 2011). The makers, "people who create, build, design, tinker, modify, hack, invent, or simply make something" are on the rise and "are moving the economy," writes *Forbes* contributor T. J. McCue (McCue, 2011). But the Maker Movement does not happen in schools, where children are simply consumers.

Product-oriented learning is to bring the Maker Movement into schools and bring students into the Maker Movement. For too long, students have been passive consumers and recipients of whatever adults give them: books, facilities, knowledge, tests, and disciplines. Schools have been built to facilitate effective consumption and create great recipients rather than makers, creators, and entrepreneurs. To implement project-oriented learning in schools will undoubtedly require serious changes to the school—facilities, staffing, curriculum, and other elements of "the grammar of schooling." The experiences of High Tech High certainly provide a rich source of lessons for other schools that aspire to take actions to cultivate makers, creators, and consumers.

There are other schools that have taken the actions to reconfigure the education environment they create for students. In the next chapter, I use two such schools to discuss the third element of a world class school: the globe as the campus.

References

The Big Picture Company. (1998). *The new urban high school: A practitioner's guide.* Providence, RI: The Big Picture Company.

Buck Institute for Education. (2009). Does PBL work? Retrieved March 25, 2012, from http://www.bie.org/research/study/does_pbl_work

Buck Institute for Education. (2012). What is PBL? Retrieved March 25, 2012, from http://www.bie.org/about/what_is_pbl/

Carmody, T. (2011, August 6). Big DIY: The year the Maker Movement broke. *Wired.* Retrieved March 20, 2012, from http://www.wired.com/epicenter/2011/08/big-diy/all/1

Dewey, J. (1998). *Education and experience: The 60th anniversary edition.* Bloomington, IN: Kappa Delta Pi. (Original work published 1938)

Experimental Economics Center. (2006). Impure altruism and warm glow. Retrieved April 20, 2012, from Experimental Economics Center, http://www.econport.org/econport/request?page=man _pg_experimentalresearch_impurealtruism

Guerrero, A. (2009, Spring). Where do projects come from? *UnBoxed: A Journal of Adult Learning in Schools.* Retrieved March 20, 2012, from http://www.hightechhigh.org/unboxed/issue3/where _do_projects_come_from/

Harel, I., & Papert, S. (1991). *Constructionism.* New York, NY: Ablex Publishing.

Helle, L., Tynjala, P., & Olkinuora, E. (2006). Project-based learning in post-secondary education—theory, practice and rubber sling shots. *Higher Education, 51,* 287–314.

High Tech High. (2012). Results. Retrieved March 20, 2012, from http://www.hightechhigh.org/about/results.php

Johnson, N. (2010). Warm glow preference. In D. Wise & J. Robin (Eds.), *Economics Illustrated* (pp. 42–43). San Diego, CA: Blurb.

Kirzner, I. M. (1999). Creativity and/or alertness: A reconsideration of the Schumpeterian entrepreneur. *Review of Austrian Economics, 11,* 5–17.

McCue, T. J. (2011). Moving the economy: The future of the Maker Movement. *Forbes.* Retrieved March 28, 2012, from http://www .forbes.com/sites/tjmccue/2011/10/26/moving-the-economy -the-future-of-the-maker-movement/

Mergendoller, J., Markham, T., & Ravitz, J., & Larmer, J. (2006). Pervasive management of project based learning. In C. M. Evertson & C. S. Weinstein (Eds.), *Handbook of classroom management: Research, practice, and contemporary issues* (pp. 583–615). Mahwah, NJ: Lawrence Erlbaum Associates.

Murphy, V. (2004, October 11). Where everyone can overachieve. *Forbes.* Retrieved March 20, 2012, from http://www.forbes .com/free_forbes/2004/1011/080.html

Patton, A., & Robin, J. (2012). *Work that matters: The teacher's guide to project-based learning.* London, England: Paul Hamlyn Foundation, Learning Futures.

PBS Newshour (Producer). (2011, June 29). Can DIY movement fix a crisis in U.S. science education? Retrieved from http://www .pbs.org/newshour/bb/science/jan-june11/makerfaire_06-29 .html

Pearlman, B. (2002). Designing, and making, the new American high school. *TECHNOS, 11*(1), 12–19.

Rubenstein, G. (2008, December 3). Real world, San Diego: Hands-on learning at High Tech High. *Edutopia.* Retrieved March 20, 2012, from http://www.edutopia.org/collaboration-age-technology -high-tech

Strobel, J., & Barneveld, A. V. (2009). When is PBL more effective? A meta-synthesis of meta-analyses comparing PBL to conventional classrooms. *Interdisciplinary Journal of Problem-based Learning, 3*(1), 44–58.

The Students of High Tech High. (2006). *Perspectives of San Diego Bay: A field guide.* Providence, RI: Next Generation Press.

Thomas, J. W. (2000). *A Review of research on project-based learning.* San Rafael, CA: Autodesk Foundation.

Walker, A., & Leary, H. (2009). A problem based learning meta analysis: Differences across problem types, implementation types, disciplines, and assessment levels. *Interdisciplinary Journal of Problem-based Learning, 3*(1), 12–43.

Wise, D., & Robin, J. (2010). *Economics illustrated.* San Diego, CA: Blurb.

Yu, T. F.-L. (2001). Entrepreneurial alertness and discovery. *The Review of Austrian Economics, 14*(1), 47–63.

The Globe Is Our Campus

Global Entrepreneurs and Enterprises

There's enough on this planet for everyone's needs but not for everyone's greed.

—Mahatma Gandhi

There are no foreign lands. It is the traveler only who is foreign.

—Robert Louis Stevenson

In February 2010 I met three high school students from Cherwell School in Oxford, U.K., at a conference in Cape Town, South Africa. Charlie, Sam, and Verity were there to present their Chicken Project business plan to an audience of educators from six countries. Their plan was to build a chicken enterprise in partnership with Gcato School in Eastern Cape, South Africa. Eastern Cape is the poorest province in South Africa, and students of the rural Gcato School come from three extremely poor villages.

The project started with a volunteer visit to Gcato taken by Verity and her family in July 2009. "Whilst visiting another school Verity and I saw a chicken shed and the idea for Gcato was born," Julie Stuart-Thompson, Verity's mom and a teacher of Cherwell, told me later. Verity had taken a business class and saw the opportunity to apply what she learned to a real-world problem. Upon returning, Verity invited Charlie and Sam to work on the project as they had taken the class together. They devised a plan to jointly operate a chicken business in the school.

According to the plan, students in the United Kingdom would help raise funds to get the business started and act as business consultants, while the South African students would set up and run the business. The business would raise chickens and sell the eggs to the local community in the beginning and gradually expand to a large chicken farm. "Once their business has flourished and the breakeven point reached, profit can be used to enhance the learning experience of the African students (new equipment, learning materials) or to fund the next phase" (Cherwell School, 2012). The project has four phases of development:

> Phase 1 means chickens can be kept in a shed for egg sales. Phase 2 introduces a second shed containing birds reared for meat sales; even more popular amongst the villagers and raises more money. With enough capital, The Chicken Project can provide phase 3, where an incubator is purchased to help with egg hatching, allowing a faster and more reliable business. Finally phase 4, the construction of a full scale industrial sized chicken shed providing long term sustainability and a thriving, successful business in poor areas. (Cherwell School, 2012)

The students made a very convincing presentation of their proposal with detailed cost-benefit analysis. They also responded well to challenging questions from the audience. In the end I was convinced and decided to make an investment in the business, which has been my first and only investment in a startup so far. And they made me the honorary life president of the Chicken Project.

Two years later, the enterprise is flourishing. Gcato School received its first batch of chickens in August 2010. But apparently they had difficulty buying unsexed chicks and some turned into non-egg layers, according to a Chicken Project newsletter (Cherwell School, 2011). In 2011, they ordered a new batch of 22 chickens. "The school now has a much clearer ordering and accounting procedure in place and the chicken-based learning has begun again for the Business and Agriculture students," the Chicken Project reported in November 2011. The enterprise expanded to two more South African schools, including the Umzamomhle Day Care Center based in Alice. The Center "seeks to equip children and youth with special needs with the skills that could make them self-reliant" (Cherwell School, 2011). The Center now has 12 chickens and has begun to sell the eggs to local businesses and at a local market. The money is used to buy more feed, making the project sustainable.

Recently the chicken enterprise expanded into Cameroon, but for a slightly different purpose: conservation. Dan Bowen, a sixth form (high school) student at Cherwell School explains the reason for expansion in an article published by the Siren Conservation Education Project *Silent Forest:*

> Cameroon is a country that suffers greatly from systemic overharvesting of wildlife that has a huge effect on the regions' ecosystems and biodiversity. The problem is twofold. Hunting (which when illegal, is known as poaching) is usually targeted at the larger more slowly reproducing species due to the value of the meat. As these large animals are rapidly disappearing from the forests, at the same time the forests are rapidly disappearing from them due to deforestation in the region. Preventing harvesting is one of the ways to stop the problem but to achieve long term success projects should try to tackle the reasons why people are poaching, by providing them with economically viable alternatives. (Bowen, 2012)

One alternative is small household-sized "chicken project pods," or moving the school-based chicken enterprise to homes. The project has started with 10 household chicken enterprises in Cameroon. "Small household sized 'Chicken project pods' in the region will hopefully allow the local people an alternative to some of their dependence on eating and selling wild meat," writes Bowen (2012).

The enterprise has moved beyond the startup phase. The three founders have graduated and left Cherwell School. More than 20 Cherwell students have now joined the enterprise. In 2011, the Chicken Project won approximately $5,000 (3,000 British pounds) in the Reaching for Gold competition that supports innovative ideas from students. Moreover, it has also convinced more people to join, including a school from another Oxford—Oxford, USA.

Oxford Community School is a public school district that serves the area surrounding Oxford, a small village located in the northern part of Michigan's Oakland County. The area is going through a rapid transition from a rural to a suburban community. Cherwell students in the U.K. Oxford might have not known there was another Oxford until the Chicken Project because the United States's Oxford does not have a world-famous Oxford University or any other reason to be known to outsiders. The connection was made by Dr. William Skilling, superintendent of Oxford Community Schools, who was also in the audience of the Chicken Project presentation in the South Africa. Today, Oxford has become a partner in the project and known to students in Cherwell.

Oxford has not only become known in England, but also in China. Thanks to its visionary and globally minded leader, Dr. William C. Skilling, who came to talk with me in 2008, shortly after he was appointed the superintendent of Oxford Community Schools. He was working on reimagining education for his more than 4,600 students. We talked about how we need to prepare students to enter the rapidly globalized world. He went back and began the work. In 2009, Oxford Community Schools's proposal won approval as a Project ReImagine by the state of Michigan, an effort to stimulate innovative education programs. "This was in recognition of Oxford's efforts for innovation in preparing students to work and live successfully in a global world," Dr. Skilling told me later.

Today the district offers bilingual programs for all elementary school students in Chinese and Spanish. All seven Oxford schools are pursuing International Baccalaureate accreditation. It established an international school in Shenyang, China, called Northeast Yucai Oxford International School in 2011, which allows American students, not only Oxford students, to spend up to three years studying at the school in China, according to report in *Education Week* (Ash, 2012). It also launched the Oxford International Residency Academy to enroll students from outside the United States to study at Oxford. Already about 20 students from China have begun their study, paying a tuition to the district. Oxford has sent over 50 teachers to China and has built sister school relationships with a number of Chinese schools. Additionally, Oxford has launched the Michigan and Oxford Virtual Academy, marketing Oxford courses online to students in other countries who want an American-style education.

The Chicken Project and the Oxford Community Schools's global initiatives exemplify the third leg of the new education paradigm: students as global entrepreneurs and schools as global enterprises. In both cases, they have moved their campus beyond their physical boundaries, just like the Oxford Motto—Oxford Community Schools: Where the Globe Is Our Campus. They are exploring and learning about the globalized world and "exporting" their knowledge, talents, and resources to other places that need them.

OPPORTUNITIES PROVIDED BY GLOBALIZATION FOR JOBS AND ENTREPRENEURS

As discussed in Chapter 2 of this book, globalization has changed the landscape of jobs and entrepreneurship. While it presents challenges in terms of competition, it also provides new opportunities. To recap, the globalized world, with physical distance and societal boundaries minimized by technology, economic globalization, and political changes, presents a number of new potentials and challenges for the entrepreneurial and creative makers.

A Global Market With Local Needs

In theory any product or service today can reach a global market of seven billion potential consumers. In fact, many products are consumed on a global scale—from the iPhone to Coca-Cola. While the market is global, the needs are very local, except for a limited number of products that may have a universal appeal. Due to cultural diversity, economic disparity, political differences, and geographical locations, different communities around the world have different needs. Consequently, what is of value and in high demand in one community may not meet any needs in other places. For example, GPS devices have become almost essential for city dwellers in developed countries, but I cannot imagine of any use for it for the villagers in China, who don't drive. On the other hand, they now need equipment to deal with the amount of garbage accumulated due to increased consumption of packaged goods. Some products may be desirable, but they are not affordable in certain communities. For instance, while smartphones are in high demand, unless they can be sold for less than $10, the majority of people in developing countries won't be able to buy one. Finally, even universally wanted products have to typically go through a localization process to better meet the local needs. Even global food chains, such as McDonald's and KFC, localize their flavors and offerings in different communities.

Thus to be able to take advantage of the global market, entrepreneurs must understand local needs. They need to know what people need and what they can afford. Responsible entrepreneurs also know what productive products and services are to local people so they are not being exploited. The Chicken Project is an example of discovering a local need and finding ways to help address the need.

A World of Investors

In the globalized world, potential entrepreneurs can also have access to investors globally. It is amazing to see the Chicken Project receiving funding support from a small community in Oxford, Michigan, thousands of miles away from Oxford, England. Through platforms and mechanisms for "crowd-funding," ordinary individuals without necessarily having tremendous amount of wealth can provide investment capital in enterprises they believe in. It is equally fascinating to see thousands of individuals who do not know each other coming together from all over the world to invest in the production of a movie or song, as in the case of *Save the Cosmonaut*. As people in less developed countries begin to accumulate more wealth, there will be more potential investors in traditionally untapped areas in the future.

The challenge is having the ability to convince others to make the investment. To realize the potential, that is, to convince people to part with their money, is not easy. To convince people from different cultures to part with their money is even harder. It requires not only a solid idea or an innovative product, but also, and perhaps more important, making the case in a culturally sensitive way so it can appeal to people in different parts of the world. This, again, means a deep understanding of others—their needs, their way of conducting businesses, and their way of communication.

A World of Ideas and Solutions

Ideas for new products, creative solutions to existing problems, or innovative models of business are available globally as well. Crowdsourcing has become a popular practice to solicit ideas, products, and solutions from the masses. Individuals, wherever they are located, could contribute to an enterprise. It is not an isolated case that the Canadian gold company Goldcorp Inc. found more gold thanks to tips from thousands of individuals from around the world, who were not their own employees. In March 2012, Zero Robotics from MIT, the U.S. Defense Advanced Research Agency (better known as DARPA, the inventor of the Internet), and NASA announced that they were looking for "computationally effi- cient code solutions for a hypothetical mission scenario which models autonomous docking or satellite servicing proce- dures" through crowdsourcing (Zero Robotics, 2012). The job is very serious. It is to program "an active satellite or 'Tender' to synchronize its motion with and capture a tumbling, pas- sive space object or 'POD'" (Zero Robotics, 2012). Anyone can participate, but teams from high schools and colleges are especially welcome.

But crowdsourcing does not have to be the only way to obtain ideas and solutions globally. Social networks, that is, circles of friends, can be extremely effective, especially to reach into a foreign market. In some significant ways, the Oxford Community Schools's global initiatives came to frui- tion as a result of Dr. Skilling's social network—his friends who provide ideas and insights.

To realize the potential of ideas, solutions, and talents that are scattered across the globe requires the ability to reach them and convince them. It also requires the ability to manage ideas and talents globally and virtually. The capacity to develop and manage a global social network of friends and like-minded individuals is certainly a major plus.

A World of Partners

While crowdsourcing may provide temporary assistance, one-time ideas, and solutions, one could also find long-term partners globally through crowdsourcing or global social net- works. Partners are for longer-term collaboration rather than a one-time transaction. Partners offer complementary skills and knowledge. For example, when the Chicken Project expanded into Cameroon, the organizers found Tanyi D. Ebai, a local park ranger in Cameroon, who understands the local culture and context and was willing to collaborate.

Oxford Community Schools found Northeast Yucai School in China as a partner.

Finding and working with international partners is in itself a challenging task. Understanding and managing cultural differences, different expectations, and different ways of conducting business are a must in creating successful international partnerships. As well, sustaining international partnerships requires expertise in languages and cultures, mutual respect, and empathy. Furthermore, international partnership means "joint-venture"—taking risks together, which requires a deep appreciation for each other's situations and demands.

In summary, to realize the entrepreneurship potentials brought about by globalization requires global entrepreneurial competency. That is the perspective, attitude, knowledge, and skills to discover opportunities, identify needs, secure investment, seek ideas, and build partners across national borders. Schools aiming to help cultivate global entrepreneurs will need to create opportunities for students to develop such competency by becoming global enterprises.

ELEMENTS OF ENTREPRENEURIAL GLOBAL COMPETENCY

The topic of general global competency has been a popular topic recently. The definition of global competence remains a "contested field," and there is no universally agreed-upon set of skills and knowledge that make up global competence (Hunter, White, & Godbey, 2006). For example, the Swiss Consulting Group, a global business consulting firm, defines global competence as "capacity of an individual or a team to parachute into any country to get the job done while respecting cultural pathways" (Swiss Consulting Group, 2002, p. 4). Fernando Reimers, a Harvard University education professor, offered a similar definition in 2008. According to Reimers, global competence includes "the knowledge and skills that help people understand the flat world in which they live, the skills to integrate across disciplinary domains to comprehend global affairs and events and to create possibilities to address them. Global competencies are also the attitudinal and ethical dispositions that make it possible to interact peacefully, respectfully and productively with fellow human beings from diverse geographies" (Reimers, 2008).

Bill Hunter and his associates reported findings of an empirical study using a Delphi technique and survey involving university representatives, human resources officers of transnational companies, United Nations officers, intercultural trainers, and foreign government officers. The study found that these individuals came to agree that "global competence was 'having an open mind while actively seeking to understand cultural norms and expectations of others, leveraging this gained knowledge to interact, communicate and work effectively outside one's environment" (Hunter et al., 2006, p. 277).

The University of Wisconsin in the United States suggests "universities need to provide the skills, knowledge, and attitude to work effectively in our increasingly interdependent world" and defines global competences as "abilities to communicate effectively across linguistic and cultural boundaries, to see and understand the world from a perspective other than one's own, and to understand and appreciate the diversity of societies and cultures. Students need to appreciate the interdependence of nations in a global economy and to know how to adapt their work to a variety of cultures" (University of Wisconsin–Global Competence Task Force, 2008, p. 3).

Harvard professor Howard Gardner proposes, without using the term global competence, that precollegiate education should prepare students to develop an "understanding of the global system," "knowledge of other cultures and traditions," and "knowledge of and respect for one's own cultural traditions," and foster "hybrid or blended identities" and "tolerance and appreciation across racial, linguistic, national, and cultural boundaries" (Gardner, 2004).

The definitions differ because the competency required can be different for different purposes, while there are some common basic concepts. What is required of an ordinary person may be different from a diplomat, just like any other discipline—math competency is different for the common citizen from mathematicians. Naturally what is required of a global entrepreneur should be different from that which is required of an ordinary citizen. It should include elements that would help one with his or her entrepreneurial activities. In addition to the common elements proposed by various scholars such as "an open mind to others, an understanding of the global nature of our world, and the ability to interact with people cross culturally," there are a few additional elements for global entrepreneurship.

Global Problems as Enterprising Opportunities

Human beings face tremendous challenges: environmental degradation; drastic climate change; natural disasters; large and small conflicts among national, ethnic, and religious groups; hunger and poverty; energy; health; aging; migration; and unemployment, to name just a few. These challenges are global problems intensified by globalization. We could complain, we could criticize others for causing these problems, or we could also try to look at them as opportunities waiting for the creative and entrepreneurial to come up with solutions. Being able to adopt a perspective that helps to examine these problems as rich opportunities for new products and services is what is needed for global business entrepreneurs, social entrepreneurs, and policy entrepreneurs. The Chicken Project founders saw poverty, and they took action to help alleviate it.

Understanding Relative Strengths and Weaknesses of Different Groups

Different communities have different strengths, so do different individuals. Likewise, they have weaknesses. Effective global entrepreneurs know how to avoid competing in areas where others are strong. Instead they would work to build a global supply chain of resources and talents. They would try to develop products and services to help improve a community's weak area and make use of what it is strong at. For example, the Oxford Community Schools's global initiatives are designed to help the Chinese improve their English by exporting American-style education while importing the Chinese to help teach Chinese to enhance American students' global competence.

Having a Global Network of Friends

Networking is considered one of the five skills (the other four being associating, questioning, observing, and experimenting) that make up the "innovator's DNA," resulting in "disruptive innovations" according to business professors Jeff Dyer, Hal Gregersen, and Clayton Christensen in their 2011 book *The Innovator's DNA* (Dyer, Gregersen, & Christensen, 2011). Christensen is also a coauthor of the well-known *Disrupting Class: How Disruptive Innovation Will Change the Way the World Learns.* They found "innovators gain a radically different perspective when they devote time and energy to finding and testing ideas through a network of diverse individuals" (Dyer et al., 2011, p. 113). Individuals from other cultures often bring drastically different perspectives that can stimulate new ideas or force one to revise, especially when the idea is to be applied in a global context. A global network of friends from different countries also provides access to resources, insider views of a community, and nuanced knowledge about a culture.

Developing a High Level of Cultural Intelligence

There is increasing interest in the concept of cultural intelligence, or CQ, in multinational corporations and business schools as businesses become more global and cross-cultural. Two management professors, Soon Ang of Singapore's

Nanyang Business School and Linn Van Dyne of Michigan State University, gather a broad collection of research studies about CQ in the *Handbook of Cultural Intelligence* (Ang & Dyne, 2008b), published in 2008. They define CQ "as an individual's capability to function and manage effectively in culturally diverse settings" (Ang & Dyne, 2008a, p. 3). Research has shown that cultural intelligence is closely related to the performance of business travelers, multinational work teams, and executives of global businesses (Ang & Dyne, 2008a). Global entrepreneurs will inevitably need to "function and manage effectively in culturally diverse settings" as they solicit ideas and capital globally and work with partners from different cultures. CQ, according to Ang and Van Dyne, includes four components: *metacognitive CQ* (conscious cultural awareness during cross-cultural interactions), *cognitive CQ* (knowledge of norms, practices, and conventions in different cultures), *motivational CQ* (the capability to direct attention and energy toward learning and functioning in cross-cultural settings), and *behavioral CQ* (the ability to exhibit appropriate verbal and nonverbal actions in interactions with people from different cultures).

CULTIVATING ENTREPRENEURIAL GLOBAL COMPETENCY

Schools as Global Enterprises

An effective approach to cultivating these entrepreneurial global competences is what is discussed in Chapter 8: Product-Oriented Learning, but in a global setting. For this purpose, we can imagine a school as a global enterprise. As a global enterprise, the school makes products for the global market and draws on expertise and resources globally. Learning is conducted around these products and services. Through participating in the activities of a global enterprise, students are engaged in entrepreneurial activities and provided the support that can help them become globally competent.

I first discussed the idea of "schools as global enterprises" in my last book, *Catching Up or Leading the Way: American Education in the Age of Globalization* (Zhao, 2009), as a way to conceptualize schools in the age of globalization. The idea was to help schools think beyond their immediate physical confinements in terms of outcomes, resources, and markets. Here I expand on the same idea for the purpose of preparing students as global entrepreneurs, with more detailed suggestions.

Make Products and Create Services for Others

When I was learning and teaching English in China, I became aware of the poor quality of the learning materials. In fact, even today there is paucity of interesting and authentic language learning materials in most foreign language classes. The official textbooks are often contrived, uninteresting, and uniform for all students, while many language teachers and learners want more authentic, personalizable, and engaging materials. In the meantime, students in English-speaking countries are asked to write essays and compositions that nobody other than the teacher reads. Wouldn't it be great to have native-English-speaking students make English learning materials for students in China or English language learners or new immigrants in America? Similarly, students in China could create materials for American students who are studying Chinese. They can even be custom ordered so that students who are interested in specific types of materials can ask students in another country to write for them. With the capacity of today's technology, students can easily create and deliver these products and services on a global scale.

These products can be carried out by students of all ages. They can be accomplished using a variety of media—audio stories, photo journals, animation, video, or simply old-fashioned books with voice narration. They can be in the genres of fiction, nonfiction, news reports, diaries, interactive games, or mobile device apps.

Equally interesting would be having students provide tutoring or instructional services to each other. For example, an Australian school in Sydney could provide instruction about the Sydney Harbor to students in the United States or Japan who are studying about it. Chinese students would be great mentors on the subject of some aspects of Chinese culture to students in England who are studying Chinese history. The Oxford Community Schools virtual academy can easily engage students as instructors in their courses for students in other countries.

The products and services do not have to be limited to what students or schools need in another country. They could serve the general public as well. For instance, with an increasing number of Chinese tourists visiting foreign countries, it would be an excellent idea to have students in destination cities to offer customized information packets and guide services.

Products and services can also be joint ventures. For example, an elementary school class can work on a global festival project. The final product of the project could be a digital picture book about how people in different parts of the world celebrate important days in their culture. Students in different countries are invited to draw pictures, take photos, write captions, and assemble them into a multimedia, multilingual product about festivals in their own cultures.

Ideas for products and services can be generated through engaging students in authentic interactions with the potential consumers. The ideas can be bidirectional. Students can come up with ideas for products and services, and test them with the potential customers. In the meantime, the potential customers could express their needs and suggest products and services that can be useful. To enable such activities, schools need to build partnerships with their potential customers.

Build a Global Network of Partners

Partners are not only potential consumers, but also collaborators and resources. In other words, they can be both consumers and suppliers. They can be readers of the books students make or recipients of courses students teach. At the same time, they can be providing suggestions and feedback to students. More important, they can be making books or offering courses to students. They can also play hosts for study abroad trips or offer internship opportunities. Individual students in one school can also seek to carry out projects collaboratively with individuals from the partnership organization, so can individual teachers and their students. Global partnerships also provide a platform for students to develop friendships with individuals from other countries and learn to work with people across cultural and physical distance. The overarching idea is that partnerships serve a full range of functions and should not be limited to just educational institutions. In some sense, partners can be considered an extended campus or branch campus in other countries.

Although sister schools have been a familiar form of global partnership, partners are not limited to schools in other countries. They can be any institution that has a need for what a school can offer or resources to help the school achieve its goals. The key to building effective and sustainable international partnership is mutual benefits and understanding. Learning to discover mutual benefits and develop mutual understanding itself presents opportunities to develop global competency.

Many schools and teachers have already embarked on the journey to build their global network of partnerships. Oxford Community Schools is one example for school-level partnerships. The Flat Classroom Project, cofounded by teachers Vicki Davis of Westwood Schools in the United States and Julie Lindsay of Beijing International School in China, has evolved into a global phenomenon. "One of the main goals of the project is to 'flatten' or lower the classroom walls so that instead of each class working isolated and alone, 2 or more classes are joined virtually to become one large classroom," according to the Flat Classroom Project website (Davis & Lindsay, 2012a). The project has attracted thousands of teachers around the world, and it now offers training and conferences.

The project was featured in Thomas Friedman's *The World Is Flat* (Friedman, 2007). And now the two teachers have written a book to help other teachers build flat classrooms (Davis & Lindsay, 2012b).

Provide Foreign Experiences and Study/Work Abroad

One of the effective ways to develop global competence, particularly CQ, is to experience being a foreigner—living and working in a context where one's own culture and language are not the dominant. Short and frequent international travels have been found to have a significant positive effect on CQ, for example (Ang & Dyne, 2008b). Whenever possible, schools should develop programs that can provide students with opportunities to experience being a foreigner.

Study abroad programs, service learning in another country, or internships are possible ways to provide students with that experience. Or in the spirit of product-oriented learning, students can have a product tour akin to book tours in foreign countries to showcase and market their products or themselves. I have been quite impressed with and written about the Ringwood experience. Ringwood Secondary College in Melbourne, Australia, organizes its senior students for a world tour. They take a show that features music, singing, dance, drama, puppetry, projection and audience interaction to their partner schools around the globe. Students in the performance group not only perform, but they also stay with the host families and attend regular classes at the partner school. This is a semester-long project, and students normally visit six or seven countries.

Teach Foreign Languages and Which Language

Being able to communicate in another language is a true asset for the future global entrepreneur. Google Translate can do the mechanics, but it will unlikely provide the human touch or cultural nuance that makes human languages different from computer languages. And offering foreign language learning to all students is fairly easy for a school that is a global enterprise because of its global partners and creative uses of technology.

Developing true proficiency in a foreign language takes tremendous effort and is a long process. Depending on the learner's native language and the target language, it can take thousands of instructional hours for an individual to achieve functional proficiency in a foreign language. But very often many schools only teach foreign languages in high schools, and students often take a foreign language for only two or three years. These language courses at most are taught one hour per day—and in many countries a school year is about 200 days—so students may study a foreign language for about 400 to 600 hours, which is far from sufficient to develop functional proficiency. In addition, foreign languages are often taught as an academic subject and thus much attention is given to the linguistic knowledge rather than communicative competence.

To help develop foreign language proficiency and use it as a way to develop cultural intelligence, schools should begin offering foreign languages as early as possible and change how foreign languages are taught. Bilingual immersion programs starting in primary grades have been suggested to be an effective way to teach foreign languages. Bilingual immersion programs provide abundant language learning experiences by teaching subject matter content in both the native and target language. They also provide students the opportunities to experience the cultural differences embedded in the two different languages so as to engage in deep cultural learning that involves confronting and surmounting difference in ways of thinking, value systems, and habits of mind in other cultures, as John Dewey suggests (Saito, 2003). This is necessary for developing high levels of cultural intelligence because of the nature of culture.

A common question schools in English-speaking countries face is what foreign language to offer because there are many possible languages, while in countries where English is not the native language, the choice seems to have been easier: English. The answer depends on many factors, among which two are essential: educational value and utility value. Learning a foreign language is first and foremost of educational value. It should be considered part of a well-rounded education experience for all students. In deciding what language to teach, we should start with how much educational value a language offers. It is true that learning any foreign language is a valuable experience, but some languages may provide more value than others especially when it comes to helping develop global competence.

What affects the value is cultural and linguistic distance. Historically, human languages have evolved and spread along different paths. As a result, some languages are more similar to each other than others. For example, English is much more similar to Spanish than Mandarin Chinese. Thus one can say the linguistic distance between English and Spanish is much shorter than that between English and Mandarin Chinese. Languages are used in different cultures. Cultures too have different distances. Some cultures are more alike than others.

Linguistic and cultural distances can have an impact on the educational value of language learning. The farther the distance, the more challenging it is to learn the language and thus it requires more cognitive efforts and resources to learn it. The extra effort and resources provide a more rigorous— hence more educationally valuable—experience. Following this logic, it is then more desirable to teach languages that are more different from the native language.

The utility value of a language can be determined by assessing how likely the language may be useful in the future. There is really no magical formula to make accurate predictions, because world affairs change rapidly and the world's hot spots can move from one country to another quickly.

However, we can attempt to guess the likelihood of a language being used by considering (1) the size of the population of native speakers of a language—the more people who speak the language, the more likely we will encounter one in the future; (2) the importance of the economies/countries where the language is spoken—the more important, the more likely that the language will be used in international business and political transactions; and (3) geographical, political, and historical proximity to the target language culture or countries—the closer the target language culture is to the learners' through migration, economic transaction, tourism, or historical ties, the more likely the language will be useful.

Schools can use these two criteria, educational value and utility value, to help decide what language or languages to offer. Of course there are other factors such as to what extent the local community has a large immigrant population and what language(s) are spoken, what resources (teachers and materials) for certain languages are available to the school, what language(s) have been taught in the school, and so on. As a general suggestion, Arabic, Chinese, Japanese, Russian, and Swahili are good candidates.

SCHOOLS IN THE AGE OF GLOBALIZATION

A Summary

The world is flat (Friedman, 2007), and the entrepreneur needs to be globally competent to succeed in this flattened world. To cultivate globally competent entrepreneurs, schools will need to transform themselves into global enterprises that make products for the global market, draw on resources from around the world, and expand their campuses beyond their immediate physical locations.

References

Ang, S., & Dyne, L. V. (2008a). Conceptualization of cultural intelligence: Definitions, distinctiveness, and nomological network. In

S. Ang & L. V. Dyne (Eds.), *Handbook of cultural intelligence: Theory, measurement, and applications* (pp. 3–15). Armonk, NY: M. E. Sharpe.

Ang, S., & Dyne, L. V. (Eds.). (2008b). *Handbook of cultural intelligence: Theory, measurement, and applications.* Armonk, NY: M. E. Sharpe.

Ash, K. (2012, February 1). U.S., Chinese schools build virtual ed. partnerships. *Education Week.* Retrieved March 25, 2012, from http://www.edweek.org/ew/articles/2012/02/01/19el-china exchange.h31.html?qs=oxford

Bowen, D. (2012). Cherwell School's chicken project in Cameroon. *Silent Forest.* Retrieved March 20, 2012, from http://www.silent forests.net/images/files/thechickenproject.pdf

Cherwell School (Ed.). (2011). *The chicken project.* Oxford, UK: Author.

Cherwell School. (2012). The chicken project. Retrieved March 20, 2012, from http://www.cherwell.oxon.sch.uk/content/index .php?page=168

Davis, V., & Lindsay, J. (2012a). About. *The Flat Classroom Project.* Retrieved March 29, 2012, from http://www.flatclassroom project.org/About

Davis, V., & Lindsay, J. (2012b). *Flattening classrooms, engaging minds: Move to global collaboration one step at a time.* New York, NY: Pearson.

Dyer, J., Gregersen, H., & Christensen, C. M. (2011). *The innovator's DNA: Mastering the five skills of disruptive innovators.* Boston, MA: Harvard Business Review Press.

Friedman, T. L. (2007). *The world is flat: A brief history of the twenty-first century.* New York, NY: Farrar, Straus and Giroux.

Gardner, H. (2004). How education changes: Considerations of history, science, and values. In M. M. Suarez-Orozco & D. B. Qin-Hillard (Eds.), *Globalization: Culture and education in the new millennium* (pp. 235–258). Berkeley: University of California Press and The Ross Institute.

Hunter, B., White, G. P., & Godbey, G. C. (2006). What does it mean to be globally competent? *Journal of Studies in International Education, 10*(3), 267–285.

Reimers, F. M. (2008, October 3). Preparing students for the flat world. Retrieved October 15, 2008, from http://www.edweek .org/

Saito, N. (2003). Education for global understanding: Learning from Dewey's visit to Japan. *Teachers College Record, 105*(9), 1758–1773.

Swiss Consulting Group. (2002). *Global Competency Report 2002*. New York, NY: Swiss Consulting Group.

University of Wisconsin–Global Competence Task Force. (2008). *Global Competence Task Force report*. Madison: University of Wisconsin.

Zero Robotics. (2012, March 6). Autonomous space capture challenge opens algorithmic crowdsourcing to general public. *Top Coder*. Retrieved March 29, 2012, from http://www.topcoder .com/blog/2012/03/autonomous-space-capture-challenge -opens-algorithmic-crowdsourcing-to-general-public/

Zhao, Y. (2009). *Catching up or leading the way: American education in the age of globalization*. Alexandria, VA: ASCD.

10

Create a World Class Education

Principles and Indicators

When a subject becomes totally obsolete we make it a required course.

—Peter Drucker

Don't limit a child to your own learning, for he was born in another time.

—Rabindranath Tagore

It's April 2012. Less than two years after the celebration of the launch of the Common Core State Standards I described in Chapter 1, U.S. Secretary of Education Arne Duncan has begun to debate with himself about the Common Core. In a statement in February 2012 on a legislative proposal to block the implementation of the Common Core in the U.S. state of South Carolina, Arne Duncan unambiguously expressed his firm belief in the power of the Common Core:

That's [blocking the Common Core] not good for children, parents, or teachers. I hope South Carolina lawmakers will heed the voices of teachers who supported South Carolina's decision to stop lowering academic standards and set a higher bar for success. And I hope lawmakers will continue to support the state's decision to raise standards, with the goal of making every child college- and career-ready in today's knowledge economy. (Duncan, 2012)

But less than a month later, he seemed to have changed his position. On March 7, 2012, he sent a letter to the Superintendent of Public Instruction Larry K. Shumway of the state of Utah, where the legislature passed a resolution that directs the state's education authority to reconsider the adoption of the Common Core (Cortez, 2012). Arne Duncan wrote to confirm his "full and unqualified agreement with" Shumway's letter, which stated that the Utah State Board of Education has the right to change, add to, or subtract from the Common Core standards and asserted the state's right to complete control of "learning standards in all areas" of public education curriculum. The letter further stated that the state has full control of assessment and has the right to withdraw at any time from the common assessment consortium. "States have the sole right to set learning standards," Duncan said in closing and thanked Shumway for the opportunity to "clarify our mutual understanding" (Ziegler, 2012).

Whether Duncan has changed his position on the Common Core is uncertain, but what is certain are the growing challenges to the initiative. Legal and cost concerns associated with adopting and implementing the Common Core are the primary reasons underlying the debate. Conservative pundit George Will challenges the legality of the federal Department of Education's actions to push the Common Core to states and schools and worried about "as the government becomes bigger, it becomes more lawless." "In its most extreme form, national control of curriculum is a form of national control of ideas," Will quotes Joseph Califano, Secretary of Health, Education and Welfare under Democrat President Jimmy Carter as a warning of the potential effect of the Common Core (Will, 2012). The Boston-based Pioneer Institute put a daunting $16 billion price tag on Common Core implementation (AccountabilityWorks, 2012).

The legal and costs debate will continue, but the outcome is already in sight. "Despite all the money and effort devoted to developing the Common Core State Standards—not to mention the simmering controversy over their adoption in several states—the study foresees little to no impact on student learning" (Loveless, 2012, p. 3). That is the conclusion of a study by the Brookings Institute reported in *The 2012 Brown Center Report on American Education*. The author of the report, Tom Loveless, senior fellow of the Brookings Institute, thus suggests:

> Don't let the ferocity of the oncoming debate fool you. The empirical evidence suggests that the Common Core will have little effect on American students' achievement. The nation will have to look elsewhere for ways to improve its schools. (Loveless, 2012, p. 14)

The "elsewhere" are Summerhill, High Tech High, Cherwell School, and Oxford Community Schools—not in the so-called high-performing education systems because of their stunning test scores. What will create my dream school for the future comes from the "alternative" schools rather than education systems. What will prepare our children for the future, not the past, comes from what has been done by courageous and visionary individual education leaders, who may have been considered so exceptionally gifted or outlandishly crazy—or both—that their actions cannot or should not be replicated by the ordinary school or educator.

But as this book has so far documented, to prepare our children to meet the challenges of the future, we must move away from the employment-oriented education to the new paradigm, which ironically has already been created. In this final chapter, I will show that the new paradigm can be replicated elsewhere. Moreover, I bring together the principles exemplified by Summerhill, High Tech High, Cherwell, and Oxford to formulate a framework for developing the schools we truly need.

THE TRIAD MODEL OF EDUCATION FOR GLOBAL CREATIVE ENTREPRENEURS

The previous three chapters discuss the three principles of a new education paradigm that aims to cultivate globally competent and creative entrepreneurs. These three principles are closely interconnected and form the core of the new paradigm. Each of them points to a direction that schools can use to take action and develop strategies.

Summerhill and Autonomy: The What

While the reformers are busy arguing about what will make our children globally competitive and ready for college and career, Summerhill and other like-minded schools have shown that following and supporting the children's passions and interests produces competent, responsible, passionate, productive, and happy citizens (Posner, 2009). Granting children their deserved autonomy in choosing what to learn rather than imposing upon them what others deem useful is necessary to cultivating creative entrepreneurs in the age of globalization.

Unique and Diverse Talents. In a globalized world crowded by more than seven billion individuals, we cannot all have the same talent and compete for the same job. Likewise, in a world where human needs are diverse, a standardized set of talents cannot possibly meet all the needs. Furthermore, in a world that is changing constantly and rapidly, a predetermined set of standardized skills and talents are not good bets for jobs that have not yet been invented. More important, in a world where human interests, backgrounds, living conditions, and abilities are diverse, it is ethically wrong and economically disastrous to reduce all the diversity into a few skills. Granting and supporting individual students' pursuit of learning enables the development of unique and diverse talents.

From Adequate to Great. While the agricultural and mass production industrial economy needs many workers with similar skills, these skills are routine, standard, and basic. As technology and economic globalization render the traditional lines of jobs obsolete and the economy is increasingly driven by knowledge and creativity (Florida, 2002; Goldin & Katz, 2008), we will need individuals with different talents and skills—but beyond what can be standardized and basic. They need to be great. Adequate is not enough. But greatness does not come from standards. Best-selling author Daniel Coyle suggests in his book *The Talent Code: Greatness Isn't Born. It's Grown. Here's How* that greatness comes from deep practice, that is, tens of thousands of hours of practice with master coaching. "But deep practice isn't a piece of cake: it requires energy, passion, and commitment. In a word, it requires motivational fuel" (Coyle, 2009 p. 93). That motivational fuel comes from the inside, not outside, of an individual. Thus only when children have the autonomy can they be driven enough to become great.

Confident, Curious, and Creative. The world needs creators: creators of more jobs, better products, more sensible policies, more effective business models, and more meaningful human services. Creators are curious people, who keep wondering and imagining. Creators are confident people, who are courageous to think and act outside the box. Creators are, well, creative people, who can come up with novel ideas and solutions. Creators cannot be planned, predetermined, or standardized. They must be allowed the freedom and encouraged to wonder and wander, to explore, and to experiment. They must not be judged against others, a standard norm, or external assessment. They need autonomy.

High Tech High and Product-Oriented Learning: The How

While reformers are pressuring schools to have their students master the skills to produce test scores so they can graduate and go to college, High Tech High has been encouraging its students to produce books, videos, and art pieces, and through which they learn what they will need to be ready for college and career. While the reformers are working hard at creating "urgency schools" (Fine, 2011), in which students and teachers are instilled the urgency to meet standards and pass tests, High Tech High has created an environment where students own the school and happily engaged in works that matter. High Tech High serves as a good example of using project-based learning as an approach to engage students in deep learning through creating authentic products and services. I have re-labeled this approach product-oriented learning because the traditional PBL has too broad of a definition.

Product-oriented learning changes the orientation of the learner from the recipient and consumer to the creator and provider. It changes the relationship between the teacher and the learner as well. The teacher no longer serves as the sole source of knowledge or disciplinary authority, but rather as a motivator, a reviewer, a facilitator, and an organizer. The learner becomes owner of their learning and is responsible for seeking and securing the necessary guidance, knowledge, skills, and support to make high-quality products. These changes facilitate the cultivation of creative entrepreneurs.

Problems as Opportunities. Entrepreneurs seek to solve—not avoid—problems. They ask questions, not find ready-made answers to existing questions. They challenge the status quo with the belief they can always make it better. Product-oriented learning asks the learner to consider problems as opportunities for actions. It inspires them to create solutions, which then motivates them to acquire the knowledge, skills, and resources necessary for creating the solutions.

Other People's Needs. Product-oriented learning compels the learner to care about others because in order to make meaningful and useful products and services, the learner must first know what is needed and meaningful to different people in different situations. It helps the learner to develop an empathetic perspective on others and the necessary skills to learn about other people's conditions and needs. An acute sense of other people's needs helps develop alertness to opportunities, which is a common trait of successful entrepreneurs.

Strengths and Weaknesses. We cannot be good at everything. Thus knowing what one is good at or wants to be good at is essential to be successful. Successful entrepreneurs know their strengths and limitations. They stick to what they are good at and "outsource" their weakness to other able people. Product-oriented learning provides learners with the opportunities to try out their interests and talents so they can decide what to pursue and what they need help with.

Perseverance and Disciplined Creativity. Entrepreneurship is not a smooth journey without bumps. It requires perseverance to go through the ups and downs. Unbounded creativity or a flash moment of enthusiasm does not lead to truly meaningful products or successful enterprises. Great ideas lead to great results only when sustained and disciplined efforts are applied over a long period of time. Product-oriented learning, through multiple drafts and peer reviews, helps the learner to develop resilience and perseverance before failure and learn about the importance of discipline and commitment.

Cherwell and Oxford Community Schools and Global Enterprises: The Where

There is a sad irony in education reforms around the world today. While the reformers intend to prepare their students to be globally competitive by admiring and adopting international standards and practices, they are in reality closing their school doors to the outside world because they want their students to focus on the core academics and raise test scores on international tests. Fortunately we have schools like Cherwell in England and Oxford in the United States. They have taken the bold action to make the globe their campus. Instead of preparing students to compete with others, they have taken the action to help their children develop the competency that enables them to benefit from helping and working with others.

Global Perspective. In a globalized world where all aspects of human life are interconnected, the entrepreneur—be it business, policy, or social—needs to see their work as part of the global economic and political network. They need to know their work affects and is affected by people in other places. Such a perspective is most effectively developed through engaging in experiences with people from other lands or living in other places.

Global Partners. In a globalized world, innovators and entrepreneurs need friends for fresh ideas, different perspectives, local knowledge, and a variety of resources. A global network of friends and partners is thus a tremendous asset. But friends and partners do not just fall from a tree in one's backyard. They become friends and partners only through interactions in various occasions when mutual interests, respect, and understanding are uncovered and developed. Therefore expanding the campus, the learning environment, beyond the physical boundaries is key to developing global partners.

Global Competency. A global entrepreneur cannot avoid interacting with people and organizations in other countries. To be effective in international settings requires a level of global competency, which ideally includes fluency in a foreign language and a high level of cultural intelligence. Schools intending to cultivate global entrepreneurs must provide the opportunities for students to learn foreign languages and become culturally intelligent.

A WORLD CLASS SCHOOL

Indicators

A community of autonomous learners engaged in creating meaningful products located on a global campus is the image of a world class school following the new paradigm. The three principles of the new paradigm have in various ways been put into action by schools around the world. Thus there are abundant examples to learn from and resources to draw upon, without reinventing the wheel.

While Summerhill may be one of the most famous examples of the "open school" or "democratic education" that maximizes student participation in school government and freedom to learn, there are many others that follow the same philosophy to varying degrees. According to the International Democratic Education Network website, there are 200 places offering this type of education in over 30 countries.[1] More than 40,000 students are enrolled in these schools (International Democratic Education Network, 2012). Writings about these schools and their outcomes have also appeared. Besides A. S. Neill's writings about Summerhill, Daniel Greenberg, one of the founders of the Sudbury Valley School in the United States, has written a number of books about the Sudbury School experience,[2] including *The Pursuit of Happiness: The Lives of Sudbury Valley Alumni* (Greenberg, Sadofsky, & Lempka, 2005). More recently, Rick Posner wrote in his book *Lives of Passion, School of Hope* about the Jefferson County Open School in Lakewood, Colorado, a U.S. public school following the democratic philosophy (Posner, 2009).

The High Tech High–style PBL has spread widely as well. The Whitfield County Schools in rural northwest Georgia, for example, began implementing the High Tech High model in 2009. "Today, daily life for the teachers and students involved has dramatically changed," observes Grace Rubenstein of *Edutopia*. "Students still take some tests, but more often they participate in multidisciplinary projects ranging from writing and producing a scientifically based murder-mystery play to enacting a Japanese tea ceremony to building an outdoor classroom"(Rubenstein, 2011). In the United Kingdom, a similar type of school called "Studio School" has been growing

---

[1] A complete list of democratic schools is also available on its website: http://www.idenetwork.org/democratic-schools.htm

[2] The Sudbury Valley School operates its own press and publishes writings about the school. Interested readers can find its publications at http://sudburypress.com/

fast.[3] Started with two in 2010, the number of Studio Schools reached 18 in 2012. The Studio School is very similar to High Tech High in the United States. According to a press release of the U.K. Department for Education, Studio Schools have these characteristics:

- All subjects are taught through projects, often designed with employers.
- They typically operate longer days and outside standard school terms—giving pupils a good understanding of a working day, and the importance of good attendance and punctuality in business.
- Along with their studies pupils carry out work placements for four hours a week, with employers who work with the school.
- Each pupil has a "personal coach," who seeks to replicate the role of a supportive line manager in the workplace. (Department for Education, 2011)

There are also abundant writings about the works of High Tech High and the Studio School, including tips for replication (Rubenstein, 2011), curriculum models (The Studio Schools Trust, 2010), and teachers guide for implementation (Patton & Robin, 2012).

Cherwell and Oxford are not the only schools that have begun to engage in expanding their students' learning space globally. The Asia Society produced an excellent resource guide *Going Global: Preparing Our Students for an Interconnected World* in 2008 with plenty of examples of schools that have done so. The guide also suggests practical strategies and actions schools can follow to expand their students' learning space (Asia Society, 2008). In Australia, the Asia Education Foundation provides a wealth of information and resources for schools and teachers to engage students in global studies.[4]

---

[3]For more information about studio schools, visit the Studio Schools Trust website: http://studioschoolstrust.org/welcome

[4]More information about the Asia Education Foundation can be found on its website: http://www.asiaeducation.edu.au/default.asp

In the United Kingdom, various organizations including the British Council have been promoting and supporting global school partners.[5]

Given the availability of excellent resources, it does not make sense for me to repeat the specific suggestions. Rather I distill from these examples and recourses a list of indicators of a school oriented to prepare citizens in the age of globalization. These indicators can be used to guide the development of such a school and used as accountability measures for a true world class education.

Student Voice: Governance and Environment

In a world class school, students should have the right and opportunity to participate in school governance and constructing the physical, social, and cognitive environment. To determine if students have a voice in the operation of a school, we could ask the following questions:

- To what extent are students involved in the development of rules and regulations in the school?
- To what extent are students involved in selecting and evaluating staff?
- To what extent are students involved in decisions about courses and other learning opportunities the school offers?
- To what extent are students involved in decisions about equipment, library books, technology, or other similar items?

Student Choice: Broad and Flexible Curriculum

In a world class school, students should have certain degrees of freedom to pursue their own interests. Thus schools must have a broad range of curriculum offerings and flexible range

---

[5]The British Council's global school partnership website: http://schoolson line.britishcouncil.org/home

to enable students to explore, experience, and experiment with their interests and passions. To determine the level of student choice, we could ask the following questions:

- How many different courses, programs, and activities are offered?
- To what degree can students construct their own courses or programs?
- To what degree can students learn from outside resources, either in the local community or through online arrangements?
- To what degree does the school provide resources such as mini grants to support student-initiated activities such as clubs or project teams?
- To what degree can students be excused from externally imposed upon standards and assessments with good reasons?

Student Support: Personalization and Mentoring

A world class school provides sufficient and easily accessible emotional, social, and cognitive support for students to personalize their learning experiences. Mentoring and advising are an essential element of personalized learning to help guide, inspire, and facilitate students' learning. To determine the level of support for students, we could ask the following questions:

- Does each student have an adult advisor or coach?
- To what degree can students choose the adult advisor or have the freedom to change advisors?
- To what degree are adults available to talk and work with students upon request?
- To what degree are students provided with opportunities to work with advisors from outside the school?

Authentic Products: Personally Meaningful or Useful for Others

Product-oriented learning indicates a significant departure from traditional learning, and the authenticity of student work is a key indicator of the product-oriented learning experience. Authenticity is defined by the degree to which the final product or service serves a genuine purpose, solves a real problem, meets a genuine need of others, or is personally meaningful. If a product only ends as evidence for measuring a student's mastery of certain content or skills, it is not authentic. To determine the degree to which product-oriented learning is the primary learning approach, the following questions can be useful:

- Is there an infrastructure for students to develop, display, or market products and services?
- Are relevant policies that govern student products, for example, policies regarding ownership of the intellectual property of student products, in place?
- What products and services have students created?
- In what ways have students' products and services been used?
- To what degree are students engaged in product-oriented learning? Or what percentage of student activities is product oriented?

Sustained and Disciplined Process: Multiple Drafts and Review

Only when students are engaged in a sustained and disciplined process of product development and marketing can they develop the skills, spirit, and understanding required for creative entrepreneurs. High-quality products can only come from such a process as well. Thus product-oriented learning should go through multiple iterations with professional standards applied and professional feedback. To determine if there is a sustained and disciplined process, we could ask the following questions:

- Is there an established process for reviewing proposals and products?
- Is there an established process and protocol for product improvement?
- Is there an established process to engage external experts from the broad community to participate in proposal and product review?
- Are there established criteria for products and proposal review?

Strength-Based: Unique and Local

Although a world class school should have a global perspective, it emphasizes local strengths—strengths of each student, teacher, school, and local community. In other words, it should build on their own strengths. To determine the degree to which a school follows the strength-based approach, we can ask the following questions:

- Does the school have unique features that reflect the local community resources?
- Does the school have unique features that reflect the strengths of its teaching staff?
- Does the school have an established mechanism for students and staff to explore and express their strengths?
- Does the school stand out in any other way?

Global Orientation: International Partners and Opportunities

In the age of globalization, a world class school must have a global orientation and operate as a global enterprise. International partners and opportunities for students to engage in international activities are good indicators of a school's global orientation. The following questions are guidelines for assessing a school's global orientation:

- How many international partners does the school have?
- How frequently are students engaged in international activities?
- To what degree are students' projects/products oriented to global issues or needs of people from other countries?
- To what extent does the school utilize international resources?
- To what extent does the school provide resources to other countries?
- Are there established channels for frequent international interactions among students and staff?

Global Competence: Foreign Languages and Cultures

A world class education also helps students develop global competencies, that is, the ability to interact with others in different cultures. Proficiency in a foreign language and general cultural intelligence are generally accepted indicators of global competence. Thus the degree to which a school is committed to developing global competence can be determined by asking the following questions:

- How many foreign languages are offered in the school?
- Can students learn a language that is not offered by the school staff?
- What opportunities are available for students to engage in cross-cultural interactions?
- What opportunities are available for students to live or study in culturally unfamiliar situations?

WHAT ABOUT THE BASICS?

The new paradigm school as described above may sound messy and ineffective to some people. Allowing students the autonomy to pursue their interests and passions may appear not attending to the basics, and product-oriented learning could look chaotic and missing the systematic transmission of predetermined content. Thus proponents of standards may quickly object to the new model of education on the grounds that it ignores the importance of the basics—literacy and numeracy. But that is far from the truth for a number of reasons. First, if the basics are truly basic, that is, essential to functioning in today's society, they are unavoidable in students' pursuit of making great products. They must be able to read and do the math to acquire the knowledge and skills to make their products, to market their products, and to convince people that their pursuits are of value.

Second, children learn more and better when they are interested and engaged. In this new paradigm of school, the basics are sought after rather than imposed upon. In pursuing their interest and passion and through making authentic products, they will be learning the skills to read, write, and do arithmetic.

Third, there is plenty of empirical evidence that in democratic schools like Summerhill, Sudbury Valley, and Jefferson County Open School, children graduate with excellent basics and much more (Matharu, 2008; Posner, 2009). High Tech High has produced outstanding results in terms of basics and percentage of graduates attending college (High Tech High, 2012).

CREATING A WORLD CLASS EDUCATION FOR THE WORLD

Recommendations

The need for global, creative, and entrepreneurial talents is clear. The brave pioneers have already laid a path, although there are still obstacles. For all schools to get there requires collective actions to remove the obstacles and take advantage of new opportunities.

Obstacles

On the way to the ideal world class education for every student are a few conceptual, institutional, and practical obstacles that must be removed. None of these obstacles will be easy to be moved aside, but it is not impossible. Chief among them are three: old definition of education success, the existing bureaucracy, and preparation of educators.

Old Definition of Education Success. In the traditional and presently dominant paradigm, educational success is defined by external agencies and measured by the degree to which a child or school successfully completes the pre-defined tasks, which typically means the level of mastery of prescribed skills and contents. In other words, it is defined as how well one "plays the game" or completes the "race course." Thus there are standards, assessments, and league tables and rankings. This mindset has tremendous psychological appeal and has been in existence for a long time. Despite its inability to cultivate the talents we need, as discussed elsewhere in this book, it will be difficult to change. To begin changing this paradigm, we need to stop pushing for common standards, common assessment, and ranking of students, teachers, and schools within an education system or internationally.

The Existing Education Bureaucracy. In almost every society there exists a large education bureaucracy that is supposed to ensure all children receive high-quality education. Although the intention that started the various elements of this bureaucracy may be well justified, quite often they have evolved to watch out for their own interest and self-survival instead of the interest of children. There are also tremendous political and financial interests invested to keep the bureaucracy going. But it has become a major obstacle for education and educational innovations. "The organizational flaw in America's schools is that they are too organized," writes Philip Howard, lawyer and the author of *Life Without Lawyers: Restoring Responsibility in America*, recently in *The Atlantic*. If America's schools, many content to be the least organized in the world, are too organized, imagine schools in other places. "Bureaucracy can't teach," Howard, who founded the nonprofit organization Common Good, continues. "We must give educators freedom to be themselves." He suggests, "scrapping the current system—all of it, federal, state, and local, as well as union contracts. We must start over and rebuild an open framework in which real people can find inspiration in doing things their own way" (Howard, 2012). I may not go this far, but to implement the new paradigm of education, the existing bureaucracy must shift to stimulate innovations and allow educators to educate instead of turning them into bureaucrats as well.

Preparation of Educators. In the *Forbes* magazine article about High Tech High, reporter Victoria Murphy asked about how many High Tech Highs could there be and was given the answer "How many Larry Rosenstocks are there?" (Murphy, 2004). It highlights the importance of great leaders in creating and leading great schools. But we have a shortage of Larry Rosenstocks in education. High Tech High had to establish its own graduate school to prepare teachers and leaders who can lead and teach in the new paradigm of schools. A real obstacle is that the dominant paradigm discourages visionary, courageous, innovative, and entrepreneurial leaders like Larry Rosenstock and rewards those who follow rules and comply with standards. Furthermore, teacher education and administrator education programs already tend to focus more on management skills and the ability to raise test scores; the push for more standardized testing and compliance is further driving innovative and entrepreneurial educators out of our schools. To prepare more innovative and entrepreneurial educators, we must first stop the compliance-based accountability approach to schools. We must not focus on standardizing teacher education and rendering it to the transmission of trivial instructional and class management skills. Moreover, we need to view teachers as leaders in a school community, not simply someone who manages and teaches in a classroom only. After all, to cultivate entrepreneurial students requires educators to have a bit of the entrepreneurial spirit as well.

Opportunities

Education also faces tremendous opportunities brought about by technological changes and globalization. However, because of the excessive focus on standards, assessment, global competition, and accountability, we have not been able to have the opportunity and resources to re-imagine and re-create our education. In other words, we have been so busy fixing the horse wagon in order to get to the moon instead of spending time and resources on inventing rockets. As a result, far too many education systems are working on becoming globally competitive by shutting the school doors to the outside world in order to raise student academic achievement, that is, test scores.

Technology. Opportunities brought about by recent development of technology have been almost completely missed in education. While technology has significantly transformed many sectors of our society—from economics to politics, from entertainment to business, and from social life to work life—it has been largely ignored in education at best or misused at worst. For example, instead of using it to create exciting learning opportunities, a massive amount of money is spent on building data systems to test and track student learning of prescribed content as well as ranking schools and teachers. Instead of using it to support student creation, it has been used to dress up "drill and kill" exercises as engaging materials. Instead of using it to free teachers from routine tasks of teaching, it has been used to force teachers to record and report student test scores. Instead of helping schools and teachers to realize the potentials of technology for education, it has been used to profit from education through low-quality online programs. Technology holds amazing potential to support the new paradigm of education in a number of ways. First, as a tool for creation, digital technology makes it much easier and less expensive to create media products, books, arts, and all sorts of other products and services. Second, as a tool of communication, technology enlarges the campus to make it possible for students to learn with experts and resources from outside the school. Third, as a platform for marketing, technology makes it possible for students to reach a global audience for their products. Finally, as a tool for collaboration, technology enables students to work with partners from around the world anytime from anywhere.

Globalization. Like technology, globalization brings great opportunities for improving education. But like technology, globalization has been ignored or misconceived in education. One of the most damaging misperceptions is the misinterpretation of global competitiveness as test scores on international assessments, which has driven many educational systems down the wrong path of education change. This interpretation is at least partly responsible for reinforcing the old education paradigm and global homogenization of learning (Zhao, 2010). The new paradigm of education can take advantage of opportunities brought about by globalization in a number of ways. First, globalization makes it much easier to build partnerships with schools in other countries. Second, globalization enables easier interactions with people from other cultures. Third, globalization creates value of local knowledge and skills because what is not valuable in one community due to its abundance can be of value in another community. Hence students in one community can more easily find needs for their products and skills. Finally, globalization makes expertise from other countries more accessible.

The Oba Project.[6] To take advantage of the opportunities brought about by technology and globalization, I am working on a project at the University of Oregon. The project, called Oba, is an online learning platform and community. As an online education platform, Oba provides a full suite of functions that include online course management, social

---

[6]More information about Oba can be found at http://www.obaworld.net

networking, portfolio management, video editing and storage, and virtual classroom meeting spaces. Oba is also a global membership community of schools and learners. It enables schools to develop and deliver online courses and other educational services to their own students and students from other schools globally. As a result, schools within the Oba community can market their courses to students in other schools. Independent teachers or education providers can also market their courses and services to students globally. Oba also makes it possible for teachers and students from different schools to collaborate on a global scale. More important, Oba enables students to develop and market their products to schools and students globally.

THE END OF EDUCATION

I bring this book to a conclusion with the title of the late cultural critic Neil Postman's book *The End of Education: Redefining the Value of School* (Postman, 1996). In explaining the purpose of the book, he wrote:

> I write this book in the hope of altering, a little bit, the definition of the "school problem"—from means to ends. "End," of course, has at least two important meanings: "purpose" and "finish." Either meaning may apply to the future of schools, depending on whether or not there ensures a serious dialogue about purpose. By giving the book its ambiguous title, I mean to suggest that without a transcendent and honorable purpose schooling must reach its finish, and the sooner we are done with it, the better. With such a purpose, schooling becomes the central institution through which the young may find reasons for continuing to educate themselves. (Postman, 1996, p. xi)

Postman would be disappointed with what's happening today in the education arena. The dominant discourse remains about the means of schooling: curriculum standards, teacher effectiveness, better assessment, charter schools, data-driven instruction, and a host of other factors that may affect student achievement, without questioning whether the achievement is meaningful. Politicians, businessmen, and to some degree the public and educators have been working hard to make better schools, not necessarily better education for children. A former teacher and doctoral student at Harvard Graduate School of Education laments on the loss of the human dimension in some schools that may be deemed successful:

> Over the last two years I have visited public schools of many varieties, and many seem to share some level of this ruthless intensity around "on-task" and "forward-driving" work. In all of them I recognize the image of the achievement-hungry school where I spent four years teaching. There, the rhetoric of urgency and seriousness loomed above all of us like a shadow. On the one hand, it cast our practices in a new light, allowing us to become more focused and driven. On the other hand, it clouded our vision, making us feel desperate to make sure that we were meeting goals and closing gaps. It was all too easy sometimes to lose track of the human dimensions that underpin the best teaching and learning: Respect, dignity, curiosity. (Fine, 2011)

This book is really about the human dimensions. It is about respecting children as human beings and about supporting, not suppressing, their passion, curiosity, and talent. If schools can do just that, our children will become global, creative, and entrepreneurial. Boston College education professor and coauthor of *The Fourth Way: The Inspiring Future for Educational Change* Andy Hargreaves commented after my presentation of similar ideas at a conference: "Yong Zhao is trying to make a link between the future and the past. What is needed in the future is the enhancement of what comes with us as human" (Hargreaves & Shirley, 2009). And he is absolutely right!

References

AccountabilityWorks. (2012). *National cost of aligning states and localities to the Common Core Standards: A Pioneer Institute and American Principles Project white paper.* Boston, MA: Pioneer Institute.

Asia Society. (2008). *Going global: Preparing our students for an interconnected world.* New York, NY: Asia Society.

Cortez, M. (2012, March 7). Legislature questions common core standards. *Deseret News.* Retrieved April 1, 2012, from http://www.deseretnews.com/article/865551701/Senate-asks-Board-of-Education-to-reconsider-common-core-standards.html

Coyle, D. (2009). *The talent code: Greatness isn't born. It's grown. Here's how.* New York, NY: Bantam Books.

Department for Education. (2011, December 14). New Studio Schools to bridge gap between schools and the world of work. Retrieved April 5, 2012, from http://www.education.gov.uk/inthenews/inthenews/a00200863/new-studio-schools-to-bridge-gap-between-schools-and-the-world-of-work

Duncan, A. (2012, February 23). Statement by U.S. Secretary of Education Arne Duncan on a legislative proposal in South Carolina to block implementation of the Common Core academic standards. *U.S. Department of Education.* Retrieved April 1, 2012, from http://www.ed.gov/news/press-releases/statement-us-secretary-education-arne-duncan-1

Fine, S. M. (2011, October 26). School "urgency" and the loss of the human dimension. *Education News Colorado.* Retrieved April 5, 2012, from http://www.ednewscolorado.org/2011/10/26/27253-school-urgency-and-the-loss-of-the-human-dimension

Florida, R. (2002). *The rise of the creative class and how it's transforming work, leisure, community & everyday life.* New York, NY: Basic Books.

Goldin, C., & Katz, L. F. (2008). *The race between education and technology.* Cambridge, MA: Harvard University Press.

Greenberg, D., Sadofsky, M., & Lempka, J. (2005). *The pursuit of happiness: The lives of Sudbury Valley alumni.* Framingham, MA: Sudbury School Press.

Hargreaves, A., & Shirley, D. L. (2009). *The fourth way: The inspiring future for educational change.* Thousand Oaks, CA: Corwin.

High Tech High. (2012). Results. Retrieved March 20, 2012, from http://www.hightechhigh.org/about/results.php

Howard, P. K. (2012, April 2). To fix America's education bureaucracy, we need to destroy it. *The Atlantic.* Retrieved April 6, 2012, from http://www.theatlantic.com/national/archive/2012/04/to-fix-americas-education-bureaucracy-we-need-to-destroy-it/255173/#bio

International Democratic Education Network. (2012). International democratic schools. *International Democratic Education Network.* Retrieved April 5, 2012, from http://www.idenetwork.org/democratic-schools.htm

Loveless, T. (2012). *The 2012 Brown Center report on American education: How well are American students learning?* Washington, DC: Brookings Institute.

Matharu, J. (2008). *Summerhill School inspection report.* London, England: Ofsted.

Murphy, V. (2004, October 11). Where everyone can overachieve. *Forbes* Retrieved March 20, 2012, from http://www.forbes.com/free_forbes/2004/1011/080.html

Patton, A., & Robin, J. (2012). *Work that matters: The teacher's guide to project-based learning.* London, England: Paul Hamlyn Foundation, Learning Futures.

Posner, R. (2009). *Lives of passion, school of hope.* Boulder, CO: Sentient Publications.

Postman, N. (1996). *The end of education: Redefining the value of school.* New York, NY: Vintage Books.

Rubenstein, G. (2011). Replicating success: Project-based learning. *Edutopia.* Retrieved April 1, 2012, from http://www.edutopia.org/stw-replicating-pbl

The Studio Schools Trust. (2010). Rooting learning in the real world: An introduction to Key Stage 4 projects. *The Studio Schools Trust.* Retrieved April 1, 2012, from http://studioschoolstrust.org/sites/default/files/Studio%20School%20Curriculum%20Introduction.pdf

Will, G. F. (2012, March 9). Those pesky things called laws. *The Washington Post.* Retrieved April 1, 2012, from http://www.washingtonpost.com/opinions/obamas-disregard-for-those-pesky-things-called-laws/2012/03/08/gIQAHIA61R_story.html

Zhao, Y. (2010). Preparing globally competent teachers: A new imperative for teacher education. *Journal of Teacher Education, 61*(5), 422–431.

Ziegler, E. (2012, March 7). U.S. Secretary of Education Arne Duncan: Utah has "complete control" of standards. Retrieved April 1, 2012, from http://utahpubliceducation.org/2012/03/07/u-s-secretary-of-education-arne-duncan-utah-has-complete-control-of-standards/#.T3xNnr9SS25

Index

CORWIN

A SAGE Company

The Corwin logo—a raven striding across an open book—represents the union of courage and learning. Corwin is committed to improving education for all learners by publishing books and other professional development resources for those serving the field of PreK–12 education. By providing practical, hands-on materials, Corwin continues to carry out the promise of its motto: **"Helping Educators Do Their Work Better."**

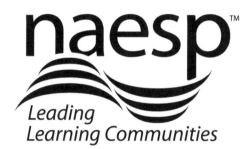

The National Association of Elementary School Principals (NAESP), founded in 1921, is a professional organization serving elementary and middle school principals and other education leaders throughout the United States, Canada, and overseas. NAESP believes that the progress and well-being of the individual child must be at the forefront in leading learning communities. Further, NAESP believes that the development of quality education in each elementary and middle school depends on the expertise, dedication, and leadership of the principal. NAESP is proud to lead in the advocacy and support for principals who serve 33 million children in grades pre-kindergarten through 8, operating through a network of affiliated associations in every state, the District of Columbia, and U.S. territories. Find details at www.naesp.org.